Douglas Fairbanks: In His Own Words

Douglas Fairbanks: In His Own Words

*From the archives of
the Douglas Fairbanks Museum*

Foreword by Keri Leigh, Curator

iUniverse, Inc.
New York Lincoln Shanghai

Douglas Fairbanks: In His Own Words

iUniverse books may be ordered through booksellers or by contacting:

iUniverse
2021 Pine Lake Road, Suite 100
Lincoln, NE 68512
www.iuniverse.com
1-800-Authors (1-800-288-4677)

ISBN-13: 978-0-595-39776-1 (pbk)
ISBN-13: 978-0-595-84183-7 (ebk)
ISBN-10: 0-595-39776-X (pbk)
ISBN-10: 0-595-84183-X (ebk)

Printed in the United States of America

"This is not an explanation of why I am writing about my own failure. It is the sheer novelty of telling the truth about myself that has appealed to me."

—Douglas Fairbanks

(From *One Reel Of Autobiography*, **Collier's** magazine, June 1921)

Contents

Illustrations

* All illustrations are from the collections of the Douglas Fairbanks Museum, except #1, which is courtesy of the Academy of Motion Picture Arts and Sciences.

Foreword

When we hear the name Douglas Fairbanks, many labels immediately come to mind: dashing swashbuckler, athlete, world traveler, actor, producer, director, Hollywood visionary, *bon vivant*. Yet there is one descriptive label rarely applied to him—*author*. This fact is somewhat puzzling considering the volume of his published writings actually far exceeds the number of films he made during his entire career in motion pictures.

The Douglas Fairbanks Museum has assembled here 50 of his very best written works, collected from our extensive archives. *In His Own Words* contains short stories, essays, quotes, quips, autobiography, rare personal correspondence, advice columns, and original screenplays penned by Fairbanks. It's a lively and engaging read, made more intriguing when one realizes that most of these pieces have not been seen since their initial publication nearly a century ago.

Reading his words all these many years later brings us a new perspective on the man that no traditional biography can quite capture. A mental picture begins to emerge of someone who deep down inside always yearned to be a writer. This was a talent he no doubt wanted to develop further, but perhaps lacked the time or confidence to write. For all of his outward self-confidence, Douglas Fairbanks was surprisingly insecure about many facets of himself and his own artistic worth. One thing for certain: Fairbanks clearly had a great love for writing, and the psychological release this exercise brings. Writing, even more so than acting, was the one creative activity that remained constant throughout his entire life, the one thing he never lost his passion for. Long after he had retired from acting, he kept on writing until his death in 1939.

Even as a lad of fifteen, young Fairbanks was already a budding playwright. The proof was found in a recently discovered theatre program from the Tabor Grand School of Acting's third monthly performance at Denver's Elitch Theatre in August 1898. Douglas wrote and performed in a short sketch entitled *Mr. and Mrs. Muffet*, played with Miss Flora Leach. The one-act play itself has never surfaced, but the program from that performance is the first documentation we have of Fairbanks as a writer. Although he would soon enough move to New York and become a star of the Broadway stage, it was another decade before his writing debut was finally published.

Our book opens with "Those Guileless Ruralites" (*Green Book* magazine, August 1912), an early short story that finds young Fairbanks heavily under the influence of O. Henry. It's a humorous tale of a sissified city boy, a mollycoddle, who embarks on a camping trip trying to impress the girl he loves with his rugged manliness. Of course, he has a lot to learn about survival in the great outdoors, and after a run-in with the local authorities, he learns never to underestimate the craftiness of small town folk again. In the process, he manages to dupe his romantic rival and win the affections of little Mildred Orman.

As this first published work demonstrates, Fairbanks was still growing as a writer, and had yet to develop his own individual voice. It's also interesting to see that he already had a framework in mind for the character he would later make famous on the silver screen. "Those Guileless Ruralites" could have easily been an early Fairbanks film, a comedy not unlike *The Lamb* or *His Picture In The Papers*, in which a limp-wristed, over-pampered socialite must go through many hilarious ordeals to make himself a man, always for the sake of a girl. This formula worked like a charm for Douglas Fairbanks; by 1920 he had refined it even further, transforming foppish Don Diego Vega into the screen's first caped crusader, Zorro. With this character, Fairbanks created an alter ego persona that enabled mild-mannered nerds like Bruce Wayne and Clark Kent to become the steel-willed crime fighters Batman and Superman.

Growing up in Colorado at the end of the 19th century, young Fairbanks had tasted the real "Wild West" and became infatuated at an early age. Throughout his life, he maintained close friendships with outlaws like world-famous train robber Al Jennings and Wyatt Earp, who reportedly made a brief cameo in one of Fairbanks' early westerns. He also had many Native American friends who became a part of his permanent film company: Eagle Eye, Tote Du Crow, and Charles Stevens, grandson of the Apache warrior Geronimo. In addition, Douglas Fairbanks was an avid collector of western artifacts, possessing several original paintings by Frederic S. Remington and Charles M. Russell, an enviable collection of vintage firearms and weaponry, even an antique bar from an authentic Wild West saloon. In his later years, he often spoke of wanting to start his own western museum, a plan that unfortunately never came to be.

Some of Fairbanks' best stories reflect his love for the American West. In a 1917 piece titled "Combining Play With Work," he describes in humorous, meticulous detail what it's *really* like to try and ride a bucking bronco, and tells a campfire story of how his pal and former 101 Ranch cowpuncher Jim Kidd taught him how to tame one of these wild beasts. Like many old-timers, Kidd was now making a few dollars working in the movies (you can see Kidd briefly in

D.W. Griffith's *The Birth of A Nation* as a security officer). In "Sunrise and Other Things" (1924), Doug writes of the joy he takes in sharing a real cowboy breakfast at 6am on a high hilltop after an exhilarating predawn horseback ride up steep, rugged California cliff sides.

F airbanks picks up the pen to tell his own life story in "One Reel of Autobiography," (*Collier's*, September, 1921), in which he comes across as remarkably candid, at times perhaps even a bit resentful of the "famous Fairbanks smile" and athletic onscreen stunts that initially brought him to fame. He expresses a serious desire to take on new movie projects that will allow him to prove his dramatic merit. By the time this piece appeared in print, Fairbanks had already accomplished the stated goal with his film adaptation of *The Three Musketeers*, hushing those critics who had previously dismissed him as a mere "grinning monkey."

Doug's autobiographical accounts were always a mix of fact and fancy, and he often avoided giving too many details of his early life—for good reason. Instead, he would invent or embellish stories to keep reporters and fans as far away from the truth as possible. Don't expect accuracy in these pieces, but *do* expect to be thoroughly entertained. A great storyteller knows that all the best tales have some foundation in fact, but if you can spin a story well enough, your audience won't care if it's true or not. With this in mind, the included 1933 "Biography of Douglas Fairbanks" becomes much easier to interpret if one reads between the lines. Another gem of (mostly) fiction is "Personal Reminiscences," from *The Theatre* magazine's April 1917 issue, published the very same month that the United States declared war on Germany.

When America entered World War I, Douglas Fairbanks tried to enlist, but was personally told by President Woodrow Wilson that he could serve his country far better by using his celebrity to aid the war effort at home. In addition to raising millions for the Red Cross, the American Liberty Loan and Canadian Victory Loan Drives, Fairbanks made a series of pro-war films for the government, and also penned a number of articles to rally the American public behind the cause. 1917's "Personal Reminiscences" is packed with Allied propaganda, as is most of his second book, *Making Life Worthwhile*. In a June 2, 1918 telegram to the *New York Times*, included herein, Fairbanks encourages every American to do their patriotic duty by investing in Liberty Bonds. He even wrote articles exclusively for the troops, such as "Listen My Children and You Shall Hear," originally published in the September 7, 1918 edition of the *Arcadian Observer*, the official paper of the United States Army Balloon School in Arcadia, California.

As might befit a silent film star, a few of the stories are told with images rather than words. Two such examples are "Why I Was Disappointed In The Grand Canyon" from the February 1918 *Ladies Home Journal,* and a spring 1919 "Photo Interview" with Douglas Fairbanks. The latter depicts a day in the life of Doug Fairbanks; being tailed everywhere he goes by scribe Alfred A. Cohn, a tired man who is desperately trying to keep up with his subject. After a thorough workout, a swim, a drive, climbing a few buildings, and being hung upside down from a balcony, the poor reporter winds up being rushed to the hospital suffering from total nervous exhaustion!

One particularly fascinating piece is a December 1919 interview that Fairbanks and his best friend Charles Chaplin gave Ray Frohman of the *Los Angeles Herald.* The often-guarded Chaplin rarely spoke to the press, and perhaps it is due to Doug's presence in the room, drawing him out of his protective shell that Charlie opens up here like never before. This intimate, relaxed conversation may well be the most honest and revealing interview either man ever put on record, and it gives us tremendous insight into what made these two creative geniuses really tick.

N ot only did Douglas Fairbanks run his own film unit (The Douglas Fairbanks Pictures Corporation) producing and starring in his own films, he also distributed them himself under the banner of United Artists, a company he founded with Mary Pickford, Charlie Chaplin and D.W. Griffith in 1919. But few of his fans knew at the time that Fairbanks *wrote* most of his films as well. He kept this fact cleverly concealed, most likely because he disdained the annoying habit of some egocentric producers to slather their names all over the credits: "Produced by...Directed By...Written By...and Starring...!"

Fairbanks was surprisingly humble for a movie star; a "King" of Hollywood, always placing his name last in the credits instead of first. Rather than accepting due credit for films he himself had authored, he more often chose to give the limelight to a secretary or typist, and even then only shared credit under a pen name. Of his many pseudonyms, the one most frequently used on his screenplays is Elton Thomas, which is actually comprised of his two middle names. *(His birth name was Douglas Elton Thomas Ulman. The last name was later changed to Fairbanks.)*

We have included within these pages the story treatments Fairbanks wrote for some of his best-known films, transcribed from the original playbooks in the museum's archives. *The Three Musketeers* (1921) is, of course, an adaptation of the classic tale by Alexandre' Dumas, written with longtime friend and collaborator Edward Knoblock. His secretary and scenario editor Lotta Woods receives co-authorship credit on *Robin Hood*, *The Thief of Bagdad*, and *The Black Pirate*, all to be found here in their entirety, complete with Fairbanks' original introductions and footnotes.

Fairbanks often was asked to contribute a brief foreword or prefatory to books by other authors, such as 1931's *Scientific Self-Defense*, written by the Shanghai Superintendent of Police, 1924's *The Truth About The Movies*, and *Young Lawyer U.N. Truth's First Case*, a novel penned by one of his cousins, E.W. Ulman, in 1922. These pieces are included here to demonstrate that Fairbanks could speak with authority on any number of subjects besides just making movies or scaling skyscrapers.

Over the years, Fairbanks developed relationships with his editors, and became a regular contributor to a few select publications. The two magazines he wrote for most often were the *Ladies Home Journal* and *Boys Life*. Doug's first feature appeared in the *Ladies Home Journal* in 1918, and from 1922–24, *LHJ* published a series of in-depth articles that tell us more about his filmmaking philosophy than any others did. "Let Me Say This for the Films" (September 1922) came out at the same time *Robin Hood* was released; the accompanying article expresses his vision of the films as a viable medium for fine art. In "Why Big Pictures" (March 1924), Fairbanks explains why as a producer, he feels justified that making million-dollar movies is well worth the financial risk. "Films for the Fifty Million" (April 1924) divulges a few behind-the-scenes secrets of how the special effects are done on his masterpiece *The Thief of Bagdad*, while "A Huge Responsibility" (May 1924) examines America's leading role in motion picture production worldwide.

In 1923, he began to write for *Boys Life*, the official Boy Scouts of America magazine. A series of six such magazine articles, compiled into a single volume titled *Youth Points the Way*, was released by the Boy Scouts in 1924. We have reproduced this rare book in its entirety here, including the original preface by James E. West, Chief Scout Executive of the Boy Scouts, Editor of *Boys Life*, and personal friend to Fairbanks. Doug contributed to *Boys Life* well into the 1930s; we've chosen a few more of his best pieces for this periodical, like 1928's "The Big Adventure," and "If I Were Fifteen" (1926), in which he takes a look back to his own boyhood.

T he year 1927 brought several major changes to Hollywood, not the least of which was the advent of "talkies." Just three months before *The Jazz Singer* exploded onto the scene, *Motion Picture Magazine* asked industry leaders, "When Will We *Really* Have Talking Movies?" Here, Fairbanks shows his obvious enthusiasm for the new sound technology, but curbs it with due caution. Like most studio heads of the day, he underestimated the powerful effect sound would have on the entire industry, and just how quickly those changes would come.

At the time, Douglas Fairbanks was 44 years old and realized that his years as a romantic leading man of the screen were coming to a close, even though he was still in better physical condition than some athletes half his age. He was instead focusing more on the goal of establishing the films as a respectable art and turning humble little Hollywood into a world class city. His civic activities included helping to finance and build Sid Grauman's Chinese Theatre and the Roosevelt Hotel on Hollywood Boulevard, as well as the new Beverly Hills Water Works, needed to accommodate all the movie stars that were now flocking to Beverly Hills and building their own versions of Pickfair.

When Fairbanks co-founded the Academy of Motion Picture Arts and Sciences that year, he was immediately elected their first president. In November 1927, the new organization published the inaugural issue of *Academy Magazine*, with an introduction by Fairbanks. In "The Academy's Plans," he lays out a vision for the future: he sees the Academy as a school, an institution of higher learning for those who want to study the motion picture arts. He calls for a central headquarters to be built, including offices, classrooms and meeting space, an in-house publishing division, a research library, and technical laboratory. Then he suggests that the Academy tap its all-star membership to make an original benefit film, with the proceeds being shared between the new organization and the Motion Picture Relief Fund (another one of his favorite causes) equally.

In his continual quest to provide a place for aspiring filmmakers to learn their craft, Fairbanks later helped to found the nation's first film school at the University of Southern California in 1929, a time when not a single American college offered coursework in film studies. Now, nearly *every* university in the world has a school of film—it could be said we have Douglas Fairbanks to thank for that.

His vision for the industry extended far beyond the geographical borders of Hollywood; in fact, Fairbanks was one of the first American stars/producers to actively cultivate overseas distribution (though UA), with nearly 40% of his overall box office revenue coming from Europe. In the article "A Huge Responsibility" (*Ladies Home Journal*, May 1924), he addresses the importance of the global market for movies, and also implores film producers to implement a standardized ratings system to protect younger viewers from offensive material. Bear in mind this suggestion was 44 years before the MPAA would establish such a ratings code (**G, PG,** *etc.*).

In an April 9, 1929 piece written for the *Christian Science Monitor* titled "Fairbanks Says Talkies Will Become Better and Cheaper," he hints at a new technological phenomenon—television—which he has become keenly interested in of late, declaring it will change the world. He also foretells a future time when movies will be ordered up "on demand" from the comfort of home, a prediction that would not actually come true until cable TV and home video arrived on the scene fifty years later.

Some of Fairbanks' personal correspondence appears in this volume, and these letters from different periods reflect the many transitions in his life. An April 1920 note to a friend accepting good wishes on his recent wedding to Mary Pickford is brimming with Doug's unique personality and hope for the future. But time changes everything in Hollywood. Seven years later, as both of their careers were fading, Fairbanks would write to a fan about Mary Pickford's rumored retirement from the screen. The old optimism is there, but now it feels a little forced. A 1929 letter to world-renowned metallurgist Francis L. Bosqui shortly before his death expresses Doug's desire to make a historical film about the conquest of Mexico. This proposed film was one of many projects that sadly never came to be, as Fairbanks was gradually losing interest in moviemaking for reasons only he knew.

This book contains a few anomalies, perhaps some surprises—but then, Doug was always full of surprises. Few know that Fairbanks wrote songs, too; usually humorous little ditties like "Oh, What A Pal Was Mary." Published in the *Wandering Minstrels Songbook* in 1920, the lyrics tell the tale of their long courtship, Mary's sensational divorce from Owen Moore and subsequent re-marriage to Fairbanks that same year, in all its controversial glory.

Another curiosity included here is a 1929 endorsement ad Fairbanks did for Lucky Strike Cigarettes that depicts him as D'Artagnan in *The Iron Mask*, Doug's sequel to *The Three Musketeers*. While it might seem bizarre to us today that someone like Fairbanks who was the epitome of good health, clean living and physical fitness was also a three pack a day smoker, that wasn't unusual at all back in the 1920s when little was known about the dangers. His tobacco habit was likely a contributing factor to the heart trouble that would claim his life ten years later.

"The Inside of the Bowl" is the only article Fairbanks ever wrote with Mary Pickford, but by the time it was published in the November 9, 1929 issue of *Lib-*

erty magazine, the marital tension between them was noticeable. Even the lead of this piece acknowledges that "there have been difficulties" and that in this case, "two heads are not better than one." These statements could have just as easily applied to the film the pair had just completed, Shakespeare's *The Taming of the Shrew*, their first (and last) onscreen pairing. Hollywood's royal couple were unraveling here, right before the public's disbelieving eyes.

I n his later years, Fairbanks absented himself from Pickfair, Hollywood, and the United States for long months at a time to purse his lifelong dream: he'd always wanted to travel every inch of the globe. Off he went to Europe, India, Africa, The Philippines, Hawaii, China, Japan, and every island in-between, even documenting his wanderings in a travelogue film called *Around the World in 80 Minutes with Douglas Fairbanks* (1931). All the constant moving about left him little time to write; this is reflected in the dramatic drop in his published output after 1930.

In the January 1933 issue of *Boys Life*, he tells of finally living out his desert island fantasy during the making of *Mr. Robinson Crusoe* (1932) on location in Tahiti and Fiji. His last article was, oddly enough, something he'd never tried before—sports writing. On March 24, 1934, newswires around the world carried what nobody at the time guessed would be Douglas Fairbanks' final missive; an all-too-brief report on England's Grand National horse races.

After his retirement from the screen in 1934, and his subsequent divorce from Mary Pickford the following year, Fairbanks stepped out of the limelight almost entirely. He remarried in 1936 to the former Lady Sylvia Ashley, and spent the next three years traveling to exotic places, truly seeming to enjoy taking it easy for the first time in his ever-active life. Soon, he would be forced to slow down; after a couple of mild heart attacks, Fairbanks was sentenced to bed rest, a fate he thought worse than death. (*"Now cracks a noble heart..."*—Shakespeare.)

For someone with a heart condition, writing is a perfect occupation that requires little, if any, physical exertion. Perhaps it was just to pass the time, or maybe Doug was toying with the notion of finally writing that novel he'd always wanted to do, but he picked up his pen and started writing again. He penned a screenplay for a film he envisioned about the travels of Marco Polo, but ended up abandoning the project and sold the rights to Sam Goldwyn, one of his UA partners. Goldwyn had Fairbanks' original story treatment rewritten, cast with Gary Cooper in the leading role, and released it in 1938 under the title *The Adventures of Marco Polo*.

In the last year of his life, Douglas was working on a story treatment for a new movie project to be titled *The Californian*, slated to star his son Douglas Fairbanks, Jr., now a top Hollywood star in his own right. But this, sadly, was not meant to be. His health took a turn for the worse; the proposed film didn't make it into production.

Early in the morning hours of December 12, 1939, Fairbanks suffered a major heart attack and died at the age of 56. His sudden death shocked the world; few had known of the heart condition that plagued him for years. Fans and friends held a vigil outside his home on the beach at Santa Monica and gathered by the thousands at his funeral to mourn the movies' fallen King.

His widow Sylvia commissioned William Cameron Menzies (the famed set designer who got his start on Fairbanks' *The Thief of Bagdad)* to build an impressive memorial which still stands today at Hollywood Forever Cemetery, holding the remains of both father and son. *(Fairbanks Jr. died in 2000 at age 91.)*

All who come to pay their respects at the great man's final resting-place will surely find some comfort in the peaceful inscription carved onto his marble sarcophagus. It is a quote from his favorite playwright, William Shakespeare, upon the death of *Hamlet*:

"Good night sweet prince, and flights of angels sing thee to thy rest."

The Douglas Fairbanks Museum is proud to present this anthology of Doug's writings to you on what would have been the 123rd anniversary of his birth. For all of us here, it's incredibly satisfying to see these rare works back in print again for a new generation of Fairbanks fans. Feels like we're letting a Genie out of the bottle!

So without further ado, allow me to step aside and give Mr. Fairbanks the podium. It's time for him to tell you his remarkable life story *In His Own Words*.

Keri Leigh, Curator
The Douglas Fairbanks Museum
May 23, 2006

Acknowledgments

First and foremost, we would like to thank *you* for purchasing this book. The proceeds for each copy sold of *Douglas Fairbanks—In His Own Words* will be applied towards educational programs, publications, and exhibitions, as well as the continuing collection, conservation and preservation efforts of the Douglas Fairbanks Museum. By simply enjoying a good book, you've become a part of our future.

This book would not have been possible without the generous support of the museum's donors and volunteers. While it would be nearly impossible to list all of their names on this page, these individuals and businesses are the true heartbeat of our museum, helping us to keep Mr. Fairbanks' legacy alive.

We would like to acknowledge the extraordinary efforts of two very special volunteers who provided endless hours of assistance on the *In His Own Words* project. Greg Jackson and Barbara Burkowsky gave us invaluable help by carefully transcribing many of the articles included herein from the original newspaper and magazine sources, meticulously checking to make sure that every comma, hyphen and period were reproduced exactly as they appeared upon first publication decades ago. Both are great fans of Mr. Fairbanks and were particularly excited by the prospect of his writings finding publication again.

A tremendous thanks is due to our Board of Directors for encouraging this book project, from the initial idea stage to the final edited manuscript. They had the vision to see this book as more than just another museum fund-raiser; rather, they visualized an opportunity to provide both an educational resource for film buffs as well as a fascinating slice of early 20th century history.

Most importantly, our shared goal was to produce an edition of Doug's best written works in a single volume. We hope that with this book, past, present and future Fairbanks fans will have a very intimate and personal portrait of the artist, the actor, the filmmaker, the creator, the adventurer, the writer, the star, the friend of millions, the man—*Douglas Fairbanks: In His Own Words*.

Introduction

By Douglas Fairbanks

There is one thing in this good old world that is positively sure—happiness is for *all* who *strive* to *be* happy—and those who laugh *are* happy.

Everybody is eligible—you—me—the other fellow.

Happiness is fundamentally a state of mind—not a state of body.

And mind controls.

Indeed it is possible to stand with one foot on the inevitable "banana peel" of life with both eyes peering into the Great Beyond, and still be happy, comfortable, and serene—if we will even so much as smile.

It's all a state of mind, I tell you—and I'm sure of what I say. That's why I have taken up my fountain pen.

I want to talk to my friends—you hosts of people who have written to me for my recipe. In moving pictures all I can do is act my part and grin for you. What I say is a matter of your own inference, but with my pen I have a means of getting around the "silent drama" which prevents us from organizing a "close-up" with one another.

—*Excerpt from the book* **Laugh and Live** *by Douglas Fairbanks, 1917.*

A young Douglas Fairbanks, then an up-and-coming Broadway star, with one of his many beloved dogs. This signed portrait was taken around the same time his first short story was published in **Green Book** Magazine, August 1912.

(See story next page)

THOSE GUILELESS RURALITES

♦

Douglas Fairbanks' first
short-story—the adventures
of a city actor in the woods

By Douglas Fairbanks

T HE guileless ruralites taught me a lesson—expensive it was, but worth more than the cost. Since then I've stopped taking snap judgment. It was this way:

People wondered why John Dornan and Henry Hemmer hooked up as partners and one always refused to appear in any play without the other. John is big and strong and husky and emphatic and rather slow and always great on outdoor sports. I'm just medium sized, rather nervous and quick, and my outdoor work consisted of sitting in the bleachers.

People wondered more when we began tagging Mildred Orman around, each willing to jump through the hoop whenever she gave the word. People couldn't understand how Mildred, attractive as she was, could appeal to two people of totally dissimilar tastes.

John almost fell out of his chair when I told him one day near the first of September that I was going with him and the Ormans on their regular camping trip,

1

and had brought a dandy shot-gun. He thought I was sick; then he asked sarcastically if I knew which end to hang onto when I wanted to shoot.

"Yep," I answered. "I've learned that much, and maybe if I'm not careful I'll kill something I'm shooting at."

When he got tired laughing and stopped long enough to speak, he wanted to know if I'd taken out an extra accident insurance policy and what made me suddenly decide to change the manner of my living.

"Mildred did it," I said. "No use beating around the bush, John. We know we are both in love with her. Now, I saw she didn't think so awful much of my form of manly exercise—fact is she told me several times that anybody could sit still and watch a ball game. Didn't catch the point when I told her only a dead one could sit and watch a good ball game. Anyway she seems to expect something more in a man who puts the ring on her finger. So I decided to try to get in the game."

"Well," (he wasn't so very pleasant), "I hope you won't shoot your fool self or any of the rest of us."

I left him alone to recover from the shock. And it was a shock. He, as well as Mildred, and everybody else that knew me at all well knew that the one thing I had against the country was the fact that it wasn't the city. It always struck me that the country was too much of a good thing, and that what little good there was about it was spoiled by the guileless ruralites that specked up its face.

"It's all very well," I said to Mildred one day, when she was telling me what a beautiful thing nature was in the country, "when you're all tired out and want to sleep twenty hours a day. But otherwise, please deliver me. I prefer to love nature at a distance and where the white wings can sweep the dust off her face and then sprinkle it every day."

I made up my mind to plunge into the life of a huntsman one day after I persuaded Mildred to admit that, aside from this one point, she thought I was rather ahead of my partner. I immediately joined a gun club, bribed the groundskeeper to give me a few lessons on the sly, and was able to shoot without getting my eyelids down, by the time the party was ready to go. The party was made up of Arthur Orman, Mildred's brother, and his wife, and Elizabeth Benton, and us three. Mrs. Orman hustled around and found Elizabeth after I surprised her by intimating I'd be glad to go if I were asked. Elizabeth insisted that she was "just crazy about camping," but she knew about as much of it as I did.

I learned afterwards from Mildred that Katie—that's Mrs. Orman—had it all cooked up to pair me up with Elizabeth, so we couldn't bore or be bored by them, which plan might have worked properly had I not preferred being with Mildred, and Elizabeth hadn't preferred John's company to mine.

The camp certainly was one grand spot. The Ormans had been going there for several years and it felt like home to them. I was willing to admit it was a beautiful location, and it would do very well so long as the natives remained hidden in the woods.

Elizabeth and I sat on a box and watched the others put up a tent and get the camp in order. That was about all we could do to help them. I tried to drive a peg in the ground, but the hatchet slipped—Arthur said I missed the peg altogether—and smashed John's finger into the soft, mossy earth. It didn't hurt him very badly—just made a nice red lump about the knuckle—but they wouldn't let me try to do anything more. John's language wasn't what it should have been—I was very glad he spoke to me in a whisper.

There was a pretty little lake in front of us, and a lot of big trees all around us—Wisconsin seems to have a good crop of lakes and trees every year. Then just beyond the woods there was a lot of open ground dotted with thickets and bunches of bushes.

"Pike and pickerel in the lake," said Arthur, explaining to Elizabeth and me the advantages of the place; "squirrels in the trees; rabbits, woodcock, snipe, plover and grouse in the open spaces."

"Where do they keep the natives?" I asked.

"Don't be an idiot," Arthur growled.

Arthur caught a couple of big pike for our dinner—he is dippy on the subject of fishing, and I was given the chance to redeem myself and told to clean one. Arthur had attended to the other but was needed elsewhere. I'd been watching him, didn't think it looked hard, and tackled the job with considerable confidence, with Elizabeth as my audience.

"Grasp him firmly," Arthur said as his parting instruction, "or he'll slip away from you."

I grasped firmly with my left hand as I raised my right aloft, armed with a hatchet, determined to cut off the head with one blow as Arthur had done so easily. That is, I intended to grasp him firmly and I thought I had him, but he squirted away just as the hatchet started down. I couldn't stop the blow, but the fish almost won the race all the same, and lost only his tail when the blade descended.

"Wasn't that clever?" I said brazenly to Elizabeth. "I wanted to cut the tail off first so it wouldn't be in the way."

She swallowed the bluff, but I heard a snicker from somebody else. That made me mad and I grabbed the pike again and pushed him back in place. He had gathered a few blades of grass, some leaves, and several grains of sand, in his mad dash for liberty, and I thought these things would make it easier for me to hold him. They didn't. He got away from the hatchet three times before I decided to keep my hands off and try to catch him while he was still. That scheme worked, although I did make a slight miscalculation and cut the head off an inch lower than was necessary.

With a sigh of relief and a look of triumph at Elizabeth, I laid aside the hatchet and took the knife. "The scales will be easy to scrape off" I thought. Arthur hardly looked at him when he did it.

But my pike was just as wily without head or tail as he had been with them. I grasped him firmly, just above the place where the tail had been, and gave one scrape. Scales and fish shot away from me together. I heard more snickers and began to get peevish. I turned the fish around, big end towards me. He couldn't slip away then, I was sure, unless he could pry my fingers apart and make the opening through them larger so his body might get through.

Like so many brilliant schemes, this one failed to work out in practice. I discovered with some surprise that the scales all grew the same way, and pushing the knife from head to tail the blade slipped over them, and almost cut my hand off. I jerked it away just in time.

Then I took off my coat and rolled up my sleeves. Elizabeth looked sympathetic. Arthur passed by and smiled. Katie turned away quickly and I knew she was hiding a grin. John Dornan snickered quite audibly and asked if I didn't want some help. I caught a glimpse of Mildred and her face had such an expression of mingled pain and disapproval that it made me desperate. I grabbed the pike again and the tail, head pointed towards me, and started to scrape to headward. The blade caught on the scales and for an instant I felt triumphant. The next second, however, in response to a vigorous pull on the knife handle, the fish sneaked out of my hand and plunked me squarely in the stomach.

Then I was mad. I didn't care what the others were thinking, looking or saying. It was me and that fish to the mat. I don't remember exactly the process, but I remember that I had him scaled and skinned as well—which Arthur suavely remarked was unnecessarily cruel—in half an hour. I had a dim recollection that at one time during the struggle I got him down and held him with my knee.

"There," said I, holding him up in triumph, "I knew I could do it."

Well, the others were so surprised at my very evident satisfaction that their smiles of derision faded away. It was a funny thing, but it seemed to me that

Mildred was much kinder to me after that. I asked her about it two days later and she confessed that she had been angry because others were laughing at me.

"But it must have been funny," I said.

"It—it was." She smiled at the memory of the scene. "But it wasn't fair for them to poke fun at you. I laughed, but I didn't laugh at you."

"No, I suppose you thought the laugh was on the pike."

I didn't care for fish or for fishing after that experience. "Why," I explained to Arthur, "I'd never get one out of the water. If a dead one is that hard to handle, then a live one must be the limit." When he remarked that I would learn how, I assured him that my piscatorial education had been neglected until too late in life.

Elizabeth also seemed to have gained a prejudice against fishing, and she positively refused to even look at the hooks and lines. Mildred took me in hand, to show me the country and where to find the game. Arthur and Mrs. Arthur naturally paired off, both being rather fond of fishing. And Dornan began to grow grouchy because he had to look after Elizabeth, who preferred staying in camp most of the time because it was "so deliciously quiet" there.

We were not very successful in our search for feathered game. Mildred bagged a couple of partridge the second day. The rest of the covey got out of range before I got my gun to my shoulder—which was the occasion for more snickers when the others heard about it. I started to say something but Mildred's eyes snapped and her tongue spoke first:

"I don't suppose any of you did a bit better the first time you flushed a covey of partridges."

And I decided since she had taken up the cudgel in my behalf, that the best thing I could do would be to keep my mouth shut.

Next day I sneaked close up behind a big fox squirrel and shot him before he knew what was happening. Mildred had been after one in another tree and hadn't seen me violate at all the rules of sportsmanship by shooting a sitting critter and not give him a chance to get away if he could, and especially a squirrel or a rabbit with a shotgun! I'd heard about squirrel stews and decided I'd try to make one for our supper. Mildred had come to my rescue to keep me from wearing myself out. I think it took me forty-seven minutes to skin and cut up the first squirrel, and then I let nearly a third of the hide get into the pot.

The others tried to poke fun at me, but when they saw me liking it and Mildred getting all fussed up, they stopped. I was beginning to think I'd better keep right on making myself look foolish and helpless. Intentionally, I made remarks on several occasions displaying wonderful ignorance. The way Mildred bristled up and fought for me, just like a mother fighting for her kid, made me feel pretty good.

Along in the second week I got so I could hit something sometimes. One day we walked considerably farther west than usual, and discovered another large cleared space. Mildred shot a brace of grouse—the first we had seen—and I was lucky enough to bring down one. Next day we packed up a lunch and started for an all-day hunt. We struck the birds a-plenty, and by noon our game bags were getting heavy. We stopped to look about and Mildred exclaimed ecstatically: "Isn't this lovely?"

"I'm willing to admit it," I answered, "in fact, it's the only country I've ever been able to work up an enthusiasm over."

"That's because you've not gotten into the spirit of it before."

"No, it's because you and I are here alone; because there are no country jays about to spoil things. There's some more."

A big covey of grouse flew up from a little thicket, darted west nearly a quarter of a mile and settled. We hurried after them. Fifty feet away they started up again. Mildred's gun got into action first, but both barrels snapped. I bagged a couple. We started towards them, when I felt a heavy hand on my shoulder and heard a deep, growling voice:

"Huh? I guess you'd better come along with me."

He was the rubest of the rube.

"Better take some more reckoning," I said with a grin, "because I'm going the other way—the way you are not going."

"Ho, ho," he chuckled, "you're one of those smart-alecky city chaps, eh? Well, you come along with me."

I started to let him have my fist when Mildred caught my arm and commanded the stranger to explain his actions.

"Well," he drawled, "you see, I'm Jim Jelly, the game warden. You broke the law and you're under arrest. Here's my star. That satisfy you?"

"No, it doesn't." Mildred retorted. "We haven't broken the law. These are grouse, and the open season doesn't close for nearly a week."

"You got another guess." Jelly grinned. "I've been watching you folks for three days. Your camp's over in Dodge county, where the grouse season runs from September tenth to the first of October. But this is Columbia County, where there ain't any open grouse season. I thought mebbe you'd step over the line," he chuckled, "ef I just waited long enough."

That staggered Mildred. I waited; feeling that she knew a lot better than I what to do.

"Well," she said finally, "it wasn't intentional; you know it. We didn't know we were in another county, there isn't any sign around to mark the boundary."

"Can't help it." Jelly was firm. "You know, there ain't anybody let off because they're ignorant of the law."

"Oh well," I wanted to get the old jay out of my sight, because he was spoiling the scenery. "I suppose it's a small fine. What is it? I'll pay you and save us the trouble of going to the justice."

"Well," he said, "that's not strictly regular, but seeing as how the lady is with you, mebbe I might do it."

He picked up the two dead birds just about the time I discovered I had not brought any money with me. Mildred was in the same boat.

"Will you walk over to the camp with us," said I, trying to be polite, "and get the money?"

"Oho, you are the smart one," he laughed his infernally irritating chuckle. "Well, I reckon not. That's out of my jurisdiction. You get in that county, and I'll lose my fee because I couldn't arrest you. I guess you'd better come along."

"Oh, don't be so stubborn!" Mildred cried. "We'll not try to run away from you."

"No, I reckon you won't," he sneered; "you city folks think you're so dinged smart. I know you, and you women are the—"

"Here, shut up, or I'll make you!" I hadn't been as mad for a year—except when I was wrestling with the pike—and I surprised the old duffer and startled Mildred. "You'll speak respectfully to her, or I'll see if I can't make you, warden or no warden."

The look Mildred gave me was enough to more than pay for all the discomforts of that trip into the woods. "Come on, and we'll see the magistrate. Mildred, you can go back to camp alone and send Arthur and John over to—where are you going to take me?"

"To jail," Jelly growled. "And you'll stay there all night, too. Your case won't be called 'til morning before Squire Hummel. Your friends can come over to Deerville to-night if they want to, but they'll not see you, Mr. Smarty. And if you give me any more of your sass, I'll prefer a charge of attacking an officer against you."

"Oh, rats!" I was disgusted. "Shut up. I may have to go with you, but I'm certain there's no law in the world cruel enough to make me listen to your yapping."

Mildred tried to calm me down, tugging at my arm and whispering in my ears, but she didn't have any effect until she said: "Henry, please, please don't.

You do not realize how vindictive these people can be. Now you must keep cool, you must, you must—for my sake—dear."

Well, of course, I couldn't resist that sort of an appeal. So I chased my anger—or rather her words chased it, because they gave me something a lot better to think about—told her good-bye and turned northward with Jelly at my side. Neither of us spoke for fifteen minutes. When we had crossed the clear space and were following a well-defined wagon road, he said:

"I hope you've got enough money in camp to pay your fine. You wouldn't like to stay in jail 'til you got it from Chicago, would you?"

"Hardly." I replied. "What will the fine be?"

Well," he drawled, "them grouse are female birds and each one is supposed to have about six chicks this time of the year. It's an awful thing to leave them chicks motherless, and our Justice is mighty apt to be severe—he's pretty fond of grouse himself. Let me see. There's $25 for each chick, $300 in all, and another $25 each for the mothers. That makes $350. Then there'll be some costs on each of the fourteen cases; say about $5 each. That's $70. Well, call it a spare $400 on the hull thing."

"But say man!" I stopped and stared at him. "I don't want to buy your whole county. I haven't any use for it, and I don't like the country anyway."

"Better not let Judge Hummel hear you talk that way," the old fellow warned; "he thinks this is the best country on earth."

"But I haven't got that much money here," I said.

"That's too bad," he said sympathetically, "but maybe you could get it by telegram. Leastways, you can fix up for a bond that way. Maybe there's a way to let you get back to your wife to-night."

It tickled my heart when he spoke of Mildred as my wife, and I didn't tell him of his mistake. Instead I asked him what might be done.

"Oh, I dunno," he replied. "I'll send Sam Sellers to you when we get to town. He's something of a lawyer, and mebbe he can help you out."

Jelly tenderly turned me over to Sam and left, after saying he would go and see if he couldn't persuade the judge to accept bail that night, so I wouldn't have to go to jail. I thanked him, and decided that I'd done him and other rural residents an injustice. Sam asked if I knew any landowner in the county, and when I answered in the negative, he said: "Well, I think I can persuade the judge to let you out on cash bond of—say, about $50."

"I haven't got that much."

"Telegraph works to Chicago, you know," he replied with a grin. "That might not get the money here before dark, but you look like you might be an honest city man, and I'll put up the $50 for your bail. You telegraph for the money and have it sent to me. Come on."

Sam Sellers was an energetic man, even if he was a real-estate-agent-notary-public-attorney in a small town. Ten minutes later we had the telegraph wires working and five minutes later I'd put up the cash bond of $50 with the village blacksmith, whom Sellers addressed as Judge Hummel. The judge was very stern when he learned the nature of the charge, and it required considerable persuasive powers upon Sam's part to make him accept the $50 cash bail. However, we were back in Sam's office presently, and I was relieved of the rather disagreeable prospect of spending the night in jail. After Sam closed the door, he spoke in a confidential whisper.

"Jelly's told me about you and your bride, and I reckon you'd like mighty well to get back to her, wouldn't you? And I reckon too, you don't relish the idea of parting with $400. That would come in pretty handy furnishing your house, eh?"

He poked me in the ribs and gave me a knowing wink. I didn't understand what he meant and told him so.

"Oh," he said, "I just thought you might skip over to your camp right now and fail to show up to-morrow. You can be out of the state before we find out where you've gone."

"You mean for me to jump my bail?"

"Well, I wouldn't put it that way," he said slowly, "and if you don't ever breathe a word of it and don't stop payment of that $75 you wired to Chicago for, why—well—my memory's pretty treacherous at times."

Once more I made a mental vow never to think harshly of rural residents, promptly accepted his offer, slipped out the back door of his office, and scooted for the camp.

I met Mildred, Arthur and Dornan about four miles out, much to their surprise and my joy. Hurriedly I told them that I had to make the train that night. I tried to evade answering the questions they fired at me but it was no use. Mildred and John wouldn't be satisfied without an explanation. When I finished my story John howled and doubled up with laughter. Between gasps, I managed to make out what he was saying.

"Caught you on that old gag, did they? Oh, Mommer! Mr. Wise Guy from the city played for a sucker by a trio of rubes, and caught to a fare-you-well. Oh, Mommer!"

Arthur confirmed John's remarks. I was so relieved to learn I hadn't broken the law that I was ready to grin even if it was a $75 grin. But Mildred didn't see anything funny about it, and she told them so, politely and in ladylike words, if you please; but in such a manner that they could not doubt her sincerity. I never knew I needed anyone to take care of me, as well as I knew it before she'd been talking fifteen seconds.

When Arthur and John hurried along ahead of us to escape further commentaries on their heartless conduct, I told Mildred I was sure she would have to marry me to look after me, and she assured me that it was her own opinion.

But never since then have I ventured even to think of the guilelessness of the ruralites, though I am deeply grateful to Jelly and Sam and the blacksmith bogus magistrate for the part they took in shaping my affairs of the heart.

Prosecute them? Hardly. Nobody would, even if he hadn't won the best wife in the world. They'd be too much ashamed.

*Fairbanks' first published foray into fiction writing was submitted to **Green Book** Magazine, who ran his short story in the August 1912 issue, a special edition devoted exclusively to the theatre. At the time, Fairbanks was a top star of the Broadway stage. His recently rediscovered writing debut gives us a fascinating glimpse into the early development of Douglas Fairbanks the writer. He would have plentiful opportunities to grow this talent upon his entrance to the motion picture business three years later.*

PERSONAL REMINISCENCES

By DOUGLAS FAIRBANKS

I FIND myself, as I sit down to write the true story of my fair young life for THE THEATRE MAGAZINE, resembling, in at least two respects, the hero martyr of other days, Nathan Hale.

At the moment when peril glares angrily into the eyes of our country, I am ready as was Hale to fight for the life of American principles in America, and like the same strong spirit, I only regret that I have but one life to write. The one I have is really not worth writing about.

The "reminiscences" of my career will make brief and sketchy reading, for I have been too busy to crowd reminiscence into any of my sixteen years on the stage. However, I suppose when the editor says "Camera, Ready, SHOOT," there is no use in putting up a kick, so here goes.

I was born in Denver, Colo., on a particularly bright and sunny morning in May, 1883. It was the proud ambition of my parents to see me a mining king, and to that end after graduating from Denver High School, Jarvis Military Academy and other centres of learning in the Colorado metropolis, I was sent to the School of Mines, in Boulder.

Before I learned much about the science, art and ethics of mining, I saw Frederick Warde in his repertoire of classic plays, and after viewing that actor's performance decided that as a mere capitalist I should be wasting my time. The call of the higher drama lured me all the way to Richmond, Va., where I made my first appearance with Mr. Warde's company in the role of Francois in "Richelieu."

I n this character, and in that of Florio in "The Duke's Jester," which followed, I failed to make any perceptible dent in the classic drama, but I probably wore the most astonishing costumes ever beheld on the native stage, being fitted out by a well meaning but misguided costume mistress in odds and ends of ancient, modern and medieval garb.

So effectively did my costumes succeed in breaking up the actors and actresses who happened to be on the stage whenever I made my entrance, that Mr. Warde released me without visible signs of pain, to join Herbert Kelcey and Effie Shannon in "Her Lord and Master," the next season.

This engagement brought me to New York, where I made my first bow in the Kelcey-Shannon company at the Manhattan Theatre on March 3, 1902.

I cannot say that Fame seemed to come my way in galloping bounds in this engagement, but I managed to hold down my engagement until the end of the season. Then I played in the support of Miss Minnie Dupree who had the courage to cast me for the role of Philip de la Noye in "A Rose of Plymouth Town." The following season found me doing my best with Miss Alice Fischer in the part of Charlie Banastar in "Mrs. Jack."

The season of 1903–4 brought me to the Lyric Theatre in New York with Wilton Lackaye in W.A. Brady's stirring production of "The Pit," a dramatization of Frank Norris' big American novel, which was supposed to be based upon incidents connected with the celebrated battle of Joseph Leiter against the whole army of brother speculators in the "wheat pit" on the Chicago Exchange. From the wheat pit I went to sea, as it were, appearing in May, 1904, as Jack Jolly in "Two Little Sailor Boys" at the Academy of Music.

In January of 1905 I opened with Jefferson de Angelis at the Lyric Theatre in "Fantana." There was no wheat pit in "Fantana," and I soon quit the role of Fred Everett in Mr. De Angelis' support, and changed my name to "Benny Tucker," which part I played in a piece called "Frenzied Finance," produced at the Princess Theatre (the old Princess on Broadway, not the present theatre in Thirty-ninth Street) in April of the same year. This was rather a busy and varied season since "Frenzied Finance" failed to achieve a long run and later on I played a part in a piece called "As Ye Sow."

An engagement at Elitch's Gardens, in Denver, followed. In my home town I played a number of unimportant parts as a member of the stock company that was a fixture at Elitch's—a company in which every Denver actor is expected to appear at least once in his career. The Denver engagement was followed by a season in the support of Grace George in "Clothes," a play by Avery Hopwood and Channing Pollock which was written almost simultaneously with Mrs. Wharton's similar conceit in "A House of Mirth," which was produced as a play at about the same time.

"Clothes" ran out a season, I believe, and then came a big milestone in my road. I was cast for the part of Perry Carter Wainwright in Broadhurst's play "The Man of the Hour" with Holbrook Blinn as Alwyn Bennett—the titular role. This was the first of those brisk, breezy parts that a young chap always likes to play, which had ever been entrusted to me, and getting a chance to play it was a big thing for so young an actor as I. I have spoken of the part in "The Man of the Hour," as being a great thing to capture, but it was while playing this part that I made the luckiest capture of my life; for in July, 1907, I married Miss Beth Sully, the fine girl who has gone the rest of the road with me.

I see they are tearing down the old Bijou Theatre at the present moment. That's a pity, for this house which others describe as a fire trap, a dingy old catacomb, and which I believe, held the undisputed championship as the shabbiest and most inconveniently arranged theatre in New York, always shines a radiant gleam to my eyes, since it was here that I began a new chapter in my professional life and became a "star." The date of this event was August 20, 1908. "All For a Girl" was the title of the piece, and I played the part of a speedy young chap named Harold Jepson. I regret to state as a chill and bitter fact that Harold's speed took him straight off the boards and after a brief run of a month, "All For a Girl" gave place to "A Gentleman From Mississippi" in which I was co-star with "Tom" Wise who wrote the play in collaboration with Harrison Rhoades.

In 1910 "The Cub" gave me the role of Steve Oldham, and this part was followed in May, 1911 by the part of "Philosopher Jack" in the "all-star" revival of "The Lights o' London" at the Lyric Theatre.

In the following August, I was assigned the role of Edgar Willoughby Pitt in "A Gentleman of Leisure" at the Playhouse, and when I relinquished that part it was to appear under the management of my good friends, Messrs. Cohan and Harris, in "Officer 666." Travers Gladwin was the name of the pestered hero in that farce and I created the role in Chicago at the Grand Opera House in March, 1912, afterwards following Wallace Eddinger in the New York production at the Gaiety Theatre.

P ERHAPS it would not be out of place to pause for a moment to maintain that Mr. Cohan has nothing on me, in the matter of star spangled patriotism. To be sure I have never written songs about the good old flag, nor have my friends ever encouraged me to sing ditties regarding it; but proud patrons have solemnly declared that the first articulate utterance of my infant lips was an emphatic "d-a-a-a" which any parent knows means "flag" and it is most religiously believed in the intimacy of our family circle, that I invariably howled and roared with all the vigor of which my infant lungs were capable whenever any attempt was made to rob my cradle of a small American flag which I cherished as my most precious belonging.

It is a poor sort of American who fails to thrill to the call of his flag to-day, and for that flag and the freedom, the liberty, the brotherhood which it represents, I am ready to abandon my profession should the need arise and with all my strength, all my power and the deepest conviction of which I am capable, I am ready to fight until it waves triumphantly as a symbol of the splendid America which our fathers founded and fought for in '76.

But to return to the field of reminiscence.

"Hawthorne U.S.A.," was the next vehicle in which I appeared as star, and it was Hawthorne which brought me down to the close of 1912.

After that engagement, I appeared with William H. Crane, Amelia Bingham and other sterling players in a star revival of Bronson Howard's master play "The Henrietta" brought up to date by Winchell Smith. A short engagement of "He Comes Up Smiling" and one or two brief seasons in other pieces, together with a four weeks' flyer in vaudeville where I tried out a tabloid version of "A Regular Business Man," brought me down to my present engagement in the screen drama.

In the "movies" I have found the most interesting and adequate dramatic expression of my career. I have known numbers of fine players who feel called upon to speak apologetically of their appearance as screen players. I am not of these. I believe that in the field of the silent drama, we have found a new medium of expression that it is yet in its infancy, but that has already created new standards in audiences, and new audiences as well, for the legitimate theatre.

The camera has brought to the far out lying territories of all countries, graphic reproductions of spoken plays set in magnificent and appropriate surroundings, at a price which has familiarized the small town man and woman with the work of the big dramatists and the big players. With Sarah Bernhardt, Sir Herbert Beerbohm Tree, E. H. Sothern, Maxine Elliott, George M. Cohan, John Barrymore, William Courtenay, W. H. Crane, the incomparable Mary Garden, besides such stars as Fannie Ward, Marguerite Clark, De Wolf Hopper, Nazimova, John Mason and a half hundred other eminent artists whom I could mention, bringing their energy and enthusiasm to the screen, there is no longer any excuse for failure to recognize the dignity of the photoplay, as it exists to-day. And I hold to a firm conviction that the photographic drama of 1917 holds the same relation to the "movie" of coming seasons that the melodrama presented by Al. H. Woods twenty years ago when "Bertha the Sewing Machine Girl," and "The Queen of the Opium Ring" measured the taste of audiences, bears to the productions made by Mr. Woods of high type melodrama to-day.

I cite Mr. Woods as one manager who has moved along in always upward lines, as I fully believe the photo drama is moving, and must move if it is to survive.

And because I believe in progress, I am glad to ally myself with that branch of the drama that is most vibrant with life—most quiveringly alert to the thought, the meaning and the message of the hour, and that is reaching with the most eager grasp and the widest vision, out into the three great fields where the active life of to-day and to-morrow finds expression: the picture plays that educate, picture plays that bring home to audiences the great, big problems with which moralists, religionists, scientists, and nations at war are grappling, and picture plays that throb with big drama.

In the latter field the speaking actor, and the newly developed school of screen actor will find their place, and the survival of the silent drama depends upon the quality of endeavor brought to its interpretation.

There's plenty of fun, plenty of excitement in the motion picture game. Sometimes I've been caught in pretty tight places. It seems touch and go at the time, but we get through somehow and then we have a good laugh at the experience. We took "The Americano" in Mexico a few months ago. The conditions down there are not ideal exactly. We had a hard time. The fights one sees in the pictures were on the level, with real Mexicans playing the other parts. I got a few good punches with my fists before it came to guns. I said "America first," and I don't think we suffered much.

Talk about excitement, in the big fight scene, which takes place in a cell after I rescue the Presidente, my opponent, a full-blooded Mexican, was instructed by the translator, to put up a real fight—and he did. Ten minutes after the camera stopped turning the same Mexican was caught knife in hand by a military officer and his staff, who were acting as our guides.

In a scene of "The Americano," it was my business to communicate with a lady, who was held prisoner in her room by the revolutionists. About fourteen feet from the balcony, was the top of a tree, forty feet high. I climbed to the top of the tree, and stood in a crotch formed by two branches, got the thing swaying forward and backward, and at the right moment, when about six feet from the house, I jumped, caught at the coping of the balcony, and drew myself up, hat in hand, at the window of the astonished lady's boudoir. If I'd missed the ledge, I never would have lived to tell the tale.

During the production of "American Aristocracy," filmed in and around Watch Hill, Rhode Island, one of the scenes called for me to jump from the mast of a schooner to the water, rescue the girl, and bring her to shore.

I received my cue, made a diving leap to the water, searched for the heroine, but, as we would say on the Bowery, "nothin' doing." I then learned that at the last moment the girl showed the greatest fear for the water and positively refused to proceed. The scene had to be postponed until another actress, replying to a hurry call, came from New York. The real calamity occurred when the new girl arrived. She threw herself bravely into the water, immediately sank and almost drowned before I could reach her. We had to try four other girls after that and only the sixth proved efficient. Finally, the rescue scene was recorded on the films to everyone's satisfaction.

At the present moment, we are witnessing a wonderful development of the screen drama, in the pictures (these are to be listed in the educational class) of scenes created by the stress of the present war. The horror of it, the magnificent devotion of the men and women who help their cause by work in the ambulance and hospital division, the whole pictured exposition of the new science of war, is a record whose value cannot be estimated. And the man who can see these scenes before his eyes—but this is not properly reminiscence. However, I cannot close without taking my stand beside the camera which has done in its share in waking our country to the dangers of a cowardly, un-American peace, and declaring again that as a man, and as a camera actor I am ready to fight for the cause that thrills everyone who sees the story of America's perils on the screen and has the need of the hour brought home to him with a truth, a force, a realism impossible in the spoken drama, and justifying at a glance the existence of the cinema as the reflection of the perils of the hour.

And when the full meaning of the present crisis is brought home to thinking Americans through the medium of the screen I feel sure enough of my country-men, as I feel sure enough of myself to say with all of them: I am ready to fight!

This article originally appeared in the April 1917 issue of **The Theatre** *magazine. While the piece gives an in-depth look at Doug's early years on the American stage, it is also quite often laced with Yankee patriotism and perhaps even a hint of pro-war propaganda. The timing of the article's release seemed almost prophetic, as the US declared war on Germany and entered World War I during that very same month.*

THE AMBASSADOR

✦

NEW YORK

(Letterhead)

My Dear Mr. Stone,

I want to thank you so much for your kindness to me during my stay. It has been a rare treat indeed to have been with you so much.

Sincerely,

Douglas Fairbanks
(Signature)

Fairbanks wrote this undated piece of personal correspondence while staying at The Ambassador Hotel in New York City. The note is scribbled by hand on hotel stationery.

DOWN TO EARTH

Plenty of sunshine and living in the open, instead of being cramped up in a poorly ventilated elaborate home is what Douglas Fairbanks preaches in his latest Artcraft film, "Down to Earth."

"If people would only forget their homes, and get down to earth, we would have less use for doctors and we would have a healthier nation," said Douglas Fairbanks in discussing the theme of his new picture.

"Animals generally are healthy," he continued, "because they live in the open and climb trees, continuously doing some form of exercising. You very seldom hear of an animal suffering from heart disease, bad cold or tuberculosis. Then it stands to reason, that sunshine and open air should be taken advantage of, in preference to afternoon teas and sewing circles.

"Walk on dirt paths in preference to brick sidewalks, and take advantage of the nourishments of mother earth. Compare the boy who has spent his life in the country, with the over-dressed chap who lives in the city. The former nine times out of ten is a picture of health, because he wallows around in the mud, and gets down to earth. The latter is afraid of soiling his kid gloves, he covers every part of his body with clothes, thereby absolutely disregarding the health advantages of sunshine. I think, we will reach an age, when people will dress more consistently to avail themselves of the sunshine and open-air benefits.

"In 'Down to Earth' we try to show these things by a process of contrast. Whether or not we have succeeded, is of course up to the public. John Emerson, who directed this picture, is a very capable student of human nature, combined with a pronounced sense of satire. He and Anita Loos are wonderful in this respect. Their combined satirical angle on life is tremendous. It isn't insulting but highly amusing. Being associated with two such capable people in the capacity of director and scenario writer, we can't go wrong very far without being checked. We all work together in the development and the producing of our Artcraft pictures and up until now, we seem to have given the patrons of the cinema the proper kind of entertainment. 'Down To Earth' is a different kind of a story, and

I feel that we will earn a myriad of sympathizers, who will agree with us, that sunshine and open air, versus the patronizing of indoor amusement, will win every time."

Excerpt from the pressbook for the 1917 film **Down to Earth**, *published by the Douglas Fairbanks Pictures Corporation in association with Artcraft/Paramount. At the time, Fairbanks was one of the few stars who had the luxury of his own production company and had complete creative control over the making of his motion pictures. He also took an active role in promoting his movies, often writing short articles like this one for distribution in local newspapers.*

The Two Douglas Fairbanks—Father and Son

ALL lovers of the father will be glad to know that the son inherits his father's smile and athletic ability. Douglas Junior is just seven, but even now he can climb trees and jump fences and perform other athletic stunts almost as well as his wonderful father. He has the same qualities that have put his father, Douglas Fairbanks, in a class with Mary Pickford and Charlie Chaplin as one of the three great moving picture stars. Douglas Fairbanks tells in the accompanying pages how he has done it.

This photo appeared in the **American Magazine**, July 1917.
(See related story on next page.)

Combining Play With Work

By Douglas Fairbanks

T
O MY mind health and cheerfulness are the greatest assets one can have, whatever be one's walk in life. They did more for me on the stage than any other quality, for I never pretended to be a great actor. And in the moving picture game they have proved immensely more available than any reputation I might have gained in the legitimate. To illustrate: Many moving picture "fans" came to me in Philadelphia—where I'd played lots of times in the legitimate—and asked me if I'd ever been on the stage.

My conviction is that reputation in the legitimate, unless it be so great as to obviate the necessity of certain artistic screen qualities, is not valuable to a moving picture actor. When a great actor has appeared in the plays that he has been identified with, his usefulness in the camera field, so to speak, ceases. But the "movie" star can go on impersonating new roles so long as new roles are being invented for him.

With me, health was natural, and when one has health it ought to be just as natural to develop one's athletic side as it is for water to run down-hill.

Walking is a great exercise. I would rather go afoot than ride any time. When eighteen years old, I walked through Europe just for the fun of it. It was done on a bet. There were three of us. We had fifty dollars apiece and we were going to make it last for a three-months trip.

We worked our way over on a cattle ship, and got eight shillings and a return ticket for the job. Then we tramped from Liverpool to London, doing odd jobs by the way, sleeping in the open and occasionally pilfering the withal to supply the cravings of the inner man—a regular gypsy proposition. Our method of stealing grub, when at sea, we thought to be very original, but we discovered later that it was a regular old "con" game, so old and universally practiced that it's a wonder any sea cook ever fell for it. It can be done only once, however, so it is practicable on none but the shortest voyages, such as crossing the Channel. On the way from Dover to Calais, two of the boys—we were going steerage—lured the cook away from his galley and I went in and "pinched" the plum duff, which was nothing more nor less than a big roll of pudding done up in a sack. I had to stick it down under my coat and, believe me, it was hot enough to make a mustard platter feel like a piece of ice!

On landing in France, we walked to Rouen, where we got a job carrying lumber and water for just enough to pay for our room. Seeing that we had to eat, and as our original store of money was likely to be depleted through idleness, we next footed it to Paris and got a job loading wooden pavement blocks on barges. The weather was very hot and we used to go stripped to the waist, but we liked the adventure of it.

Three years ago, I got the *wanderlust* so bad that I couldn't stand it any longer, so I just "beat it." I took a steamer to Cuba and walked across the island from Havana to Batabano, about one hundred and twenty miles. I took a cow-puncher with me, who had chanced to come East for the first time in his life to visit relatives. In fact, he'd never been off the range before. I had known him there as a very retiring fellow, a man who never exploited his views, and while he was a very companionable, lovable chap, I'd never put him down as knowing very much except about cattle.

But when we started to walk down there in that tropical country, he opened up like a flower, if I may use a metaphor. The novelty of the sea voyage and the strange country stimulated him, loosed his tongue, and I found that he knew a lot about plants, trees, insects, in short, the fauna and flora of Cuba; and also that he was deeply read in international affairs as well as in American politics and economics.

Later, I walked all by myself across Yucatan.

About three months ago a friend and I broke away from the routine of screen business in Los Angeles and, taking a pack mule, tramped to Hallett's Peak, then dropped down into Middle Park and crossed the Great Divide. Then, recrossing the Divide, we made our way into the Medicine Bow range in Wyoming. It was wonderful—the birds, the animals, and everything, right close to nature. Such an experience gives a man a mental and moral house-cleaning.

I have always had a longing to walk from Barcelona, Spain, to Madrid. They say it's a wonderful trip, that few strangers make it, that there are many old things and customs and little communities of primitive peoples that have never been written about. You could get a thrill a minute on a trip like that!

I like the moving picture business much more than the legitimate. Apart from one's love of nature and for outdoor work, it gives you an outlet for your ingenuity. You are not repressed as you would be on the regular stage.

The managers used to be afraid of stunts on the stage until Brady rather dubiously decided to put a fight scene into "Hawthorne of the U.S.A." It went all right, but an actor can't put up as good a fight every performance of a play as he can for the movies, where he can afford to take a chance on being laid up for a while.

The climbing of buildings is interesting. I never look at a structure without figuring out how I could climb up the side of it. This practice is not from any burglarious proclivities, mind you, but just because it's part of my business.

You remember in "Les Miserables" how that phenomenon of physical strength, Jean Valjean, by sheer muscular force worked his way up an angle formed by two brick walls and escaped? That is the greatest stunt ever described.

A lthough my father was a New Hampshire man and my mother a Virginian, where riding is accepted as a matter of course, and I was born in Colorado, I had never ridden one of those wonderful creations of the devil known as a "bucking broncho" until I began picture work in California. To stick onto one of those creatures, one must be a combination of sailor, bareback rider, freight brakeman, and lots of other things, so multifarious and unexpected are his motions. He can move in more acute angles than any other beast in the world.

A good "outlaw" will go two and a half or three feet into the air and then land stiff-legged, and you must be off your saddle just enough to take the jolt. When he jumps, he'll throw his head back and knock you over the other end of him if you don't look out. Or he pitches and throws you over his head. Or, while in the air, he humps his body up round and rolls from side to side with the most awful "seasicky" motion. You might hang on if you could grip the pommel of the saddle like grim death and think of nothing else, or if you were permitted to keep both feet in the stirrups. But that wouldn't be ethical. You have one foot in the stirrup and with your free foot you keep scratching your mount's ribs with the spur. At the same time you fan his ears with your sombrero with one hand and, with the other gripping the rein, you try to hold his head up.

I was pretty well discouraged by my semi-aeronautical broncho-busting attempts when Jim Kidd, who later proved to be guide, philosopher, and friend, came along and took me in hand. Kidd was a remarkable type of plainsman and cow-puncher. He was quite as interesting a character as Roosevelt—in fact, he was much like the Colonel in many respects.

Kidd was quite a philosopher, and I would as soon consult him as read Herbert Spencer. He was the philosophy of life generally. He taught himself never to worry. "Life at its best," he used to say, "is simply a different way of doing things." And another, "We have wonderful houses here, but the ground I sleep on is both enough and good enough for me." Once he said, "I take every man to be a gentleman until he proves himself otherwise." Or, if he should meet a man and there would be a discussion, he would say, "You are a gentleman. Now, show me."

We were riding on the Mojave Desert one day and I said, "How do you like it out here, Jim?"

"It don't make much difference where you are, it's who's with you," was his answer. And how true that is!

Jim never could stand for the ill-treatment of a horse. I heard him say once to an Indian who was abusing his broncho, "If you don't get off that horse, I'll bust you high, wide, and handsome!"

And the Indian *got*, too!

By the way, I got a good many titles for "The Americano" from just such remarks of Kidd's.

A curious thing about this man was, he was very forgiving. He had a quick temper, but a most remarkable sense of justice. He would always find a good excuse for someone who had offended him. He used to say, "Give me two hours and I'll find the right solution!" He had learned his philosophy on the round-up.

Jim never was a heavy drinker except toward the end, and then bad health drove him for consolation and relief to John Barleycorn. Previous to that he used only to drink for companionship.

He took a fancy to me because I was a tenderfoot. I had a great affection for the old man. He was getting on toward seventy and I used to have to look after him.

One night toward "the end," he came to me and said very confidentially, "Doug, if you want anybody killed let me know!"

I told him that I didn't have any work of that kind laid out or in contemplation at the moment, and he went away. But the next day he wrote me a letter saying, "I was drunk last night and maybe I meant what I said and maybe I didn't—but I guess I did. But I just wanted you to know I would do anything in the world for you."

Jim's memory used to betray him at times when he was too deeply in his cups. He gave his horse to me one day, and then went and sold the same animal to somebody else. As a matter of fact, I owned everything Jim had. He gave me his saddle and chaps, but these were buried with him when he died. I still have his hat.

K idd was sixty-seven when he died, but he was as spry as a boy. And he didn't know what fear was. Eight months ago he played for me in a picture. He rode right into the midst of a fight, and he was supposed to be killed, falling off his horse right in the mix-up of stampeding horses and fighting men!

We sent Kidd back to Wyoming, his beloved state, to be buried. Two hundred and fifty cow-punchers in full regalia rode down to the depot to "see Jim off." And there was his horse with the empty saddle reversed. It was a very impressive sight, that was!

Working in moving pictures has other compensations than giving the actor an opportunity to exercise his gifts. The greatest thing about pictures is the friends he makes. People recognize him wherever they see him and don't hesitate to come up and grab his hand and call him by his first name wherever they happen to see him. The chances are that if the movie actor should go down to the bottom of the sea, some fish would recognize him at the "pier" or at the "Park."

I get all sorts of letters from all over the world. Some of them are very interesting. For instance, here's a sample: "My dear Doug: If you will send me a picture of yourself, I will send you a picture of my pet rat."

It gives you a weird feeling, and a darn good one, too, to get letters from Russia and other parts of the world you have never visited, letters of gratitude from some poor devils that have seen your pictures. Imagine how I felt when I received a notification from Wales that I was the winner in a popularity contest in Cardiff!

But, best of all, in moving picture work is the consciousness of having given an economic quality to the happiness you impart to millions of people. For while the "tired business man" goes to the movies to get a laugh, he builds better than he knows. He not only gets his laugh, but he exercises the emotional side of him, irons out his emotions, so to speak. By so doing he is better prepared to meet life's battles. That's a feature that we haven't sufficiently dwelt upon in our dissertations on what is called the "commercialized American," but it's very true and very important.

A man relaxes when he laughs, and relaxation means emotional strength. It isn't the laughter *per se* that gives us the strength, it's the exercise of the emotions.

This is clearly proved by the fact that we feel just as refreshed by a good cry as we do by a good laugh.

Some persons' emotional nature is so dried up that they can neither laugh nor cry. This was particularly demonstrated in "The Habit of Happiness." The picture shows the teaching of a lot of "bums" in the bread line how to laugh. In making this picture we went to one of the famous bread lines and got a lot of the most sorry, sordid subjects we could find, and took them to the studio. These men's lives had been so hard that they had forgotten how to laugh. It was a physical impossibility for them to do so. They had actually to be taught now.

Their sense of humor had been almost killed by their half-starved, half-frozen, always-hunting-grub-and-shelter, catlike existence.

Nothing but rotten stories amused them, only the drastic quality of the sordid would touch what might be called their risibilities. Their case was analogous to that of the fabled drunkard who could not be reached by anything short of kerosene or turpentine!

We paid these tramps money; we gave them baths; we filled their stomachs, made them practice laughing, and at the end of four days they were different men.

This was what emotional exercise did for them. And let me tell you right here, that it wasn't so much the money they needed as human association!

Laughter doesn't always mean the same thing. Some men laugh from the sheer delight of living. Others laugh at wit or humor or a good order. Others laugh at tales of treachery or cunning, where one man gets the better of another through meanness.

It's absurd to try to look into the future of the moving picture industry, because the future always moves along perfectly logical, but, to the human mind, unexpected lines. There's no telling what ramifications may flow from the moving picture craft.

Not long ago we thought that no subjects but those which lent themselves to the most vivid kind of pictorial exploitation could ever be used. But now we find, as we develop screen language, that we are bringing the high comedy, hitherto tabooed because of the importance of dialogue, into use.

In one of our pictures we have a scene where I sit at a table opposite a man for five minutes, and we do nothing but talk by gestures—the turning of a hand, the lifting of an eyebrow, the tense gaze, the act of half rising from a table in a threatening way, the clenching of the fist, the pointing to the door or the looking toward the window and taking out the watch to denote expectancy.

In fact, we are getting more and more to use the very gestures, grimaces, and the like that they use on the regular stage to accompany and emphasize spoken words, the kind of pantomime that the frequenter of the gallery sees and understands, when he can't hear the words.

There is now on foot a scheme to suggest sentiment or emotions by odors and perfumes. There is an odor for every emotion, if it could only be found out. A certain Italian is now working in Italy on a "symphony of odors." You know how you associate an odor with some place. Heliotrope, for instance, has a wonderful effect on me. Should a symphony of odors be scientifically developed, we may get as much from it as from sight. They will be able, in conjunction with what you see on the screen, to shoot out an odor into the auditorium which will produce the same effect as sad music, such as Beethoven used to play. Belasco tried it when he used incense in the "Darling of the Gods."

This piece ran in the July 1917 edition of **The American Magazine**. *We've also included on the next page a brief-but-memorable sidebar by Booth Tarkington which accompanied the original article.*

Booth Tarkington

Sends us this word about
Douglas Fairbanks

FAIRBANKS is a faun who has been to Sunday-school. He has a pagan body which yields instantly to any heathen or gypsy impulse—such as an impulse to balance a chair on its nose while hanging from the club chandelier by one of its knees—but he has a mind reliably furnished with a full set of morals and proprieties: he would be a sympathetic companion for anybody's aunt. I don't know his age; I think he hasn't any. Certainly he will never be older—unless quicksilver can get old.

Since he has gone into the movies, millions of people have been wondering why he wanted to waste his time running for the Vice-Presidency of the United States; and in vast tracts of the country Mr. Hughes lost votes because the people feared that if they elected him and his companion on the ticket, Fairbanks would seriously neglect the movies for four long years.

Few of us would care to do the things that Fairbanks likes to do. For my part, if I were fairly certain that I could sit on a fleck of soot 381 feet above the street on the façade of a skyscraper, I wouldn't do it. In fact, most people wouldn't do it, and their judgment in the matter is praiseworthy; but the world's gayety is considerably increased because there's one man who would do it, and does do it, and *likes* to do it!

Fairbanks would do that sort of thing if he had to pay for the privilege. If the movie people had really understood him they'd never have given him a salary; they'd have charged him a fixed sum every time he risked his neck on their property. Their films would have been just as popular—and think what they might have saved! But everybody's glad they didn't think of it, because everybody likes this national bit of property, called Fairbanks, so much.

—**Booth Tarkington**

WHY I WAS DISAPPOINTED
IN THE GRAND CANYON

By Douglas Fairbanks, Himself

I CAN define my disappointment in a sentence: I couldn't jump it. I had blandly believed, encouraged, I may add, in my belief by various moving-picture directors, that I could jump anything. Here, on the rim of the world, I met defeat. And I went down gladly. Impressions? Unconveyable. A very famous man has explained that. "When the Creator made the Grand Canyon," he said, "He failed to make a word to cover it." I am comforted by the thought that mine is not the least deficient vocabulary. As for my companion, Jones, it was quite different. When I asked him what he thought of it he replied: "The Canyon? Oh, the Canyon's all right, only my camera ain't big enough." It was a four-by-five camera. Truly, I felt for Jones.

TO MEET me at the Canyon, Jones drove all the way from Gas City, Indiana, in a green Ford with red wheels, taking pictures of prairie dogs, jack rabbits and sagebrush by the wayside. Nights he'd lock the steering gear so the front wheels wouldn't slew, curl up in the tonneau and "letter run," as he said. Thus he was able to make excellent time across the plains. Arriving at the rim of the abyss, Jones realized what he was up against with his four-by-five camera. The pictures he took for the folks back home had about the same relation to the Canyon that a photograph of the gravel bank in Gas City would have. So these are not Jones' pictures, but Mr. Warrington's, taken for Jones' sake, for without such evidence he could not prove that he was out there at all.

*This story is only two paragraphs of text, as it was primarily published as a photographic spread. You can see a few of these amazing photographs on the following pages, exactly as they appeared in the February 1918 issue of **Ladies Home Journal** magazine.*

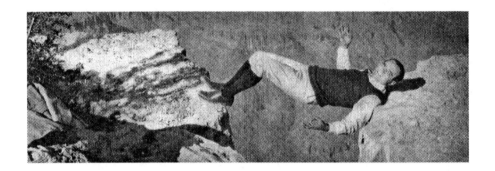

Jones Said: "If You Can't Jump It, Lie Across It." I Made the Attempt,
With This Result.

(Original photo caption by Douglas Fairbanks. Photograph by Charles Warrington)

Here I Feel Part Like the Colossus of Rhodes and
Part Like the Old Man of the Sea

(Original photo caption by Fairbanks. Photograph by Charles Warrington)

A Million Feet From the Top and the Same From the Bottom is the "Plateau."
I Call it a Bracket.

(Original photo caption by Fairbanks. Photograph by Charles Warrington)

All Words Failed Me, Except Those of the Cow-Puncher
Who Said "Golly, What a Gully!"

(Original photo caption by Fairbanks. Photograph by Charles Warrington)

THE LIBERTY LOAN DRIVE

Hollywood, Cal.

To my mind the Liberty Loan is nothing short of an inspiration in every way symbolic of our glorious nation. Every loyal American, from the small wage-earner to the wealthiest citizen, is today privileged as never before to do his bit in financing his country. What could promote a finer or more united spirit? I am proud of my privilege to invest, and when my country calls me I will be equally proud of my privilege to enlist.6

—Douglas Fairbanks

*This is a telegram sent to the **New York Times** by Douglas Fairbanks on June 2, 1918. While Fairbanks Sr. was never an enlisted soldier during World War I, he served his country by making short films in support of the war and touring the nation in a series of fund-raisers for the Liberty Loan Drive, the Canadian Victory Loan Drive and the Red Cross. He also frequently wrote of the Allied war effort in his news-paper and magazine articles. Doug's books **Laugh and Live** (1917) and **Making Life Worthwhile** (1918) were extremely popular titles amongst the boys fighting "over there" on the battlefields of Europe.*

Do you know a soldier boy in camp or going to the front? Send him a copy of

"LAUGH and LIVE"
By DOUGLAS FAIRBANKS

It will give him something to go by—something to cling to— something **to** *come back* **with.**

Put a copy in his "comfort box"— or mail direct

All Bookstores   **$1.00 Net**

BRITTON PUBLISHING CO., New York

Advertisement for the book **Laugh and Live**, August 11, 1917. Several versions of the ad were circulated in American newspapers at the time, suggesting the book as a perfect gift to our soldiers fighting WWI. And indeed, many "comfort boxes" contained a copy of **Laugh and Live**.

LISTEN MY CHILDREN AND YOU SHALL HEAR

BY DOUGLAS FAIRBANKS

You can promote success by being cheerful, the same as you can promote your pleasure by being successful. You can attack it from either angle.

Some of our big men take life too seriously. Abnormally developed people that attain the big heights are bound, as a rule, to neglect one side. If you ever develop your right arm, your left arm is bound to suffer. Get a sort of general medium of development. When a man becomes a wonderful something or other, or a great this and that, other things in his nature are bound to suffer by the law of average. The even tempered man, who is usually the well-set-up man, is not a specialist. When you begin to specialize or develop along one line, the law of average will come into play and something else will suffer. It is like the balance of the scales—as the scales go up on one side, they must go down on the other side.

Cheer should not be paramount in our nature, for then something else might suffer, although cheer might be applied to every sensation we have—cheerful charity or cheerful sympathy. You can add cheer to anything like salt and pepper. It may be just a means to other things. It is not a condition separate and apart. You set out to develop cheer and laughter along with the other things. If you develop grace in athletics you add attractiveness. When a boy in high school I went to Richard Mansfield and asked his advice. I told him I was in high school and wanted to be an actor. "You go home," he said. "Study dancing, fencing and languages—develop yourself."

"What has that to do with acting," I asked him.

"Acting is innate," he answered. "You can act or you cannot. But spend three or four years equipping yourself, so if you do happen to be successful and meet big men, you can meet them on your own ground. If you grow up and succeed at one thing you should develop all around so that you can take your place."

Mansfield was a very accomplished man. When he became the greatest American actor of his time, he was able to meet the musician as a musician, and talk his language and he could mingle with a great painter and understand him. He fitted into any walk of life. It was the same way with Irving. He was sufficiently developed to understand and sympathize with other great men in every walk of life.

Therefore you should equip yourself for success in every way. The inner accomplishments are just as necessary as the outward ones. The means of doing a certain thing is the development of all things in your brain, and this is just as essential to the successful person as to excel in his one line.

The smile, backed up by a sense of humor, is the most necessary condition of the brain. The brain requires laughter as much as the lungs require air. Allow your sense of humor to run round and consult with reason and the other cells of the brain, and you will find that you get much better results.

Everything in life is made up of positive and negative. Do not expect when you meet a strong man that he will be all positive. Everything has its negative quality.

A sense of humor is simply making light of things that are distasteful to you. All that people need to have is an objective which is fundamentally good, and nature will take care of the rest. If your objective tends toward self-indulgence, your life is wrong. Have your objective well defined and want it badly, and you will get it.

Meet your trouble with a smile. Grin and bear it. When you have a problem to meet, you don't need to set your jaws and grit your teeth and be unhappy. If you have any kind of problem to meet you can lighten your weight, brighten up, smile and get your results more effectively by the latter attitude, which is just as forceful. Lighten your manner and you will lighten yourself. There is just as much snap to a punch which is delivered in high spirits as one delivered in low spirits; in fact, more.

An endeavor to be successful is a very healthful way to succeed. Jack Johnson and Jim Corbett did not frown, they smiled; perhaps that is why they were champions. Look at Roosevelt—the most famous thing about him is his smile and his phrase, "De-lighted." His mouth is set in a smile, not in grim determination, but in cheerful determination. People don't like a grouch. They like cheerful things. Sunshine is always welcome.

If an individual will force himself to smile until ten o'clock in the morning, he will automatically smile the rest of the day. Cheerfulness is a training just like physical and other training.

The byword of "cheer" is the best you can wish everybody. To be cheerful it is necessary to be happy—one reflects on the other.

—Doug.

*This article was originally published during the first World War in the September 7, 1918 (Vol. 1, No. 6) edition of the **Arcadian Observer**, the official paper of the United States Army Balloon School in Arcadia, California.*

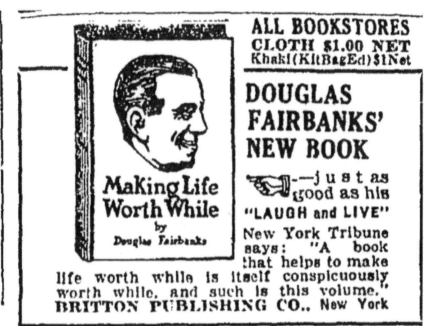

Advertisement for Fairbanks' second book, **Making Life Worthwhile**,
November 17, 1918.

DOUGLAS FAIRBANKS'
OWN
PAGE

I F YOU are familiar with baseball—and the chances are nine in ten that you
are—you know the meaning of the expression, "the breaks of the game."
Given two baseball teams of equal strength, victory will invariably perch on
the banner of the side which "gets the breaks."

It's much the same on the stage or in business. Many a good player has been
sedulously avoided by whatever fate it is that deals out fame, because the "breaks"
have been against him. Conversely, many a mediocre—or even worse—player
has tasted all the fruits of victory because he "got the breaks," as they say on the
diamond. But don't think I'm going to classify myself, because I'm not. Give it
any name you like—even modesty.

Just where I would have wound up had it not been for a strange quirk of fate,
of course no one can tell, but it was the misfortune of a fellow player that gave me
the big chance I was looking for. Perhaps it was an indiscretion rather than a misfortune. But whatever it was, the victim of the circumstance found himself in jail
on the day we were scheduled to treat the natives of Duluth, Minn., to a rendi-
tion of "Hamlet."

Now I'm not going to tell you how the star couldn't show up and I stepped
into the breach and soliloquoyed all over the stage to the thunderous applause of
the Northmen; that would be too conventional. Strangely enough I hadn't set my
sights that high. But I did want to play Laertes and my colleague having run afoul
of some offense which was the subject of a chapter of the Minnesota Penal code, I
played it that night.

Well to make a long story short, I played the part so well that it only took
about ten years more to become a star on Broadway, the ultimate goal of all who
choose the way of the footlights. Seriously, however, that was my chance and I
took full advantage of it. In succeeding articles I will tell more about the climb to
the top.

Perhaps the greatest pleasure I get out of my work for the screen is contained in my daily mail bag. And from time to time, I intend on this page to refer to some of the most interesting letters that come to me from all over the country—not only from this country, but from such far off places as Australia. By the way, I believe they are more enthusiastic over the screen in the Antipodes than they are in this country, proportionately speaking.

One of the most frequent questions I am asked to answer is that relating to success in athletics.

It may sound strange to some of those who have been following my work on the screen, but I was a failure as an athlete. In college at the Colorado School of Mines I did not excel in any particular branch of sports. I went in for nearly everything, but the student body never wrote or sang any songs about me. I never came up in the ninth with the score three to nothing against us, with three men on base and put the ball over the fence. I never even ran the length of the whole field with the pigskin and scored the winning touchdown with only fifteen seconds of play left.

Then when I went to Harvard later I was still active in athletics but while just about able to get by in most of the games, I never got the spotlight in any specific instances. It might have been different had I remained, but the call of the footlights was too insistent.

There is one rule which every athlete must follow to be successful. Be clean in mind and body. For a starter, I know of no better advice.

I am not much given to preaching, but if I ever took it up as a vocation, I would preach cleanliness first and most.

The boy who wishes to get to the front in athletics must adopt a program of mental and bodily cleanliness.

Perhaps the greatest foe to athletic success, among young college men is strong drink. Personally I have never tasted liquor of any sort.

It was my mother's influence that was responsible for that as I promised her when I was eight years old that I would never drink. I might state, parenthetically and without violating a confidence, that my family tree had several decorations consisting of ambitious men who had sought valiantly, if futilely, to decrease the visible supply of liquor. I do not wish to take a great amount of credit for my abstention. Really, more credit is due the person who has fallen under its influence and fought his way out; but I know that the keeping of this promise has had a powerful effect on my life and career.

*This brief excerpt from Doug's 1918 book **Making Life Worthwhile** was syndicated as a column to several local newspapers and national magazines. The Douglas Fairbanks Museum has one such magazine article in our collections, the name of which is unfortunately not recorded. The detached pages carry no identification stamp other than a date of Spring 1919. In addition to publishing the column written by Mr. Fairbanks above, the magazine also included a four-page "Photo Interview," included in it's hilarious entirety over the next few pages.*

A PHOTO INTERVIEW *with* DOUGLAS FAIRBANKS

By Alfred A. Cohn

Let's Go!

"Are you set, Al?" said Mr. Fairbanks.

"Yup!" answered Mr. Cohn.

"Aw right; start your pencil."

"I believe that the motion picture industry has a wonderful future. I like it particularly because it keeps oneout in the open."

"If it's all the same to you, let's stroll around the lot; I can talk better in motion. We won't waste any time going around to the stairs".

A Pair of Suspenders "As an art, the photoplay has not begun to come into its full fruition. More and more the public, now initiated into many of the mysteries of cameraland, demands not only artistic photography but suspense and surprise; and a good seasoning of comedy".

"Just drop easy-like. Nothing can happen that a bottle of arnica won't fix".

Look Out Below! "The chief difficulty these days is the lack of suitable stories, although half the world is writing so-called scenarios".

"Now let's hike over to the Subway".

5745 Minutes from Broadway "California offers exceptional opportunities to the producer of photoplays. (Los Angeles papers please copy.) Every conceivable locale in the world can be duplicated here, and so forth. We loll in Venetian gondolas or take the subway for Harlem, 3500 miles away".

Drawing by D. Fairbanks. "In this game of life the fortunate ride" (Hear! Hear!) "at the expense of the less fortunate. The big idea is to do it cheerfully no matter how humble the task".

Steady: On the Right! "What we, as a nation, need most these days, is more balance—more poise. We Americans are too susceptible to panic and hysteria, particularly in a time when absolute balance is required".

"Let's take a spin in the little old boat—got ninety out of her yesterday out in the country—and go for a swim up in my back yard. Got a lot more to tell you and a swim would put you in shape for it.".

They're Off at Hollywood! "Another great fault with us, as a people, is our insatiable demand for speed. We want it everywhere—we even dine too rapidly because of our fear that we will miss something somewhere. Why can't people take it easy? Speed merely serves to speed the end of existence. Funny I can't get more than 80 out of her today".

The Ole Swimmin' Hole. "What do I think of the future of the moving pictures? Well, I think none of us can visualize it. In a few years—as a matter of fact the industry is now merely in its infan—"

"Better look back and see if I didn't say that once before."

"According to the rules, it goes only once in an interview. Some pool, isn't it? Had it built to save beach trips".

At the End of the Rope

"Good cheer and real companionship do not come in bottles and the door to fame is never swung on double hinges."

"Gee, Billy Sunday couldn't do better than that, could he? And talking about Billy—"

A Sunday Stunt on Saturday

"The man with a message for the world will get it over if he is earnest and conscientious, and can impress his sincerity on those who listen."

"it's mighty handy to have a press agent and a valet around (standing, left to right) one can always be sure of their enthusiastic applause at the right time".

Another Interesting Point

"I aim to have some real purpose, some theme behind each photoplay I produce; not a lesson conveyed in some conventional way but with a coating of sugar as it were, over it."

"Come on over. These are only wooden spikes anyhow and couldn't hurt much".

Off (or over) To the Front

"There is a fallacious belief that pull is required to make a success on the shadow stage. That belief is rapidly being—"

"Don't holler or you'll drop the pencil. Beyond this shack lies Flanders".

In the Wake of the Boches

"With many who get up in the world, the big problem, though they do not realize it, is to get down again—down to the level of the man who views life—"

"Now don't get nervous. The bombardment is over and these Belgian buildings are sturdy affairs. It won't fall, unless I shake it".

The End of a Perfect Day

"As I was saying, when you fell, life is just a game of give and take and—"

"Call up the Receiving Hospital, Naka, after we slide him in, I want to go a few rounds with Spike".

An Interview With Charles Chaplin and Douglas Fairbanks

(When Charlie Chaplin, creator of ludicrous film divertissements that assuage the cares of a troubled world, was treated to a "pre-view" of Ray W. Frohman's interview with him for The (Los Angeles) Evening Herald—the first authentic interview Chaplin has granted for over two years, and the first dialogue between Chaplin and Doug Fairbanks ever recorded—Chaplin, the laughmaker, *LAUGHED* and said:

"This is the first artistic interview I've ever had.

"It is one of the very few articles ever written about me that really reveal me to the public."

Blushing over the praise of himself he had read, the comedian added that "perhaps the writer was a little too sympathetic!"

And then Charlie, who, as his "big brother" Doug says, "can't concentrate," pleaded to keep the "copy" "to read it again more leisurely so that I can enjoy it more.")

◆　　　◆　　　◆

If the KIDS could vote, CHARLIE CHAPLIN would be our next PRESIDENT!

And if it's true, as Doug Fairbanks told Charlie in my presence, that in Sweden and Denmark, too, they consider Charlie in a class by himself, he may yet be King of Scandinavia!

In fact, when the League of Nations gets to working and the Brotherhood of Man is a reality, my guess is that it's the internationally popular Charles Spencer Chaplin who'll be the first President of the World—in spite of his feet.

Even at RIVAL studios, publicity men paid to lie for Charlie's competitors—if he can be said to have any—say freely, "Nobody's ever had the vogue that Chaplin has."

The peerless Douglas Fairbanks himself says:

"There is only ONE king in pictures—Chaplin; and only ONE queen—Mary Pickford. The rest of us must be content to be pretty good and compete with *EACH OTHER!*"

No wonder my kneecaps vibrated as I chatted over an hour with Charlie Chaplin—and Doug Fairbanks, too, at the same time—out in darkest Hollywood.

There we were, all in the same small room for one admission: Charlie and Doug and I—the king of comedy, the nonpareil light comedian, and a dictographic nonentity—talking our heads off, or, rather, talking Charlie's head off!

Everybody knows Charlie joined Essanay in 1915, knows about his million-dollar contract with First National, and that he's now "on his own" and one of "The Big Four." Everybody's seen every Chaplin comedy from "The Bank," "A Night Out," "A Woman," "His New Job" and "Police" up through "A Dog's Life," "Shoulder Arms" and "Sunnyside."

In fact, since they say "Chaplin doesn't work" and call his producing concern out on La Brea "the century plant," we've all been content to go to see him, and him alone, over and over again in the same films!

So I didn't hash over with Charlie the well known facts of his pictorial biography.

Doug and Charlie, with an occasional interpolation from me, talked and talked of Charlie's views on art and books and plays, on beautiful women and sunsets, on the Grand Canyon and whether or not a desert is beautiful, and everything else from cabbages to kings, from "Hamlet" to Doug's new funny overcoat; and on Charlie's professional methods and unprofessional soul—for he has one—and what he says he's trying to do to pictures and is doing and is going to do.

And Eureka! Now I can tell the world for the first time WHY Doug smiles and smiles and smiles that famous smile of his!

It's BECAUSE HE HAS PRIVATE "PREVIEWS" OF UNRELEASED IMPROMPTU CHAPLIN COMEDIES, every time he and his friend get together.

For Charlie, I think most of us agree, on the screen is "the funniest man in the world."

And at times during our chat he was twice as funny as that!

And Doug—when he's "kidding" and playfully baiting Charlie and leading him on conversationally, or waxing Rabelaisian, or mimicking a noted English author for Charlie and then registering a lobe-to-lobe grin—is funnier than Charlie!

And I might have been funny myself, for I was weak and helpless from *laughter!*

Through the flimsy cheesecloth curtain of a window I saw for the first time—and recognized—the little smooth-shaven face of the off-screen Chaplin. It was thrust forward in a sort of cataleptic grin toward Doug, who was uttering one of his introductory "Do you know, Charlie's" in the deadly-serious resonant tones that he affects toward his little friend.

"Hah!" quoth I to myself, waxing Shakespearian, "I have thee on the hip"—and I was upon them.

It was the REAL Charlie Chaplin.

I do not mean the Chaplin you see on the screen, the last of the royal jesters, with all of us as his patrons, the beloved vagabond, who has been paid the sincerest flattery, that of imitation, by more people than any other man who ever lived—by little kids all over the globe, by folks at masquerades, by "would-bes" on "amateur nights," by "rival" screen "comedians," both Caucasian and Oriental.

That Charlie, with his most active flexible cane and his dogs, his oddest derby constantly being tipped to cops—until the psychological moment arrives—and to fair women, his trick moustache and his loose-fitting shapeless trousers, and the biggest feet in Filmland as well—that Charlie every man, woman and child under the stars knows.

He has probably been kicked and shot in the pants—on the screen—more than any other living man.

The camaraderie this humblest screen character displays toward policemen and burglars, until the moment arrives for him to destroy them—for he can pick up his feet quicker than any man in Shadowland—is world famous. A captivating smile, an artless blush—and then an agile hoof—is the way Chaplin on the silver sheet, broke in a saloon or restaurant, handles striking policemen before they strike.

And you are aware how chivalrous he is toward the fair sex; how his matchlike—not matchless—figure, and his inimitable—not immaculate—garb have captivated many a beautiful heroine.

He can get more fun out of stepping in a waste basket—but what's the use? You know him.

Let it suffice to say that Chaplin's smirks, shrugs and sucking together of his cheeks, his characteristic Chaplinesque gestures, his personal accoutrements and mannerisms are the most individual, distinctive on the shadow screen.

But those, as Doug opined to Charlie and me, are merely "the externals, the trappings" of his screen art.

"Our most subtle comedian," he has been called by the critic of an eastern magazine, the veteran of a million reviews.

"Vulgar," say some folks who have seen Charlie spout food on the screen amidst the medley of mock romance, mock tragedy, mock adoration, mock courtesy that he "spills" in the comedies he ORIGINATES.

But no "highbrow" has ever been able to sit through a Chaplin comedy without bursting involuntarily into spontaneous "Hah hahs!" right out loud; and cultured, intellectual college professors—wasn't Professor Stockton Axson, brother-in-law of President Wilson, one of them!—have publicly proclaimed him an ARTIST.

However, the Chaplin I talked with, as I said, was not the screen Chaplin.

Neither was he the make-believe-real Chaplin who USED to talk to interviewers before he made all the money he wants and decided that he didn't need any publicity. That Chaplin, I have one of his intimates' word for it, used to turn on the phonograph in his room and chat engagingly, ALWAYS CAMOUFLAGING HIS REAL SELF.

The Charlie Chaplin who talked to me is the real, honest-to-goodness, personal, unprofessional, actual Charlie Chaplin, I give you my word for it. He was as artless, as "off his guard" as a three years' child who doesn't know the camera's there when you snapshot him.

Charlie, you know, when it comes to being interviewed—which he hasn't permitted for YEARS—is what Fielding's eighteenth century bailiffs would have called "a shy cock."

When famous newspapermen representing papers from all over the country with President Wilson's party called on him, Charlie stuck his head in the door, took one look, said he "had to have some air," and "ditched" them all—went out for an auto ride!

When his own casting director, Edward Biby pleaded with him for an HOUR A MONTH for nation-wide magazine interviews, saying it would be worth a million dollars to Chaplin, Charlie merely waved a hand airily and said: "Oh, no, that's all right, that's all right!"

But I found him a delightfully interesting conversationalist, a sensitive little aesthete who's well-read and well versed in art, a cultured little chap with artistic sensibilities, a rather deep thinker—though I won't vouch for the soundness of his theories—and withal a somewhat shifty or shifting one.

Where the "shifts" came in, the mental sidestepping from one "highbrow" subject to another or from high to low, the "sacheting" to use a dancing term, of the gray matter in instinctive—and courteous—reaction to the conversation of others, were with Doug Fairbanks.

For when talking with Charlie, the jovial "Smiling Doug" Fairbanks is not merely magnetic—he is HYPNOTIC! He holds his friend Charlie in the hollow of his hand.

"I've been dreaming of London," mused Charlie, who was born near there only 31 short years ago and was in vaudeville there—for he became identified with the theater when he was seven years old. "I tried to show it to someone, but there was always fog or night or something—I couldn't show its beauties. But I would say 'WAIT—you'll see it.'"

Charlie said he hasn't been back in dear old Lunnon since he attracted favorable notice in "A Night in an English Music Hall," as the lead in which he came to the United States before he made his picture debut, some years ago.

But, pause! I didn't tell you how the real Charlie looks!

He's a slender sapling, this artist in the neat gray-checkered suit and black knitted tie and yellow-tinted pleated shirt who lolled in a Morris chair chatting so naturally and vivaciously. He has curly black hair with touches of gray—a young man's gray—at the temples, and vivid blue eyes, and sensitive features like the person of high-strung temperament that he is.

When he shows his perfect teeth in a grin—a charmed, fascinated, hypnotized grin—at his master, Doug, he has Lewis Carroll's Cheshire cat "backed off the boards."

At times when his eyes shine and his face glows as he gets talking of his professional or aesthetic enthusiasms, Charlie becomes almost beautiful.

And when he gets really "worked up," his disreputable LITTLE black shoes with the grayish tops twist, and his supple figure writhes, as his right hand helps him to express himself by graceful, powerful gestures.

"I became a star when I'd been at Keystone SIX MONTHS," said Charlie in response to my question. "I was there about a year. No, that's not the world's record—with some people it takes only one picture. Look at the way Betty Compson's salary jumped after her work in 'The Miracle Man.'"

"Did I have 'awful struggles,' or fights with bosses to MAKE them star me? My struggles were over before I went into pictures."

"After one picture the public fell on its face and worshipped him," said Doug. "I'm an admirer of yours, Charlie, even if you are a friend. And when I see you on the screen there's something goes from you to me, I feel an interchange.

"It isn't what he DOES, or even how he does it, that makes you laugh," "enthused" Doug to me. "When you watch his pictures it's the human dynamo WITHIN that you see. And evidently what he's giving us is what the public wants."

"What I put into my pictures is what I WANT to do," supplemented Charlie.

"Before I went into pictures, I felt repressed, I wasn't in my proper sphere. Now for the first time I'm doing what I want to do.

"I get a feeling, from a play or somewhere, and then THINK OUT WHAT I WANT TO DO."

Sometimes, say folks at his studio, where his own people never dare disturb him when he's "on the set" or on the job mentally, Charlie sits for as long as eight hours in solitude thinking up something the world—for his audiences are numbered by the hundred million—hasn't laughed at!

"I got a feeling from reading Thomas Burke's 'Limehouse Nights,'" continued Charlie, "and the result was 'A Dog's Life'—working it right out, going through natural experiences and having the consequent reactions. It is a translation, though not in Burke's language or style, of course.

"There is beauty in the slums!—for those who can see it despite the dirt and sordidness. There are people reacting toward one another there—there is LIFE, and that's the whole thing!

"Look at Rabelais. Vileness? That's only his SUBJECTS, BUT—!

"Writers have no STANDARDS of beauty. What IS beauty? It is indefinable!

"Beauty is all WITHIN," continued Charlie after Doug quoted "Hamlet" by the yard. "I DON'T THINK ANYONE HAS EVER PAINTED A BEAUTI-FUL WOMAN!"

"Artists today put on the canvas a 'Follies' type—which people call beautiful. That sort of beauty is merely external. Look at the old masters, such as Van Dyke, and you see old women with their faces screwed up with wrinkles. It's the beauty that's WITHIN that counts."

When Doug called him an admirer of Basil King's novels, Charlie did not dissent; and when Mark Twain was mentioned Charlie said: "Ah, now you're getting me back on my favorite topic.

"I've been reading Waldo Frank's book of essays, 'Our America,'" continued Charlie. "He is DEEP! You think when you start out it's the ordinary fervor, but when you get into it—! And I caught something of myself in what he wrote about me."

"Me, too," said Charlie, showing his dimples in a smile of assent, when Doug remarked that he thinks the mouth is the most expressive feature—though Charlie said he's seen some women with small mouths who were uglier than other women with large mouths.

When Doug said to him: "You are not responsible for what you are able to do," meaning that Charlie's ability to produce mirth-provoking comedy is God-given, Charlie modestly remained silent, making a gesture of instant, impersonal agreement.

Dimpling, he admitted that he "hates it more than anything else when they call me sentimental." Whether he meant in real life or reel life will ever remain an unsolved mystery.

We talked of sciences. "A scientist must be a lover of life," said Charlie.

Do you know that Chaplin has none of his excruciatingly funny stunts worked out on paper in advance, nor even the plot of his comedies prepared in "script"? He admitted it.

"He takes an idea, a theme, and works it out by himself as he goes along," said his admirer, Doug, to his face, uncontradicted. "He's a remnant of an aristocrat going through all those adventures. Reel after reel WITHOUT SUBTITLES—ACTION!"

"You are more HEART," returned Charlie, regarding Doug's screen work.

And then Charlie sprung NEWS of a new departure in Chaplin comedies! Said he:

"In the one I'm making now there's a whole reel of drama before I appear. I've got pathos, human interest, tragedy, humor—we've had that before—EVERYTHING in it! Yet it is all pertinent, constructive of the plot. It's a comedy DRAMA. That's what I'm going to do from now on.

"Edna (Edna Purviance, his leading lady) is an OPERA SINGER in this one! I didn't have her commit suicide."

It was a soul-wrenching effort NOT to call him "Charlie" but—

"Mister Chaplin," I asked, "isn't it a terrific constraint for a sensitive man of artistic sensibilities and tastes like you to play a vagabond, a TRAMP?"

At that, Doug Fairbanks exploded:

"Why, he's naturally a BUM!" said Doug, uncontradicted by the smiling Charlie. "When he has a clean collar on it's Tom Harrington (Charlie's secretary) who's responsible!"

Entirely aside from his alleged bumminess, "Spencer," as Doug called him once, fervently declared that he LIKES the smell of idoform—"the hospital smell," as it is popularly known.

He averred that the reason why people aren't particularly fond of the fragrance of the skunk is simply because their ancestors for generations haven't liked skunks, and they think of the odor that's going to get on them.

"You," he added, turning to Doug, "are particularly sensitive of odors."

But we were getting quite Rabelaisian, weren't we! Perhaps I'd better tell you at once that Charlie also talked familiarly of Bill Sikes and Nancy, and thinks that "Los Angeles will eventually be a great artistic center."

And ONCE Charlie's eyes blurred.

There were tears in them.

The face of the man who, say some who know him, works not for money but as a creative artist, and plans to retire from money-making screen work in about five years, trembled with silent emotion—whether modest shame or gratefulness, I know not.

It was when Doug quoted someone as saying that people regard Charlie as the one and ONLY, "than whom" there is no one like.

Something about that tribute touched the droll comedian's heart.

PRAISE OF CHAPLIN MADE CHARLIE WEEP!

CHARLIE CHAPLIN became, for that moment, a TRAGEDIAN!

*This rare interview with Douglas Fairbanks and Charles Chaplin originally appeared December 2, 1919 in the **Los Angeles Herald**. Journalist Ray W. Frohman managed to capture the real essence of both men in a relaxed, informal interview environment, which is part of what makes this story so engaging. The quotations are remarkably accurate, a rarity in the days before portable tape recorders when most journalists were armed only with a notepad. The fact that this interview was recorded to a Dictograph ensured that every word was printed exactly as spoken.*

Douglas Fairbanks

(Letterhead)

Dear Rupert:

Thanks for the good words. They count a lot because you say 'em.

Come to see us. You know well I'd be down to see you if I were not a hundred percent submerged in the finishing of this picture.

My finger is still out of commission, which accounts for the mechanics of this note.

Mary joins me in appreciation of your good wishes.

As always,

Doug
(Signature)

April sixteenth,
Nineteen twenty.

*The addressee of this informal letter is unknown, but "Rupert" was obviously a close friend who wrote to congratulate Fairbanks on his recent wedding. (Mary Pickford and Douglas Fairbanks were married on March 28, 1920) The casual tone of this letter feels more like a conversation; Fairbanks apologizes because the note is typed and not written by hand, blaming a broken finger. (Doug tells the whole story in **The Big Adventure**.) The film he mentions making in the letter above was, incidentally, **The Mollycoddle.***

Oh What A Pal Was Mary

By Douglas Fairbanks

Mary of mine, Mary of mine,
Bright shining star in the movies,
Shines every day, lives down the way,
Where I do the movie maneuvers.
At Reno, of course, she got a divorce,
That's why I love her so.

First Chorus.

Oh, what a pal was Mary
Oh what a gal was she,
Her name once was Moore
But its Moore no more,
Since Reno gave her to me.
Pride of my life is Mary,
We honeymooned o'er the brine,
I was right in the whirl
With lords, dukes and earls,
And Mary, old pal of mine.

Mary of mine, Mary of mine,
Whom I never played with in childhood
In the movies it seems
That she is a dream

That never run wild in the Wildwood,
But she gets the cash
And we cut a dash and
That's why I love her so.

Second Chorus:

Oh what a pal was Mary
Oh what a gal is she
She played in the pictures as Pickford and Moore
But now she plays Fairbanks with me,
Pride of my heart is Mary,
While my arm round her waist entwine,
She don't need the mon,
What we need is a son,
Mary old pal of mine.

*Fairbanks wrote songs, too—usually humorous little ditties like this one, published in **The Wandering Minstrels Songbook** in 1920. His recent marriage to Mary Pickford (and their respective divorces) was then controversial front-page news and a subject ripe for the comedic plucking. He also has a little fun with Mary's former husband, actor Owen Moore.*

One Reel of Autobiography

By Douglas Fairbanks

Sometimes I wonder whether, if you could sneak up on one of the men who are held up before the eyes of the world as successful businessmen, scientists, artists or what not, you would not discover that beneath the outward mask of success he wears a surprisingly disgruntled and twisted look; whether he might not be found dreaming disconsolately, like anyone else, of what might have been, painfully exhuming old aspirations which he had one by one sentenced to death, wondering if there is any market where one may barter fame for a good digestion and turn bank balances into a recipe for happiness.

This is no doubt a melancholy thought, and it should be, for it is the preface to a melancholy story. There are times, I may as well confess, when I have thought of myself as a success. It is a bit of egotism for which an actor with any kind of a following may be pardoned, for he is particularly responsive to what the public thinks and readily falls into the habit of taking himself at their valuation. When millions of people insist that you are great stuff as an actor, it is sometimes difficult not to add one more to the circle of your admirers and include yourself. I know of no subject on which a man stands so ready to be convinced as this—on which he receives arguments with such an open mind and such a disposition to admit that, after all, they may be right.

But just as I have almost convinced myself and decided to accept the flattering verdict of my friends, the sinister truth breaks in and spoils the picture—the truth that, measured by even the most generous standards of success, I must be classed as a terrific and unquestionable failure, if this is a source of any satisfaction to the reader.

And I am sure it is, for if the reader will indulge himself in a moment's honesty, as I am trying to do, he will be forced to admit that nothing gives him quite the same acute, if secret, sense of satisfaction as to hear of the adversity and misfortune of someone else. It gives him very little pleasure indeed to read that Mr. So-and-So was a bank president at the tender age of thirty, with an income beyond all the dreams of avarice, or that Mr. What's-His-Name rose brilliantly to the peak of his profession while fumbling with his first moustache. When he considers that at the same age he is lucky if he can look the landlord in the face and buy his wife a spring hat, he feels like going down to the river brink and ending it all then and there. What he wants to read about is someone who is worse off and harder up than he is, whose life is an unbroken chain of disappointments and failures. As he regards this poor wretch stumbling blindly and unsuccessfully through life, his pulses begin to quicken, something like a glow of satisfaction steals over him, and he decides that the world, after all, is not such an over-rated place to live in. If I were a magazine editor, and wanted to gain the real interest and approval of my readers, I would publish nothing but stories of failure.

But this is not an explanation of why I am writing about my own failure. It is the sheer novelty of telling the truth about myself that has appealed to me.

Perhaps the reader can stand about one reel of concentrated autobiography in which I explain myself. I will promise not to take him back to early life on an Ohio farm or struggling youth in a dingy boarding house on the East Side of New York. The dismal drama begins, as a matter of fact, on a sunny June day in a New York club some years ago. If I hadn't made the colossal blunder of eating lunch at that club, there would be—as the fiction writers say—no story.

It so happened that I had lunch on that fatal day with a fellow actor who had a great reputation as a wit. He had just heard a new one which, as he told it, struck me as tremendously funny. It was not one of those stories which cause one brief explosion of laughter and are promptly forgotten when someone else says: "That reminds me-" It was the kind of story that keeps coming back to you with some lingering phrase long after you have dismissed it and, with a kind of cumulative force, seems funnier every time you think of it.

I went to the midweek matinée performance of "All for a Girl"—one of the first plays in which I had been starred—chuckling over this story. I ought to explain that I had reached a point in my career when it seemed that my ambitions might soon be realized. My training had all been in classic and serious roles. My father was a Shakespearian scholar of some note, and to our home in Denver there came at one time or another almost all the great actors of the period—Mansfield, Booth, Barrett, Robson, and many others. It was under the influence of these men and my early Shakespearian schooling that my ambitions took a definite direction. My first engagement was with Frederick Warde's company of Shakespearian players. Since that time I had been diverted to comedy roles, but I felt that this diversion was only temporary, and I was merely waiting for an opportunity to resume more serious parts.

My First Step Aside

As I say, I strolled over to the theatre on this bright June afternoon, never dreaming that this silly story which caused me so much amusement was to wreck all these fine plans and completely ruin me. They say that in everyone's life there comes one important turning point. Well, this was the turning point in mine.

Somewhere along in the second act the one really serious and dramatic moment in this play occurs, and I was naturally expected to maintain a grave demeanor. There was absolutely nothing to laugh at. But at precisely this moment that accursed story, which I thought I had successfully banished, leaped back into my mind with sudden perversity and seemed twice as funny as it had before. My face broke out into a broad grin—not a stage smile at all, not a mere mechanical registry of mirth, but a genuine convulsion which spread itself wantonly over my whole face. I felt terribly about it, but I couldn't help it. The more I tried to control myself the worse I got. I was sure that I had ruined the play. It had been going badly enough, anyway, playing to smaller and smaller houses, and so close to the margin of complete failure that only a little shove was necessary to send it over. I knew I had given it this shove. When I walked off the stage at the end of the performance I was all ready to be told what several people thought of me. I braced myself for the ordeal, but it didn't come.

You can believe it or not, but I was received with open arms and congratulated. "Great stuff!" everybody told me. "It's marvelous how you did it!" When I came to I discovered that I had broken all amateur and professional records for smiling. Mr. William Brady, who was producing the show, was just as bad as the others. He wanted to know why I had been holding back on him and concealing this marvelous smile until it was too late to do the drooping fortunes of the play any good. Advertisements were promptly prepared counseling the public to *Come and See the Famous Fairbanks Smile.* I now think that the public response to this appeal represented correctly the proper valuation of the smile. It brought in box-office receipts of thirty-seven dollars and fifty cents, and shortly after this the play failed and was withdrawn.

But the harm was already done. Up to the time of this unfortunate matinée performance I had conceived myself to be a fairly serious-minded person and had never once fancied myself particularly as a smiler. I had never supposed that my smile was any different from anybody else's. But a conspiracy in which the public maliciously took part was organized to ruin me. Friends told me my smile was immense. Dramatic critics spoke of it warmly and analyzed it carefully as if smiling were an art which I had personally invented.

Now, I was at that time young and impressionable, and this furor which I had caused by a purely inadvertent and accidental smile was too much for me. The smile, if I may so describe it, went to my head. I began to take myself seriously as a smiler. I began practicing it before a mirror to see if my face was all that it was cracked up to be. I enlarged it and perfected it until I could have got a job anywhere as an advertisement of a tooth paste. I admitted freely that when it came to the matter of smiling I could give anyone else a couple of teeth and win, going away. I smiled with Tom Wise in "The Gentleman from Mississippi," in "The Cub," and half a dozen other plays and through twenty-one screen productions before the terrible truth burst upon me.

I had gone too far! I could not stop smiling! This constant misuse of the facial muscles had grown beyond all control. No effort of the will could restore my face to its natural expression—it was practically frozen into a permanent grin. I was sentenced to go through life, for all I could see, grinning like a madman, and nothing could stop it. The most melancholy thoughts, the most serious situations were without the slightest effect.

Woes of a Warped Face

I can never forget an afternoon on Broadway when my affliction was in its most acute stage. I met a fellow actor coming up the street with a mourning band on his arm and a generally grief-stricken look on his face—a man who up to that moment had been one of my best friends. In answer to my query he told me sadly that he had just lost a member of his family. I went through a moment of terrible anguish, for I knew what was coming. I made a superhuman effort to control myself, but I knew in my heart it was hopeless. I felt a premonitory twitching on the overworked muscles around my mouth and knew that I was lost—that nothing in this world or the next could prevent the fatal convulsion.

"Ha-ha!" I shouted, fairly bursting with laughter. "You don't say so." I still remember most painfully the shocked and bewildered look in his eyes as he turned away and crossed me forever off the tablet of his friendship, although I think it dawned upon him that something was wrong with me and that I was more to be pitied than censured.

There were countless other like instances which the reader must really excuse me from relating.

Some time I hope to meet one of those cheerful idiots who write songs and poems about driving away care with a smile—and when I do I won't answer for the consequences. One of us will be carried way on a litter. I have no doubt that a beaming smile is all right on occasion, that it may even add to the gayety of the party and take rank with some of the other social graces, but when it comes to being perpetually harnessed to one of them, to going around with a warped face, showing your teeth at other people's troubles and laughing at grief—it is an unspeakable affliction. Imagine, if you can, going through life without any serious relief whatever.

Still, I have only hinted at the real tragedy. I believe that if I had taken some heroic remedy during this early phase of the illness I might have been cured. During the first years it might have been possible to restore my face to normalcy.

But no one would permit this for a moment. When I came to the full realization of what this smile had done to me—how it had wrecked the serious career which I had planned and played havoc with all my real ambitions—when I wanted to attempt a different sort of part, which would give my face a rest and give me an opportunity to be serious again, friends, producers and associates laughed at me. I might not be much of an actor, they as much as hinted, but as a smiler I was a knockout. The public, I was told, wanted to see me go on smiling, and I must do it however gloomy it made me feel. I do not know that I can seriously blame the public for their unconscious cruelty, for it was something I had started myself. So the ghastly thing went on. I kept on smiling. Measured by film length, I have smiled over twenty miles. And I feel as if I had smiled twenty thousand.

Do it Again, Mister

Some deep thinker has said that troubles never come singly. I am quite ready to endorse this discovery as genuine. If anything further was needed to complete my alienation from the career which I had planned, to send all my early hopes and dreams of a serious success scurrying into the offing, it was another innocent diversion which I introduced into my pictures without any suspicion of the consequences. It was not unpremeditated and accidental, like the smile, but contained a serious and sound idea back of it. I am speaking of my "athletic" stunts. When I first started these I had not the slightest ambition to win fame as an acrobat. I thought I was using a rather obvious, perhaps crude, form of symbolism, but apparently I had a complete monopoly of this idea—no one else guessed it. In my efforts to portray the type of American boy about town, I was trying to catch the real spirit of youth as I conceived it to be; the spirit that takes short cuts and dashes impetuously at what it wants, that doesn't take the time to walk around obstacles but hurdles them—the fine, restless, impatient, conquering spirit of youth that scales whatever hazards are in its way, and rejoices in the fight.

To represent this on the screen I had to rely mostly upon a physical method. I had to indicate as well as I could a mental attitude by a physical one. I did not mean for a minute to develop the idea that all my heroes were professional gymnasts who spent the greater part of their time dangling from chandeliers and jumping from roof tops. It was not bodily agility, but litheness and exuberance of spirit that I wanted to indicate. It was not always easy to show them jumping over mental obstacles, but it was comparatively simple to show them surmounting physical ones.

But I am afraid that this pretty philosophy miscarried somewhere. It is probably too great a jump from philosophy to acrobatics. If I were suspected of having a real idea back of all this gymnastic exercise and boisterous behaviour, it was that I wanted to show off, or needed exercise, or something of the sort. The fact was that no-one cared why I was doing those stunts; but they liked to see them done. If I leaped upstairs via the balcony instead of going up the usual way, the least worry anyone had was why I was doing it. What people wanted was to see me jump up to the higher balcony.

My Dawn of Hope

Again I weakened. I found that I had once more started something I couldn't stop. If the public wanted acrobatics, I decided that I would give them what they wanted. I would show them what I really could do if I tried. I quite forgot, myself, why I had started all these tricks. They began to possess me, almost as completely as the smile. No one thought of presenting a play to me that did not contain new and varied opportunities for me to be "athletic". I am only a fair athlete, but I am carefully trained and have some specialties that I can probably do as well as anyone. I did them and invented new ones. I romped, jumped and skylarked through one play after another.

Perhaps the reader can begin to perceive the tragedy in all this. It really is not pleasant to realize that you have jumped and smiled yourself out of a serious career, that you began with serious intentions of becoming an actor and that some perverse fate has turned you into a smiler and an acrobat. It is not a thought which exactly leads one to review his life with complacency and approval.

I probably could not speak of this matter as calmly as I do were it not that I am now almost confident that this gruesome chapter of my life is finished. The smile has at least partially relaxed its merciless grip, and there is a fair prospect that I can now go through life in just as mournful a fashion as I like. The gymnastic spell has left me too, and I am free. I hesitate to recount how it happened, for fear that the reader will think I am fooling. But it is too serious a matter to fool about.

Anyone who has seen "The Mollycoddle" or "The Nut" must have noticed that something strange has happened. In "The Mollycoddle" the smiles are only occasional and sustained for but a brief period of time, and in "The Nut" they have disappeared almost altogether, like the last few flickers of a lamp that is going out. In the play which I am now producing, "The Three Musketeers", there is hardly a smile. D'Artagnan—thank Heaven—is not a smiling person. He takes himself and the world seriously. When he does smile, it is not a polite and affable expansion of the features, but a snarling, warriorlike affair—like the smile on the face of a prize fighter who has just knocked out his opponent.

This, briefly and without any decoration of the facts, is how it happened: Not long ago I engaged a very solemn-looking director who, judging from all appearances, had never smiled in his life. His face was positively cavernous in its gloom. It was a great pleasure for me to look upon this solemn man, although the pleasure was not unmixed with envy. I felt that I would have given almost anything I possessed to change expressions with him.

During the long months which it takes to prepare a picture it was this man's duty to watch me faithfully, study my expression, and guide me to the best of his ability. He had to look at me, poor fellow, for at least four or five hours every day. But I could see that after a few weeks his work was beginning to tell on him. Some subtle change was taking place. His face lost by degrees a little of its grimness, and even a ghost of a smile now and then flickered across it. He didn't seem to be smiling at anything in particular, but in a forced and distracted way, as if it pained and distressed him. Once I caught him smiling broadly when an overhead light crashed to the floor, just missing one of the cast by a few inches.

It was not, however, until the last days of the production, when he came to work with his face set in a fixed and terrible grin and chuckling to himself like a madman, that I realized what had happened. He had actually caught my smile. Looking at me constantly for months had been too much for him. Unhappy man that he was, he had entirely absorbed my expression. I could not at this time extend to him quite the sympathy he deserved, for I had been too busy studying an adverse phenomenon that had happened to me. I had lately been able to go whole hours without smiling. My face was straightening out day by day, and permanent relief seemed in sight. What I didn't realize at first was that not only had he caught my expression, but I had caught his!

The last time I saw this miserable man he was jumping over tables and chairs and trying without much success to walk up a perpendicular wall, grinning all the time to himself as if he enjoyed it.

I'm a Poor Guide

As I have gone on with this pitiful story the conviction has grown on me that I have not been writing what I was expected to write. I was expected, I am sure, to tell youthful aspirants how they might become successful movie actors by a few well-spent hours every night by the light of the kitchen lamp, and from my own experience to deduce certain principles of success which could be applied equally well by the artist, the writer, the salesman and the drug clerk. Now it can readily be seen from what I have already said that I am not at all equipped to pose as a guide in the pursuit of success. Moreover, I don't understand how anyone can seriously set out to prescribe his own rules of conduct for the rest of humanity. It would be just as sensible to prescribe a suit of Arbuckle's clothes for the citizen of average stature. There are some people no doubt who find it stimulating to rise at six-thirty and take a glass of hot milk as a preparation for the strain of a long day's work; but I am sure that there are others who could do much better to sleep until eight.

But I Might Say—

But if I *were* permitted the privilege of advising the world how to live and achieve, I know what I would say. I would suggest that we all stop listening to advice and paying attention to rules. We are all soaked and groggy with advice. We are so full of information on how to do things that we are inclined to over-look the fact that the principal thing is to do them.

I know hundreds of potential playwrights and authors and actors who go around positively bristling with fine inspirations and ideas. But there is just one little detail in the program of achievement that they overlook. They forget to write their plays, or they never take the plunge and start learning to act. There is only one law of achievement which I know anything about, and that is that there should be some balance between intake and output; that there is no real achieve-ment in the simple process of absorption, the filling up with high-minded ideas and intentions; that the more important part of the process lies in giving them some kind of useful outlet. Imprisoned and ingrowing ideas and inspirations are of very little service either to ourselves or to the world. Even a half-baked idea which is expressed and set in motion is better than half a dozen better ones stored away like useless furniture in the mind. I would add that success is not a result of rules or other people's advice. It is a matter of enthusiasm and strong desire. If you have these, you will discover all the rules that are necessary without asking some one to tell you about them. It is an old one, I know, but still holds good that any reasonable desire, if it strong enough, will be realized.

These things—I hope it is distinctly understood—are in the nature of what I might have said if I had felt in a position to mount the platform and admonish the world how to amble along in the general direction of achievement and success.

*This article originally appeared in **Collier's** Magazine for the week of June 18, 1921.*

The Three Musketeers

As interpreted for the screen from
ALEXANDER DUMAS'
Immortal Novel by

Douglas Fairbanks
And
Edward Knoblock

"All for one—one for all!"

In 1626 Louis XIII reigned over the fair land of France. Never had the French Court appeared so brilliant; fetes, masks, hunting parties, state dinners, court balls followed one another in uninterrupted sparkle. The King was young and distinguished; the Queen—Anne of Austria—beautiful, gentle and in the fullness of her youth. To the outside world the royal palace and its flower-bright gardens seemed an enchanted spot of laughter and revelry. But to the initiated few, to those favored with the pass-word leading beyond the precincts of the Louvre, the glittering walls told a very different tale.

Shadowed corners appeared to harbor whispering couples; lifted tapestries revealed secret doors; ciphered letters slipped from hand to hand; handkerchiefs conveyed signals and sent riders galloping on breathless messages to the four corners of the kingdom. In a word, Intrigue, like a stealthy cat, crept through the vaulted halls of splendor, sneaking up the broad stairs, edging along the gilded panels of the corridor and winding its way into the very sanctity of the Queen's apartments.

And what was the cause of all this plotting and counter-plotting? Who was the instigator of this mysterious intriguing, which slowly but surely began to poison the King's mind against the Queen and well-nigh wrecked their marital happiness once and for all? Who but one man, a schemer of consummate skill, of boundless ambition, of profound intellect and relentless decision—the Minister of France, Cardinal Richelieu.

Armand Jean du Plessis, Duc de Richelieu, was at this time at the height of his power. He held the destiny of France in his hand, much as a potter does a piece of clay, molding and bending it according to his whim and purpose. And even as Richelieu molded the kingdom, so did he mold the King. For Louis was vain, weak, jealous, easily aroused, little given to reflecting on the consequences of his impulses. Nor was there any one to restrain him or reveal to him the Cardinal's ultimate aims, save one person alone—the Queen. Her clear, shrewd instinct of woman could not be deceived by Richelieu's suave diplomacy. She saw through his tricks again and again, fully realizing that his pandering to the King's weaknesses was merely a means to establish himself all the firmer as the supreme, undisputed master of France. Richelieu quickly grasped the fact that he could not hoodwink the Queen; that her wit was proving the sole stumbling block to his ambitions; that in her he had found an opponent who would have to be vanquished if he wished to retain his position as the sole power behind the throne. Hence his enmity to the Queen; his pursuit of her; his determination to undermine her influence over the King, and, if need be, to ruin her reputation in order to achieve his ends.

By subtle insinuations he had already begun to effect an estrangement between the King and his unfortunate consort. Hints dropped now and again by the Cardinal caused Louis to regard his wife with suspicion; the habit of corresponding with her brother, the King of Spain, was seized upon by Richelieu as a pretext to rouse doubts as to her loyalty to France; her pride and self-control were misinterpreted by the King as indifference to his affection. It wanted but something concrete, some fact which the Cardinal could turn into a definite accusation to cause a permanent breach between Louis and Anne. It was this fact that Richelieu was waiting to find; carefully he bided his time until the occasion should present itself. Sooner or later he counted on entrapping the unsuspecting Queen.

And this occasion did present itself. For Anne, neglected as she now was by her husband, passed most of her days in the seclusion of her apartments, surrounded only by the most intimate of her ladies-in-waiting. True, she appeared at court functions whenever the King commanded. To the world she seemed to smile her gracious, royal smile by the side of her delighted husband. But in spite of this public attempt at masking her feelings, there was an emptiness in her regard, an unsatisfied searching for an indefinable something, which could not escape the eye of the sympathetic observer. And such an observer did at last come upon the scene, greatly to the Cardinal's satisfaction, for in him he saw the instrument which was to serve the Queen's undoing.

It was at one of the receptions of the Foreign Powers that the Duke of Buckingham, envoy of Charles First of England, first was presented to the Queen. He was known far and wide as the handsomest man of his time; the most accomplished of courtiers, of unbounded wealth and of noble tradition. One glance at the Queen revealed to him his destiny. He read the secret sorrow hidden in her bosom; in a moment his impulsive nature flamed into a romantic passion. Henceforth his duty, as he deemed it, stood out in shining letters. Somehow, somewhere, he was determined to tell her of his devotion and try to bring a little happiness into that sad existence of hers. As yet his plans were confused. All he knew was that his whole being trembled at the thought of her; that he was ready, if need be, to lay down his life for his divinity, if by such a sacrifice he might bring back peace and contentment to her empty heart.

During his brief sojourn in Paris he sought every means to convey his sentiments to her. The guards of the palace were bribed; the tradesmen, who submitted various goods and trinkets to tempt royal taste, were approached in order to convey flowers to the Queen. And chance favored him; for he soon learnt of a certain Constance Bonacieux, a charming young girl of impressionable, romantic nature who happened at that time to be Anne's favorite seamstress. Constance was living with her uncle, a mean, miserly creature. Nothing was easier than to grease the fellow's palm and thus to come in touch with the niece. Did she not know full well how unhappy her royal mistress was? Had she not often seen her wipe away a secret tear? Buckingham's ardent compassion for the poor Queen's lot could but appeal to a girl of Constance's temperament. Before long she had become Love's messenger, carrying Buckingham's perfumed notes to Anne whenever a fresh command of frills and furbelows took her to the palace.

The Queen, although surprised and shocked at the boldness of Buckingham's declarations, could not help being touched by the sincerity of his devotion. After all it would have been more than human, had his words not aroused some sort of response in her neglected heart. Yet she realized, at once, the utter hopelessness of his passion; that it would lead to nothing but unhappiness and peril. She never answered him, neither by written word nor by spoken message. But still she could not resist receiving his letters. It was so sweet to know that there was someone who cared for her in this empty world of formality and pomp. Besides, what could a few letters matter? Buckingham would be returning to England in another week and the whole episode would relapse into a charming memory—like the sudden meeting of two pairs of eyes from coaches that pass on the high road.

Buckingham left and the weeks passed, but still from England came those ardent notes with a persistence that began to disturb and distress the Queen. The thing must end. She wished it had never begun; it was wrong, absurd, impossible. What would be her position if the King found out? Thank Heaven he had not. And yet, had he? For an event had taken place which filled Anne full of dread. Buckingham had been proposed by England as Ambassador to France, and for some reason or other King Louis had refused to approve of his nomination. Nay more: he had threatened Buckingham's arrest should he set foot in France. What was the reason for this? Surely some political one, unknown to the Queen. For not a soul had learnt of Buckingham's letters; nobody knew of them save Constance. Even the ladies-in-waiting surrounding the Queen ignored the arrival of these secret missives. Besides, if they had known, they could be trusted—one and all.

But it was here that Anne happened to be mistaken. For amongst her most intimate associates was one, Milady de Winter, a beautiful English woman who smiled and curtsied and existed apparently only to do the Queen's bidding. But beneath all this devotion there burned a very different purpose. This grace, this readiness was nothing but a means to an end. Milady de Winter was the paid spy of the Cardinal. Not a word, not a move, not a look of Anne's but was reported to him faithfully within the hour. The Queen was sold to him, body and soul; long ago she had become his unconscious prisoner and Milady her jailer.

And that is why this glittering court of France, which so dazzled the world, was in reality a dungeon; that is why its laughter and music rang hollow, and why the fuse laid by intrigue was ready at any moment to be lit by the Cardinal. Any hour, any instant, the explosion might take place, leaving behind it nothing but a mass of wreckage upon which Richelieu counted to climb still higher and higher.

On a certain sunny afternoon King Louis had laid aside affairs of state and invited the Cardinal to a game of chess. The King prided himself on his play; he generally won. This was not so much due to the excellence of his game, as to the fact that his courtiers considered it good manners to lose to their sovereign. Richelieu, however, had no such scruples or politeness. As his moves began to corner the King, it flashed across his mind that he might use the game in order to bring home the purpose on which he was ever intent;

namely, the widening of the breach between the King and Queen. Had not that morning Louis received a request from England suggesting the withdrawal of his opposition to Buckingham as Ambassador to France? And had not Richelieu already sown fresh seeds of doubt in the King's mind with regard to Buckingham's persistence in wishing to come to Paris?

In the Queen's chamber, at the other end of the corridor, sat Anne, surrounded by her favorite ladies-in-waiting, listening to the plaintive tones of a lute. And now the music had ceased, and Milady was expatiating on the beauties of English melodies and the charm of English life in general, not so much because she really felt what she said, but in order to watch the Queen's emotion at the mention of Buckingham, whose name she skillfully interwove in her recital. But the Queen, save that her sad look might have grown a trifle sadder, did not betray herself by word or gesture. She listened with a faint smile on her lips, her thoughts far away.

Were they wandering over there to England, to that ardent lover who was waiting in vain for a sign from her? Or were they in Spain, the country of her birth and childhood, at her brother's court, her sole refuge for sympathy and consolation? Who knows?—

At that very moment Constance, the little seamstress, entered the Queen's apartment, a bandbox upon her arm. One glance of the eye showed Anne that the young girl was bringing her some important message. So, as soon as Constance had artfully spread her laces and frills to attract the attention of the ladies-in-waiting, the Queen readily consented to their examining the filmy wares. In the meantime Constance hurried to the side of her mistress and placed a note in her hand, unobserved by all save the ever-watchful eyes of Milady. Again a letter from Buckingham! With difficulty the Queen restrained her emotion as she recognized his crest on the handkerchief enveloping it. Secreting the missive in the folds of her gown, and dismissing her ladies, save Constance alone; she broke the seal and read:

Madame, my Queen:

I beseech you bid me hasten to France, that I may shield you from the Cardinal's persecutions with all the strength of an ardent devotion, which you, alas, have ever scorned.

Your majesty's most humble slave,

Buckingham.

For a second Anne hesitated. Should she answer this letter? Should she point out to Buckingham the madness, the futility of this proposal? Should she implore him, command him—not to write again? What could such letters as his possibly do but cause her misery and unrest, only making her realize all the more the utter emptiness of her existence. Evidently she decided to resist the temptation of writing him, for, with a sigh, she reduced his note to ashes. Yet now she turned to her desk and, seizing a quill, began hurriedly to pen a note. Had she changed her mind?

Meanwhile Milady lost no time in hurrying down the corridor to appraise the Cardinal of the secret delivery of a letter to the Queen, which no doubt came from Buckingham. It was impossible at that moment for Milady to approach the Cardinal in person, for he was engaged at chess in the King's apartment. But there were always ways of communicating with Richelieu. Father Joseph, his right hand man, had secret instructions to glide about the corridors of the palace in order to pick up any news which was to be conveyed to the Cardinal. Milady, therefore, whispered her information to Father Joseph, who carried it to the chess table by means of a slip of paper containing a powder which Richelieu had been ordered to take.

No sooner was the Cardinal in possession of the fact, than he began to play more than ever upon the King's jealousy. One analogy after another was hinted at skillfully by him as he moved his knight to threaten Louis' queen. At last the King was wrought to such a pitch of rage that he flung out of the room and into the chamber of poor, startled Anne. He insisted on seeing all her correspondence, and finding nothing incriminating in her desk, turned to search her person. Scornfully, Anne drew from her bosom the letter she had just written, handing it to him before he could accomplish the threatened indignity. Louis hurried from her presence into the corridor and opened the letter with trembling fingers. A smile of relief and amusement lighted his face as he beckoned to the Cardinal, who, at the other end of the hall, was awaiting the storm which he had aroused. As he approached his royal master, Louis could not refrain from saying to him, "Little about Buckingham, much about you, my lord Cardinal."

Richelieu's face, ravaged by care and illness, plainly showed annoyance as he read the letter addressed to the King of Spain, in which Anne begged her brother to use his influence with Louis to rid her of the persecutions of the Cardinal. Yet His Eminence was far too shrewd to allow the King to believe that this annoyance was due to the fact that the letter contained no reference to Buckingham. On the contrary, he pretended to be greatly relieved that the only reference in it was to him alone and that it in no way betrayed the honor of the King. But the thing that Louis failed to observe was that the Cardinal retained possession of the note with Anne's signature; nor did the King remark the smile which played upon his enigmatic features as his crafty mind plotted fresh plans to ruin the Queen.

And Richelieu would have succeeded but for the fact that Fate is stronger than the strongest of human calculations. For someone unknown as yet to any of the actors in this tangled drama, someone with all the force and directness of youth, was about to appear on the scene, and so confuse and confound the best laid plan of the Cardinal's, that he would at last be driven to throw up his hands and to cry, "Hold! Enough!"

Far down in the vine-clad south of France, in the ancient town of Tarbes, a young man's heart was beating high as he made ready to leave the home of his fathers. His keen eye flashed forth a spirit of unusual courage and daring; his trim, erect figure proclaimed a body under perfect control. He looked the very essence of his time—a blade of steel personified. His name was D'Artagnan. He sprang from as proud a race as any in Gascony. But evil days had fallen on his noble house; poverty was driving him forth in search of fortune. And so the parting hour between him and his father had come; a word or two of advice, a slim purse, a venerable horse of saffron hue, one more embrace, and the uncaged young hawk fluttered forth on the wings of adventure.

"Three things I would have you bear in mind," the elder D'Artagnan had said. "Loyalty to the King; reverence to the Cardinal and devotion to the Queen; but above all—FIGHT! Fight all the more since duelling is forbidden; for thus shall you doubly prove your courage!"

Hence it was that the youth, as he ambled along the road, glared ferociously at any passer-by who chanced to smile at the contrast between the heavy, lumbering horse and the slight figure of his rider, dressed in a forgotten fashion, but bearing himself with all the pride and dignity of a cavalier of the King.

Whilst D'Artagnan is trotting his many weary miles along the highroad to Paris, we return to Richelieu and his machinations. The letter of the Queen was still in his possession. With its aid a scrivener soon forged a note, apparently written by the Queen, begging Buckingham to come to Paris. It wanted but the seal from a signet ring to make the counterfeit complete. This, by a clever ruse, the Cardinal managed to obtain. Then, giving the sealed note to the Count de Rochefort, one of his creatures, he ordered him to take it to an inn at Meung, a spot some leagues to the south of the capital. Here he was to pass it to Milady, who would meet him there and thence convey the note to London to the Duke of Buckingham.

Now it chanced that on the very day that de Rochefort was impatiently awaiting Milady's arrival, D'Artagnan rode into the courtyard of the self-same inn. To
a man of the world like de Rochefort, the sight of the slim youth on his huge yellow horse could but present a droll spectacle; nor did he hesitate to laugh uproar-
iously.

Thus far on his journey our young Gascon had managed to frown down the
smiles provoked by his appearance; but to be laughed at by one whose dress and
bearing proclaimed him a gentleman and a courtier, was more than he could
endure. Choking with wrath, he sprang from his horse, and seizing de Rochefort
by the arm, he wildly demanded an explanation. At this moment Milady's coach
drove up before the inn and de Rochefort, contemptuously waving the young
man away, ran to pay his respects to her. The insult was too much for D'Artagnan. Hurling aside two stable boys, who tried to restrain him, he rushed after de
Rochefort, flung him from the carriage against which he was leaning and with a
rapid apology to the lady, drew his sword from its scabbard, determined to
demand satisfaction from the stranger. Our hero had a wrist of steel and the agility of a panther; it might indeed have gone hard with de Rochefort had not an
army of domestics and stable boys, marshalled by the landlord, pounced upon
D'Artagnan from behind and, despite his fierce struggles, pinned him to the
ground.

In the confusion de Rochefort managed to pass on the note for Buckingham
to Milady with the Cardinal's instructions to take it to London without delay.
Milady nodded consent and drove off hurriedly in one direction, whilst de Rochefort, mounting his horse, stepped back towards Paris. At last D'Artagnan managed to shake off his captors and brandishing his sword wildly, called in vain on
his enemy to give him satisfaction. He was gone. But D'Artagnan, mounting his
ancient quadruped, swore vengeance against the mysterious dark man with the
scar on his cheek. Some day he vowed he would meet him again and make him
pay for his insolence to the full.

*J*t was market day at the gates of Paris. The crowd was thick, pushing hither
and thither. Shopkeepers and street-vendors were shouting their wares; cau-
tious bourgeois, with their plump wives, stood bargaining at the various
stalls; masked ladies nodded from their chairs to plumed cavaliers; coaches
of the nobility sent the rabble scattering as they rattled by, regardless of the shins
and bones of the lower orders.

Through all this hurly-burly rode the young Gascon, amazed. For the first
time in his simple existence had he seen such a world of animation and swing. So

this was Paris; this busy, hurrying, scurrying, chattering whirl that eddied before him? This was the place that was to offer him his future? He gazed and gazed, drinking in the scene before him, an astonished smile on his features. Here at last he felt that he was face to face with life.

It was not long before D'Artagnan had grasped the difference between his own provincial attire and that of the tasteful Parisians. In less than half an hour he had exchanged his old horse for a hat with a dancing feather, and in less time again he had discovered lodgings, fortune leading him to that self-same Master Bonacieux, whose pretty niece, Constance, was seamstress to the Queen. And yet perhaps it was not entirely a matter of fortune, for whether D'Artagnan lodged in one house or another, was settled for him quickly enough by a glimpse of the lovely eyes of Constance, who chanced to be loitering in the doorway of her home.

The next morning our hero was standing in the presence of monsieur de Treville, Captain of the King's Musketeers, with a letter of introduction from his father to this old friend of his. De Treville happened not to be in a good humor and for the following reason: great rivalry existed between the King's Musketeers and the Cardinal's Guards. There was constant friction between them; brawls, challenges, duels were of daily occurrence. Just at the moment of D'Artagnan's arrival, de Treville had been advised of some fresh quarrels between his men and the Cardinal's. Bidding D'Artagnan be seated for a moment, he summoned the three ringleaders, Athos, Porthos, and Aramis, and gave them a very stern lecture. Yet in spite of the severity of his words, his tone clearly showed his affection and pride in his men; nor could he suppress a fatherly smile as, like so many schoolboys, they left the room after his admonitions.

At last, giving his attention to D'Artagnan, he kindly but definitely told the young man that the latter's lifelong dream of becoming a King's Musketeer could not be realized until he had served a thorough apprenticeship in some other regiment. D'Artagnan had been greatly impressed by the three musketeers: Athos, with his dignified and noble bearing; Porthos, of mighty bulk and gorgeous raiment; Aramis, with his elegance and refinement of manner; so that the thought of not being admitted at once into their glorious company came to him as a double disappointment. He turned from de Treville to the window in order to master his bitterness, when suddenly, as he gazed into the street below, his eyes fell upon the dark man with the scar—the hated man of the inn at Meung. With a cry he rushed from the room.

In the hallway he brushed against Aramis, who but lately had been wounded in a fight and therefore could not help uttering a cry of pain. Before D'Artagnan knew it, he had engaged himself in a duel for one o'clock on the following day outside the walls of the Carmelite Convent. Hastening down the steps to regain lost time, he became entangled in the broad cloak of Porthos. In trying to disengage himself, he managed to reveal to the laughing bystanders that this elaborate garment was covering his patched and torn baldrick. D'Artagnan's apologies were in vain. Porthos, whose vanity had been severely injured, insisted on satisfaction; the time was set for a quarter past one of the next day and also by the walls of the Carmelite Convent. At last, gaining the street, our hero found that his enemy from Meung had vanished. As he started to return to de Treville's hotel, he observed Aramis is conversation with a lady. The latter had dropped her handkerchief, and Aramis had intentionally placed his foot upon it, in order that he might keep it as a souvenir. D'Artagnan, in his innocence, hoped to integrate himself with at least one of the Musketeers by calling his attention to the lady's handkerchief. But Aramis, angry that his flirtation should thus be interrupted, had soon added himself to D'Artagnan's list of combatants. His hour was fixed for half past one, the meeting place the same.

The following day D'Artagnan betook himself to the duelling ground happy in the thought that though he was unable to become a Musketeer immediately, he would probably gain the honor of being killed by one of their glorious kind. Finding Porthos and Aramis present to act as seconds to Athos, D'Artagnan apologized to them in the event that Athos should get the better of him and so prevent him from offering the other two satisfaction.

The Musketeers could not help but admire this young fellow's courage and courtesy. Here was a foe worthy of the traditions of their regiment; they could pay him no higher compliment.

Our Gascon and Athos had scarcely crossed blades when a company of the Cardinal's guards, five in number, advanced upon the party with drawn swords, calling upon them to submit to arrest. For duelling had been but lately forbidden by edict, and the Cardinal's Guards had the right to arrest anyone transgressing the law. But sooner than suffer such an indignity the King's musketeers were ready to defend their lives at the point of the sword. As the Cardinal's men approached the three swordsmen, D'Artagnan came to a quick decision. In a flash he had cast in his lot with the Musketeers; in another the Cardinal's Guards closed in. The fight was one of fire and fury. The five men of the attacking party lay either disarmed, or wounded or dead, their leader de Jussac, a victim to D'Artagnan's magic swordsmanship. This hour of triumph sealed the friendship of the Three Musketeers and D'Artagnan forever. Swaggering arm in arm, the victorious quartette strutted back heroically through the streets of Paris.

As they passed an apothecary shop they decided to procure some ointment for the wound in Athos' shoulder. They were still engaged in bandaging it when Bernajoux, the captain of the Cardinal's guards, broke in upon them and began accosting roughly. He was held to be the greatest swordsman in France, a kinsman to de Jussac, for whose defeat he had come to seek vengeance. No time was lost by D'Artagnan in accepting his challenge. Out flashed their swords then and there and hotly the battle waged, first one then the other having the advantage. At last the bold, original method of D'Artagnan began to prevail. Over tables, chairs and counters he drove his gasping opponent out into the street, where he pinned him against a wall, disarmed him and sent him scurrying frantically down the alley, an ignominious figure of bewilderment and defeat. With a cry of joy, the Three Musketeers raised their young comrade shoulder high and bore him in triumph to his lodgings. Henceforth their motto became: "All for one, one for all!"

The news of the fight spread like wildfire all over Paris. It reached even the ears of the King himself. The Cardinal came to him, complaining bitterly of this unknown young Gascon who had killed his best swordsman. While the king effected to sympathize, he secretly congratulated de Treville on the skill of the Musketeers and expressed his desire to see the fire-eating young fellow who had in so short a time become the talk of the whole town. Nothing was easier, as de Treville had foreseen this contingency and brought the four friends to the palace with him. But when he went in search of them, D'Artagnan could nowhere be found. The trouble was that he had caught sight of pretty Constance as she passed down one of the corridors of the palace, a sewing basket in her hand. D'Artagnan could not resist running after her, completely forgetting de Treville's command to hold himself in readiness should the King command him to his presence. What was therefore the young man's surprise when in the midst of ardent love-making to Constance, he felt himself firmly seized by the ear and led off by de Treville to his impatient sovereign. The King received our madcap Gascon most graciously, and after a few admonishing remarks to him and his friends, bestowed on the four a well-filled purse.

This gift was indeed most welcome for the lively quartette had a hearty appetite and a heartier thirst; they went the rounds of the taverns of the town as men did in those days. Alas, the money did not hold out forever. Some of it was spent on refurnishing their wardrobe; some on enjoyment, some on gambling in the hope of making up for their light-hearted extravagance. They were put to many expedients, and put their servants to them as well, in order to make both ends meet. D'Artagnan had engaged a valet called Planchet, who soon served his master with utmost devotion, ready for any adventure he might propose. And many indeed they were, those adventures of D'Artagnan and the Three Musketeers, which bound them still closer in friendship.

So time slipped by whilst our young provincial learnt the ways and means of Paris life. And day by day his love for the fair Constance deepened and ripened. The heavens had indeed been kind in leading him straight to her heart. He longed to woo and to wed her. And yet he felt that he, a penniless cadet, had no right to do so; at least not until, by some exceptional act of valor and daring, he could establish the complete confidence of his superiors and so lay a solid foundation to his career. But where was the occasion to come from to prove his worth? He had shown well enough that he could fight; what he needed now was a cause to fight for. Was that cause ever going to present itself? How? When? Where? With all the impatience of youth, D'Artagnan began to fret and grumble and often at the end of a long day would fling himself wearily to bed and toss and turn till his healthy nature at last found repose in sleep.

Meanwhile the Duke of Buckingham in England had received the forged letter purporting to come from the Queen, and overjoyed at its contents, had secretly hastened to the French capital. Here he waited hidden in obscure quarters until he might fly to his beloved Anne. The Cardinal knew that he had left England but was unable to discover his whereabouts in Paris. From various reports of Milady he felt confident that Constance must be acquainted with the hiding place of the Duke. Richelieu therefore dispatched de Rochefort and a body of guards to the Bonacieux house to wring the information from her. If need be, the roughest, cruelest methods were to be put into execution to force the wretched girl to speak.

In the dead of night D'Artagnan was suddenly aroused by a woman's screams. He sat up and listened. Yes, it came from the floor below. Constance!—In a flash he had sprung from his bed and, sword in hand, plunged down the narrow staircase. He tore open the door only to find Constance struggling and writhing under the torture of the Cardinal's ruffians. Like lightning his sword played amongst them. In another instant he had set her free and dragged her through the battling mass out of the room, flinging the door to, behind him. As he held her in his arms the furious blades of his attackers pierced the worm-eaten panels of the oak. In another moment he had thrown her over his shoulder like a limp rag and leapt up the stairs to his room, bolting and barricading the door between him and his aggressors. The Cardinal's Guards were hot on his trail. Already they were pushing their way into his room when, D'Artagnan trusting to the skill and strength of his splendid body, climbed through the window with his precious burden, out over the steep roofs and along the leaden gutters till he managed to find a way to freedom by dropping into a silent court, while his baffled enemy stood gaping at his prowess in wonder and rage.

Constance was still clinging breathlessly to her lover's arms, while D'Artagnan was trying to calm her, urging her to seek refuge in some convent for the night. But the young girl would not listen to his proposals. As the clock in the bell tower struck the hour, she seemed suddenly to control herself and told him, with a strangely definite manner, that she was forced to leave him, as she was proceeding on a most important errand; so important and mysterious in fact, that she besought him not to follow her. And with a smile and a kiss blown from her delicate finger-tips, she slipped past him round a corner, before he was able again to argue with her. Fearing for her safety, he could not help but disobey her instructions, and followed her cautiously from afar. What was his surprise to see her suddenly met by a man muffled in a heavy cape. The two seemed to confer for a moment and then proceed toward the bridge leading to the Louvre. D'Artagnan's jealousy flamed up within him. Forgetting all of Constance's orders, he rushed after her and pushing between her and the unknown cavalier, was about to draw sword, when the young girl, staying his hand, warned him that he was attacking no less a person than the Duke of Buckingham. In a moment he was on his knees begging his Grace's pardon and putting himself and his strong right arm at his service. The Duke was only too glad to accept this offer, for Constance was leading him to his longed-for meeting with the Queen. It was as well that some one should stand guard at the small private gate to her apartments during this dangerous interview. So D'Artagnan sat him down like a faithful watchdog by the side of the door, much to the amazement of the old Swiss guard who was on duty there for the night.

In the meantime, Constance conducted Buckingham up the little winding staircase into an antechamber of paneled oak, where she bade the Duke wait till she had notified the Queen of his arrival. A moment later he was ushered into the presence of the woman for whom his whole being longed, heart and soul. Anne stood like one frozen, not believing her eyes when she saw the Duke actually before her. Buckingham, after fervent avowals of his devotion, seemed equally amazed at Anne's cold attitude; all the more so after receiving her letter summoning him to Paris. In vain she protested that it must be a forgery.

"Even if it is, so much the better. For it has brought me to you and you to me!" exclaimed the fiery lover.

Anne, moved as she was, refused to listen to his entreaties.

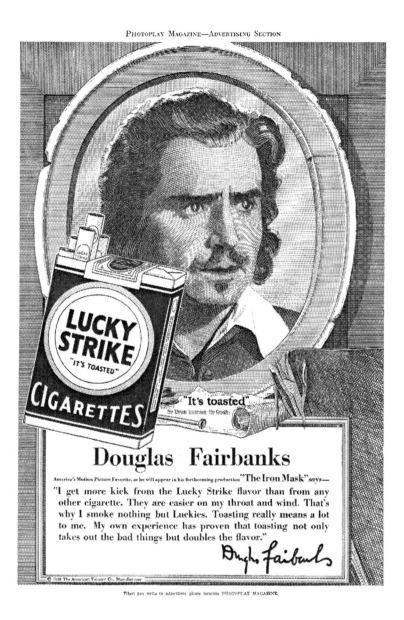

Endorsement ad for Lucky Strike Cigarettes, **Photoplay** Magazine, 1929.
Fairbanks appears as D'Artagnan in **The Iron Mask**,
his sequel to **The Three Musketeers**.

"You see me at the risk of my honor, at the risk of your life!" she cried, and with an imperious gesture urged him back into the ante-chamber. There he turned and began to plead again. But all his eloquence, all his charm proved of no avail. Still the Queen pointed to the door—still her only word was, "Go!"

At last, realizing that entreaties were in vain, as a drowning man grasps at straws, he begged:

"If you must needs send me away at least give me something for remembrance; something that you have worn which I may wear always to feel your presence close to me."

Partly to rid herself of Buckingham, partly out of pity for his despair, she snatched from her bosom a diamond clasp of twelve perfectly matched stones, and thrusting it into his hand begged him begone. He faced her once more, pressing his lips to her fingers and vanished, the secret panel which led him from the anteroom to the private stairs, closing behind him.

She breathed a sigh of relief. It might be folly to have given him the diamonds, a present the King had but lately bestowed upon her. But at any rate, Buckingham had left, was out of her life forever. Henceforward she would not be in constant dread of some fresh folly on his part. Despite the loss of his devotion she felt singularly free, at peace once more. As this thought flashed through her mind, she turned to regain her inner apartment, when suddenly she was arrested by a glimpse of a bony hand emerging from the huge chair standing by the fire, its back to the room. Then slowly the arm appeared and the gaunt figure of Richelieu arose and faced the Queen. Somehow he had learnt of this meeting; somehow gained admission to her room. He had seen and heard all. Breathless she faced him, but even as a cat plays with a mouse, he uttered never a word, giving her no inkling as to the use he would make of his knowledge. With a look of inscrutable scorn he strode noiselessly from the room, leaving Anne to all the alternate horrors of fear, shame and despair.

*J*t was not long, however, before she was to learn the worst. A week passed, seven days of suspense, seven nights of sleeplessness. Then, as nothing seemed to happen, the Queen made up her mind that she must control her emotion in order not to collapse entirely under the strain. One afternoon she was doing her best to forget her desperate situation by trying to fix her attention on some needle work. Constance was by her side showing her some new intricate stitch. As Anne's nervous fingers passed the silk to and fro through the canvas, she began to persuade herself that the Cardinal had evidently decided to relent. It was apparently sufficient for him to know his secret of hers and to taunt her with the knowledge of it if he chose to do so. After all, what greater revenge could he wish for? She felt certain that had he meant to do more, he would have sought out the King at once. The thought soothed her. She was convinced the incident was closed. She breathed more freely; she began indeed to become absorbed in her work.

There came a knock on the door. It was the King himself, smiling, gracious, the charming husband of former days. Evidently he did not know. The Cardinal had not spoken. The Queen rose to greet him. He nodded pleasantly and announced:

"I have come to remind you, Madame, that the State Ball will take place in a very few days. I wish you to honor me on that occasion by wearing the diamond clasp I recently gave you."

The blow had fallen. It was clear to Anne that behind these words spoke the Cardinal. He had not relented. He had sworn her undoing; he meant to accomplish it. With all the self-control she was able to master, she nodded acquiescence to the King and looked up, meeting his eyes calmly. But as she raised her glance she caught the shadow of the Cardinal on the door of her room. Her suspicions were confirmed. Four more days and she would be ruined. Four more days to live; after that—

She curtsied as Louis left her presence; but once the door had clicked in its lock, her knees gave way under her. Had it not been for Constance she would have fallen to the floor. She turned to the young girl in despair. Was there no way out of this terrible situation? How was she to get back the diamonds? For on the return of the jewels depended her reputation—the whole of her future. Was there no one else she could trust? No one ready to come to her aid amongst all the false courtiers and spies that evidently surrounded her? She looked at Constance with her large beseeching eyes, no longer a Queen, only a woman appealing to another woman in her bitterest hour of distress.

And suddenly there came to Constance the thought of a man who could indeed come to her rescue; the one person in the world who seemed as sent by Providence to save the Queen's honor—D'Artagnan. Anne looked at her in surprise; the name had only vaguely reached her ears. Who was the man? Could he be trusted? Would he dare risk his life on such a perilous errand?

Then Constance told all she knew of him. She explained how, in a week, he had become the talk of Paris; how he had guarded the private entrance to the palace on that fateful night of the Queen's meeting with Buckingham; how he was the soul of chivalry and daring; how, in fact—and here Constance blushed and faltered—she would sooner place her faith in him than in any other man alive, because—well—he loved her.

Anne could not help being moved at the devotion of her little seamstress. Here was a young girl ready to stake the life of her lover to save the Queen's honor. Indeed Constance's belief in his powers must be great, that she would be willing for him to take such a risk. Upon this forlorn chance Anne built her one and only hope. Seizing a pen and writing a hasty note to Buckingham with the request to return the fatal diamonds, she dispatched Constance to approach D'Artagnan without a moment's delay.

Our Gascon was sitting at home in his attic, killing time. When was the great occasion to come which would prove his character of as true a temper as his unerring steel? If only he might come across his cursed enemy with the scar; even the accomplishment of revenge were better than seeing the long days slip by one by one. He had chalked a rough image of the dark man of Meung on the wall of his room and practiced lunging at its breast. Athos watched his young friend's ill-conceived impatience with all the indulgence of an older brother. He knew very well that D'Artagnan the youth, and D'Artagnan the lover, were boiling and bubbling like molten metal to pour themselves into one mould and thus to form D'Artagnan the man.

And now the moment for which our hero had been praying at last arrived. A knock on the door, and Constance stood before him with her royal mistress's desperate story. In a flash D'Artagnan saw that here was his long-awaited chance; his Queen and his sweetheart could be served with one and the same stroke, and in a cause as perilous and bold as any adventurer could desire. In fact, for one man alone, the mission was too dangerous. To undertake it single-handed, was courting disaster. His three faithful friends must come with him. Four men would have to leave for one man to reach the destination. He needed but Captain de Treville's consent to secure their leave of absence, which he knew would be granted immediately since its purpose was to thwart the plan of the Cardinal.

Athos, who had been a silent witness of the scene, fully agreed to all of D'Artagnan's suggestions. In another instant he was hurrying off to find Aramis and Porthos, with the understanding of meeting D'Artagnan at Monsieur de Treville's house within the hour. And now came a tender farewell between the two young lovers; for Constance began suddenly to realize the dangers to which she was exposing her beloved. And D'Artagnan, who but an instant before, was all fire and flame, now dreaded the thought of separation from the lady of his heart. Earnestly he pleaded for a kiss upon that sweet mouth of hers; but Constance, fearing that she would no longer control her tears should once his lips touch hers, held out the promise of this prize on his return.

As they hurriedly reviewed their plans once more at the head of the staircase, down on the floor below, stood a man intent on catching every word of theirs. It was Bonacieux, Constance's uncle, who, unbeknownst to her, had been won over by the Cardinal's gold to pry and report on all the movements of this Gascon. Here indeed was a tidbit for Richelieu! Before D'Artagnan had given Constance a final parting embrace, Bonacieux had hurried off to the Cardinal's palace as fast as his vicious, fat, old legs would carry him. So that even ere his journey had begun, D'Artagnan was betrayed and watched, checked and counter-checked at every turn.

De Treville had soon given his consent to the expedition. The three Musketeers hurried ahead to the gates of Paris in order to procure horses, whilst the kindly old captain detained the fiery Gascon to give him some parting advice. D'Artagnan had scarcely left his presence and hurried into the street to join his friends, when he was pounced upon by a squad of the Cardinal's guards. There was no possibility of escape; he was hopelessly outnumbered.

It was not long before he stood facing the Cardinal himself. The latter had posted men with carbines behind the tapestries of his study ordering them to shoot as soon as he gave the signal by dropping his handkerchief. But for the moment His Eminence was indulging himself in the luxury of questioning and examining this unknown young fellow from the provinces, who somehow managed to block and foil his every plan. He could not help being impressed by the quickness of D'Artagnan's mind, his direct, ready answers, his amazing disregard for the oily rules of diplomacy. A growing doubt as to the wisdom of his own indirect methods and the eternal surprise of the older generation at the younger, crept into his heart as he listened to the youth. But the vanity of age and success soon made him dismiss all ideas of comparison. After all, D'Artagnan was first and foremost a swordsman, and if there was anything to be learned from him, it was in the noble art of self-defence.

And so Richelieu began to question him about the brilliant thrust by which our Gascon had overcome Bernajoux. This suited D'Artagnan's purpose admirably, for his keen eye had detected the barrel of a pistol between the folds of the curtain by the door. So in the midst of demonstrating his famous lunge and parry, he suddenly turned. Attacking the man concealed behind the draperies leading to the staircase, he fought his way through the guards outside, down the steep steps and into the street. Breathless, he hurried to the gates of Paris, where his friends had already begun to give him up for lost. In a flash, the whole party, including his loyal servant Planchet, were galloping at full speed along the high-road to Calais.

Our four friends thought themselves safe at last from the persecutions of the Cardinal. But their trials had only begun. For Richelieu, foreseeing all eventualities had sent de Rochefort ahead along the Calais road with strict injunctions to place every possible obstacle in the way of their progress. No methods too brutal were to be spared to prevent D'Artagnan or his three companions from reaching Buckingham or returning from London with the jewels.

Thus it was that our brave Gascon found himself compelled to drop his loyal confederates one by one. Soon after leaving Paris, a group of pretended road menders held them up, indignant at some fancied insult. While they were parleying, Aramis suddenly observed a man behind a wall leveling a pistol at D'Artagnan. Leaping upon the miscreant from his horse and rolling down a steep bank with him, he cried out to his friends to hurry on and leave him to take care of himself. Further along, at the crossing of a stream, the three remaining friends discovered a bridge blown up and were only able to cross it by Porthos holding up the shattered rafters on his mighty shoulders. In turn they were forced to leave him behind, half-fainting from the intense strain he had undergone. As they stopped at the inn near Calais to refresh themselves for a few moments, Athos managed to fling himself into the fray just in time to hold off a band of the Cardinal's hirelings. D'Artagnan and Planchet escaped meanwhile through the window in the roof and once more pursued their frenzied ride to Calais. They reached the port only to learn that, by order of the Cardinal, no vessels were allowed to sail for England. Here again D'Artagnan's ready wit was called into play; with the aid of his servant he managed to ferret out a fishing vessel and at the point of his sword forced the fisherman to set sail under cover of dark. Thus, in spite of Richelieu's precautions, our hero succeeded at last in reaching England.

But a messenger from the Cardinal had arrived in London before D'Artagnan with instructions to Milady to approach Buckingham at a fete' he was giving that night at his palace. She was to do her utmost to steal the diamond clasp, which he would undoubtedly be wearing, and bring it back in all haste to Paris. That evening Milady, on pretense of bringing him messages from the Queen, found it only too easy to hold the Duke's attention. During the performance of an Italian ballet she leant upon the arm of his chair and, under cover of her fan, managed to cut the diamonds from his breast. Buckingham, quite unconscious of the loss, rose to greet some other guests, and Milady, snatching the opportunity, pushed through the throng and hurried toward the street. Even as she passed out of the palace gates, D'Artagnan travel-stained and breathless, crossed her on the threshold. He looked at her in surprise; her face and furtive manner struck him as oddly familiar. Where had he seen her before? Suddenly he remembered that this was the woman in the coach at Meung, where he had first encountered his enemy, the dark man with the scar. The man had passed her a letter; they were confederates—he was sure of that. What was she doing here? He turned to one of the attendants to ascertain her name. "Milady de Winter," he was told.

A few moments later he was closeted with Buckingham, to whom he presented the letter of the Queen. The Duke realized at once that the jewels, however dear to him, must be restored to her without delay. His hand went to his breast; the diamonds were no longer there. Who had taken them? He turned a despairing look toward D'Artagnan, when suddenly the image of Milady flashed across the latter's mind. It was clear to him that there was but one person who could have stolen the jewels—Milady! He communicated his suspicions to the Duke, who, recollecting various instances of the evening, felt at once that D'Artagnan was on the right track. Everything must be done to render our hero assistance in regaining them and reaching Paris in time for the State Ball. So Buckingham placed in his hand a ring which would procure him fresh relays of horses all the way on his return journey to the French capital and bade him Godspeed.

The ship which bore Milady back to Calais was about to set sail when D'Artagnan leapt on board. She had retired to her cabin, feeling that her stroke in obtaining the jewels had earned her a good night's rest. Nor was she disturbed by anyone till just before the arrival of the ship in the French port. Not until dawn did D'Artagnan effect an entrance into her cabin. After a violent struggle, in which Milady made several vicious stabs at him with her dagger, he finally succeeded in wresting the diamonds from her. But so tenaciously had she clutched her prize, that in his effort to make her relax her fingers, he was forced to imprint his teeth upon them. Not until then was he able to secure the jewels. Meanwhile the crew, hearing her cries for help, began to batter in the cabin door and were about to hurl themselves upon D'Artagnan, when he plunged through the window and out into the sea and swan ashore, in spite of the pistol shots which made the water spurt about him.

Once on land, D'Artagnan thought it safer to choose a roundabout route to Paris. Thus Milady and de Rochefort, who joined her at Calais, reached the city before our hero. They went at once to Richelieu to inform him of the failure of their expedition. At this news the stoic calm of the great Minister deserted him and he burst into a paroxysm of rage. But, determined to snatch victory from defeat, he gave orders that every gate to Paris be guarded, and a double cordon of soldiers be stationed around the Louvre, in order to make it impossible for D'Artagnan to reach the Queen.

His precautions were, however, in vain. For our wily Gascon, on arriving at the gates of Paris, felt convinced that he would not be allowed to enter the town peaceably and so sent his servant, Planchet, disguised in his hat and jerkin, to distract the attention of the Cardinal's men from his own movements. Meanwhile he himself floated down the Seine and into Paris on a raft covered with faggots. Stealthily he made his way to the river-gate of the Louvre.

He had gained admission to the private entrance and was mounting the secret stairway, when de Rochefort, with his guards, pounced upon him. A violent combat ensued—the most violent in all of D'Artagnan's varied experience. But once again his brilliant swordsmanship stood him in good stead, and at last he found himself conqueror, though wounded and half-fainting. By a supreme effort of will, he dragged himself up the stairs, through the anteroom and staggered to the curtains that led to the Queen's chamber.

The Court Ball was in progress. Anne had delayed her entrance as long as she dared, seeking by a profusion of other jewels to hide the lack of the diamond clasp which the King had commanded her to wear. But Louis noted its absence directly as she seated herself by his side on the throne, and sternly bade her return to her chamber without delay and deck herself with the jewel. Not daring to tell him the truth, she withdrew trembling with fear. What was her relief on entering her chamber to catch a glimpse of D'Artagnan behind the curtain and to receive a signal from him that all was well. Milady de Winter too had observed his gesture, and while the Queen, overcome with emotion, sank into a chair, Milady managed to reach the curtains and, passing her hand through them, she whispered, "Your Queen." Luckily D'Artagnan recognized the mark of his teeth upon the outstretched fingers; but for that he might have been balked of his success even at the eleventh hour. Quickly extracting the clasp, he passed Milady the empty jewel case, which she, all unconscious, brought triumphantly to Richelieu. The moment she had left the room the Queen stepped forward to receive the diamonds from D'Artagnan who offered them to her on bended knee. Never had sovereign been served more loyally by subject. Words could not express what Anne felt toward D'Artagnan for his splendid devotion.

Meanwhile Richelieu, in order to make sure that no friends of D'Artagnan might assist him in the return of the diamonds, had caused the arrest of the three Musketeers and of Constance. But realizing at last that he had been outwitted at every turn, he decided that it would be more politic to make friends with a man who had undoubtedly a great future before him. So he sent for D'Artagnan and reunited him with his friends and his sweetheart. And in order to win him over completely, he offered him a position in the guards. De Treville, however, had been able to impress the King so favorably with the merit and skill of the young Gascon, that he had obtained the King's consent to admit him at once to his Musketeers.

Before D'Artagnan, therefore, could reply to the Cardinal's offer, de Treville had arrived upon the scene and placed upon the young man's shoulders the cape of the Musketeers, which proclaimed him one of the company to which he had so ardently hoped to belong.

Thus, with Constance by his side, surrounded by his three friends to whose glorious regiment he had just been admitted D'Artagnan was summoned to the ball. Before the whole court the King distinguished him by special favor, and Anne's eyes shone upon him in silent gratitude. But dearer than the smile of his gracious Queen were the smiles of his beloved Constance and the handshakes of his three loyal friends, Athos, Porthos and Aramis. And to the end of their days their motto ever remained: "All for one, one for all."

*Fairbanks' written adaptation of the classic Dumas story was published in a 35-page illustrated softcover book produced by the Douglas Fairbanks Pictures Corporation in 1921 to accompany the release of **The Three Musketeers** film. Text transcribed from original book in the Douglas Fairbanks Museum archives.*

Fairbanks working out the story treatment of **The Three Musketeers** with
Edward Knoblock on the front lawn of Pickfair, 1921. Notice the then-barren
hills of Beverly in the background.

YOUNG LAWYER U.N. TRUTH'S FIRST CASE

✦

FOREWORD

"Thrice is he armed that hath his quarrel just."

—Shakespeare

YOUNG LAWYER U.N. TRUTH'S FIRST CASE is the Story of a young member of the Legal profession who, though knowing he had no case for his client, kept bluffing along with most consummate skill, tact and energy.

U.N. TRUTH'S eloquent and patriotic oratory in his Opening Speech was for the sole purpose of deceiving the Jury; his objections were frivolous and trivial; his cross-examination of First Mate Liynd was a vain and unsuccessful attempt to break down the testimony of a reputable and reliable witness—and, with the usual attendant results; his summing up was filled with acrimony, acerbity of temper, and all the bitter vindictiveness which so often characterizes the losing attorney.

Happily the Legal profession contains many men of the highest and noblest character, and if here and there may be found a man of the U.N. Truth type exercising disingenuous and devious methods with the uninitiated, the fault is not with the Profession but with the Individual.

Douglas Fairbanks
(Signature)

Fairbanks penned this Foreword in July 1922 for a book written by one of his cousins, Emory Washburn Ulman (1861–1925). Although E.W. Ulman was himself a lawyer, the main character in the story, "U.N. TRUTH," seems to be a very thinly veiled reference to Fairbanks' own birth father, H. Charles Ulman. His father, a former Union Army captain, eminent New York attorney, and Shakespearean scholar, abandoned the family when Douglas was only five years old. He later had his name legally changed to Fairbanks and rarely spoke of his father again.

Let Me Say This for the Films

By DOUGLAS FAIRBANKS

A great joy is seldom definable. Usually it cannot be molded into words at all until after there has been some little reflection: but the night that I saw *The Birth of a Nation* I knew that I wanted to be in the pictures. I had much the same sort of vibration or thrill that I had when I saw the Grand Cañon for the first time. I do not seriously mean that this picture seemed to me so great as the Grand Cañon, nor that it impressed me so mightily, but both left me wordless.

Accordingly, when D. W. Griffith offered me a ten weeks' contract I was quite willing to leave the stage for a while. Now that I am in the pictures, I like the work much better than the theater. I suppose, however, I would find the same joy in any medium that would give an excuse to exercise my good health and vitality. And the films satisfy my desire to keep in motion in a constructive way.

As preparation for the theater I had studied elocution, Delsarte, fencing and Shakspere. When I first went on the stage I played in the classic drama for a time with Frederick Warde, and I once achieved for my work in *Hamlet* this notice from a critic: "Mr. Warde's supporting company was bad, but worst of all was Douglas Fairbanks as Laertes."

Not so much on account of this notice, but because of the fact that acting in Shakespeare meant playing on the road, I gave up my youthful ambition. I wanted to stay in New York. I wanted to be a success. Accordingly, instead of the classic roles I played modern young men, young men about town and alert young reporters, as in *The Gentleman from Mississippi* and in *The Cub*. For five years I went from one play in New York to another. I had had enough of the road. And the lines that I had studied with the hope that I might one day declaim them in the theater have proved very useful to paraphrase for captions and titles in the making of my film plays.

My first picture was suggested by one of the plays I had appeared in on the stage. W. H. Crane, Amelia Bingham, Patricia Collinge and I had played in a modernized version of Bronson Howard's old play, The Henrietta. Crane acted his familiar role of the owner of the famous mine, and I was Bertie, "the lamb." This character had originally been played by Stuart Robson in theatrical partnership of Robson and Crane, and under the title, *The Lamb*, this old character, placed in a new story, became, under Griffith's supervision, my first motion picture.

A Big Order

The early part of the film was quite orderly, but toward the end one or two stunts were introduced, and it was the response of the audiences to these that filled with athletics the scenarios of my next pictures, *Reggie Mixes In*, *His Picture in the Papers*, *Double Trouble* and *Manhattan Madness*.

But this quick action which proved effective on the screen—heretofore it had been considered that the camera recorded best only motion of exaggerated slowness—was not, so far as I was concerned, a new thing. I had always been interested in stunts and in games and had always worked at them; at first because of mere energy and vitality and the desire to keep in motion, and then because I found the work was good for me.

Long before *The Lamb* I had done similar stunts on the stage; in fact, it was this sort of thing that commended me to my first New York manager, William A. Brady, who always liked bustle, speed and energy in the plays that he directed. In a later play in which I appeared, *Hawthorne of the U.S.A.*, I made my first appearance by vaulting a wall, and at the end of the third act I sprang from a balcony to the throat of the villain.

Recently a little boy of about five, who had been admitted to the studio in Hollywood, came up to me: "Are you Douglas Fairbanks?" I owned up. He did not seem convinced. He hesitated and then pointed to one of the studio buildings. "Jump over that house," he commanded.

The athletic side of my film work has, I fear, been misunderstood by others in addition to this very youthful critic. Now I am tickled to death that athletics brought me recognition in the films; in fact, for a time I was so pleased that I lost sight of the purpose of these stunts and may have overdone the effect. Never were these things intended for an exhibition of physical prowess or as feats attractive in themselves. Just as a smile reflects good nature from within, these things reflect the indomitable spirit of youth.

Youth, it has always seemed to me, travels in lines of straight action, and if a fence is in the way it is to be vaulted. Gates are made for the old, as staircases are gauged for them. Youth does not take one step at a time.

And I have been playing young heroes.

I did not consciously as D'Artagnan in *The Three Musketeers* perform a single stunt that D'Artagnan himself might not have done. The standing slide down the balustrade, after the audience with Richelieu, has been objected to by some critics because it is not in Dumas' story, but Dumas' hero might well have done it, and to my way of thinking it was not out of character. Exhibitors tell me that this proved one of the most popular bits in the picture.

The slide was liked even in France, where there was much minute criticism of the film—criticism which so often ended with the words: "*Jamais Dumas; toujours Douglas*" (Never Dumas; always Douglas).

All this, of course, was very friendly, for the American film has won many admirers, not only in France but the world around. The correspondence of any studio will amply prove this. There is another proof of the vogue of the American films, and that is that both the English and the German producers, because of the popularity of the American films, have been forced to produce plays of our West and stories of our frontier. I have seen some of this in which cowboys use English saddles and wear cloth-fringed chaps of the Kit Carson period. But in spite of these oddities of equipment and weird incidents that would cause American audiences to howl, the drama has been generally sound enough and the background so pleasing that the films have sold fairly well.

I do not mean to imply that our own pictures of the West have always felt the urge or responsibility to be accurate and truthful. In a country of vast distances, with many miles to ride, cow-punchers do not always travel at top, dare-devil speed. They may draw their guns quickly but they are themselves slow in movement, gracefully so.

Films and the West

One of the finest achievements of the films, it seems to me, has been that they have revived an interest in our West. The color and romance of the old West were the result of conditions that had changed, and it did not seem worth while for the few remaining cow-punchers to keep up an interest in a thing which was lapsing. But the films revitalized a vast sort of local pride, and today you will not find every cow-puncher looking longingly at the trains that go to the cities.

A few years ago I took one of my films, *The Mollycoddle*, and a projecting machine up among the Hopi Indians in Arizona. Part of the picture had been taken in this same country, and many of the one hundred and twenty-five Indians who saw the film "that night" had the year before loaned color to this very picture in the making. We were naturally a little apprehensive over this effort to please. Six of our audience had never seen a white man before. The captions, of course, were to count for nothing and part of the film dealt with city and harbor life.

But little things, quite too subtle for this audience, as we thought, got over easily. There were just two things which really puzzled, and they were the appearance in life of some Indians who had died since the taking of the film, and the destruction by an avalanche of their village. This had been photographed minutely and a replica destroyed in California.

From the universal appeal of the Western story, I deduce one of my beliefs in the great future of the motion picture. There is this simple story of physical action told in pictures which can be appreciated and enjoyed by the world over. It has appealed to a circulation larger than any book or paper ever had. And it can appeal to persons who do not know and may never know the English language.

We have, then, this one extreme, the picture that has universal appeal, a pictorial common language.

Now science teaches us that where there is one extreme, there must be the other. Some day someone, some engineer, some writer, or whatever he may be, will figure out a way to reach this vast audience with subtler things and to teach less obvious lessons. I do not know where this man is to come from. He may be working now in another capacity in one of the studios, or he may, from mere observation of the films and thought about them, be studying the forming of new technic or method of his own which will change picture writing.

I am not seriously worried about the future of the films. They have made a place for themselves and they have already accomplished much. They have brought remote sections of the world into touch with the big cities. In an age which loves and prizes concentration they represent the highest form of concentration. A million-dollar production can be put in a tin can and exhibited not only in the big cities, as with theatrical entertainment, but in Roundup, Montana; Skull Valley, Arizona; San Luis Potosi, Mexico; and Bono, Indiana.

There are such places.

All Know What is the Matter

The whole industry has been overextended, and for a time too many pictures were released. "Get the money and forget the future" seemed to be the slogan of many of the companies when the films could still rely, in some measure at least, upon the fact that they were new. The public went to see almost anything. Now, and quite rightly, the public wants to know what it is paying to see. This state of feverishness in which the industry found itself was not the condition of America alone, but of the whole world. There are even today more film theaters in the city of Stockholm than there are in Los Angeles.

When the industry has found its natural place in the scheme of things, it is my belief that then nothing can hurt it any more than the theater has been hurt in periods of depression, except of course bad pictures.

The drama cannot be taken away from people altogether, once they have had it; and the films have educated millions of people who never before had any sort of entertainment to stimulate the dull routine of their lives.

It is obviously easy to have one's own idea of what constitutes a good picture and still fail to please the General and Mrs. Public, particularly Mrs. Public. The film fans, the people who read the trade papers and want to see all the pictures, are valued friends, but they do not make the difference between a half failure and a big success. It is the ordinary public that makes itself felt by staying away, and by the time that opinion can be recorded we have spent our money. And perhaps some that we hoped to make.

Of course, everyone knows just what is the matter with the films—the painter, the architect, the actor, the writer, the exhibitor, the critic and millions of fans the world over.

Learning Day by Day

We like to hear from everyone and every day's mail brings suggestions. A woman thinks that the entire fault is with the scenarios, and she has never been able to sell one; she has one now on the theme that orphans are unlucky. Another woman thinks that the trouble with the film business is because she is not employed; she is in the late thirties, the mother of five children, but still can pass for twenty-five. She has been rebuffed and demands to know how she can get into the films. Is there any way—"except by committing a crime?" A large man who is too heavy for hard work is willing to try the movies; his qualification is that he can float for twenty-six hours. A small man wants to sell his specialty; he can climb ropes over rocks. A young woman can sing and dance, and she would like to try the screen; so, too, her little sister, who is also talented at the age of six. And lastly, there is the man who is modest enough. He just wants a job. He has read every book and has had every experience for the actor. He signs himself in capitals: "I for Success."

Seriously, I have talked to many artists, and I find that they feel that the film is lacking in beauty. The painter would have every scene that we take composed as a painting is. The backgrounds and the costumes should be selected for sheer beauty. This is all very well and it is part of the business of the movie and one of the things that it can do best—that is, to present beauty in a large way; but if there is too much of it the story must inevitably suffer. This has been, from *Cabiria* on, one of the great faults of the Italian films. It is not so much that the stories are involved, but that the story often has to get out of the way for masses of people and scenic trappings.

I found when we started to do *Robin Hood*, on which we are now at work, that the lot was filled with artists. They all had sketches and suggestions for bits and sequences of beauty that would reconstruct on the screen the period in which the valiant and generous Richard, Little John, Maid Marian and the Earl of Hunting-don lived. They were enthusiastic, and we became so. We constantly found our-selves getting into the cart with them, and meanwhile our drama was suffering. I think we stopped this enthusiasm just about in time, and let background and beauty and costume take their proper places in relation to our drama.

A great many persons would have had us go to England to film this story, but I had rather construct my castles in California. Where a locality has not changed much, there is often a gain in the employment of the actual, and Sherwood For-est might help us considerably for many of the *Robin Hood* scenes.

It was quite worth while to take advantage of the beautiful country in Virginia for an essentially out-of-door film, such as *Tol'able David*; but even for the film-ing of the most modern stories I should ordinarily prefer the artist's interpreta-tion. I am not certain that in the carefully filmed new version of *Sherlock Holmes* a great deal was gained by the scenes actually taken in London. A painter will inject more feeling, eliminate a lot of unnecessary, irrelevant and uninteresting things and emphasize the particular quality that is needed for the projection of the story. One of our greatest achievements has been the progress we have made in the building of sets. We know that we make mistakes, but we are getting more and more of the period that we wished to recreate.

In taking some of my earlier pictures we did a great deal of location work, and went to the actual places where the action was supposed to take place. In making *The Mollycoddle*, for instance, we went north of Holbrook, in Arizona, among the Hopi Indians. We had the cooperation of the Indian Commissioner in Washing-ton, but it took us about a week to interest the Hopi chief sufficiently to be friendly to our project. And it was not Washington that won him over. He heard that I had with me some very fine horses and he very much wanted to see them. After a proper amount of reserve, he finally consented to dine with me in my tent. We were allowed to film what we wanted and some dances were done spe-cially for us. Effective though the actual proved in this case, I think that if I were do to *The Mollycoddle* over again, I had rather idealize it just a bit and rely a little more upon the imagination that some of the great painters have put in depicting the Indian and the West. You cannot get what Frederic Remington saw and painted by merely photographing the actual.

The Actor Misses His Lines

The actor is just as certain as the painter and the architect that he knows what is the matter with the film. He should be given a greater opportunity to create character. There is an often-voiced complaint that, since scenes are not taken in the actual sequence that they are in when the story is finished, character cannot be logically developed. For the actor who has been trained in the theater this may be confusing for a time, but it should not be lastingly a detriment to his work. In certain studios the actual order is maintained, and I do not believe that the resultant acting is any different because of this fact alone. I do believe, however, that the actor should know why he is doing the things he does, that he should know where he is riding and from where. Stage training, if it produces grace and freedom and a mobility of face, is of great help in the pictures; but the conditions are entirely different under which the acting is done, and this should be understood from the outset.

One of the great difficulties that the actor from the theater finds in adapting himself to the camera is that he misses the lines. He has nothing to get his teeth into. Everyone by now has heard of the story of Sir Herbert Beerbohm Tree and his difficulty in acting *Macbeth* without anything to read. I was working at the Fine Arts Studio at the time and often stood behind the cameras watching Sir Herbert acting and listening. This charming man, who had a great deal of humor, could never be convinced that acting was not acting wherever it was done and that lines could be unnecessary where there was acting. Almost every night Sir Herbert would get permission from Griffith to use some of Shakespeare's text, only to have the director the next day cut in upon him when he was just beginning to warm up to the situation.

There is a lurking danger in the use of lines which are not to be printed as titles in a picture. Noises which accompany action, such as chortles and grunts and whoops, are fine stuff and almost invariably get over, and it is usually safe to explode vocally.

These things are just as much of a help as the music which is played in the studio during the taking of the pictures. Now you cannot rely alone upon music to get the right feeling, but it does play upon the emotions to a certain extent. To visitors this music always seems strange, but it not only plays upon chords that we are playing upon but serves to deaden extraneous noises—such little things as the dropping of a hammer, or the rasping of wires and the drawing of nails. Some film actors do not want this music, and the use of it is a good deal a matter of habit. Soft music would not incite me to tears. I could cry from the sheer thrill and excitement of doing a picture, but not from any of the artificial aids.

A Portrayal of Inner Feelings

When the musical program that goes with the films in exhibition is carefully considered, it should carry out some of this same claim upon the emotional chords that were played upon when the film was in the process of making.

I do not hold with the view that there is no chance to act in the films. In *Forever*, the film version of *Peter Ibbetson*, which was for some reason foolishly renamed, I saw George Fawcett, a fine actor long in the theater and with whom I had played on the stage, give as the old French colonel more of the sweetness, gentleness and nobility that I know to be George Fawcett than I have ever seen him give in the theater. Surely such an impersonation is acting.

Another proof of the fact that acting can be done in the films is the work of Charles Chaplin. I do not believe that he could be so funny in the theater. He would miss the intimacy of the screen, and yet he is funnier than any comedian that I have seen on the stage.

Persons connected with the legitimate theater have so often pointed out that stars are made so easily in the movies that four or five good pictures will make a great favorite, whereas anyone to attain prominence in the theater must work for years. I suppose that four or five really good stories or novels would make a writer fairly successful. These might be published in a few years and yet that writer's career can scarcely be said to date from the writing of the first of those stories. There is something that went before. And so with the person who appeals to the public through the films. He must be a positive type, well molded and well trained. He has something which is not possessed by everybody, as a singer must have a voice. All training and technic will not take the place of a voice of good quality. And for the pictures something more than the mere physical quality is needed, otherwise the acrobats who went into the business in the early days—most of whom, if they stuck, are now getting ten dollars a day, when they work as extra men—would have been immediately successful. A peculiar kind of portrayal of inner feelings and of thought by outward expression is necessary for the films. Advertising and exploiting cannot make stars. Where are some of the movie stars of a few years ago?

Many of the critics of the films think that too many captions are used and that the justice or reason for the very existence of the movies breaks down when the spectator is asked to read, if not a whole book, at least a short story during five or six reels.

Now it is true that very often things appear in captions which should have been told in pictures, and again long scenes are given which could have been covered by a sentence or two. The caption can be a help as the illustration is to the book, and no matter how clever a book is I like good illustrations.

I do not even object, as some persons do, to titles and captions which seem to come from outside; that is, a note by the film editor or by someone who interposes an objection or makes an explanation. It seems to me entirely a matter of the way in which the producer gets his best results. No general rules can be laid down which will fit all films any more than professional coaching can make all people play golf the same way.

The One Thing: The Story

When everything else is considered, there is obviously only one vital consideration in the making of pictures, and that is the story or the drama. Now, there has been drama in the pictures from the beginning.

In the days when the motion pictures were still called cinematograph and were exhibited as sheer novelty at the end of variety bills and along with the wax works at the old Eden Musee in Twenty-third Street, New York, one of the most popular of the limited number of subjects in this new business of picture writing was the onrushing locomotive, headed directly at the camera.

To many spectators that locomotive was but a mechanical demonstration of what a new invention could record, and just as devoid of entertainment values as the agricultural reports that are received today by radio must be to many auditors who listen to them intently because the radio is new.

But those early pictures, which seemingly told mere motion, really were, to my way of thinking, unbeatable drama. The locomotive itself, a thing invented for the good of humanity, was drama. It stood for commerce, achievement, success. It carried with it destruction, and always there was danger. And it was this dashing locomotive that suggested to poets and artists and a few business men that there was something to work and play with and something to exploit when simple pictures in motion were no longer novel.

I did not sense this possibility myself until I saw D. W. Griffith's production of *The Birth of a Nation*. To be sure, I had seen about a year before another big film, D'Annunzio's *Cabiria*, which was made in Italy. In this there was great beauty, fine photography, and splendid handling of crowds. But the story was left dormant on the screen, a thing for the spectator to figure out for himself with no chance of turning the pages back, as he may with the printed story which is confused in the telling.

For my own part, the ideal film story must have youth and romance, told in the lines of quick action. More than that, there must be something back of the story, some reason for its being, some peg upon which it hangs. The picture must mean more than what one actually sees. He must feel it, too, and feel it so that he cannot be rid of the story by merely leaving the picture theater.

Whether this be drama or beauty or acting, or a combination of all—everything should conspire to create a lasting impression.

There are several periods of the world's history that have always interested me especially—the Roman, the days of chivalry, France, almost any of the later history, and California under Spanish rule. And I had always wanted to do *The Three Musketeers*, but I was a little reluctant to undertake a costume film. The impression of the business was that a costume story just would not do.

Every now and then someone of the overhead—I mean someone from the business office—would come in to tell me that an exhibitor, or group of exhibitors, wished to talk to me. Among other things I always asked them how they would feel about booking a period or costume play in their theaters. They were immediately apprehensive. They were sure their patrons, when they saw the billing up in front of the theaters, would walk to the next movie palace. I sent some men out to ask questions and they made a unanimous report against the undertaking. No costume picture need apply.

Having made sure that I was wrong, I went ahead. I felt that if there was enough good melodrama the interest could be held in spite of dress. Also the people must be kept human. Costumes change, but customs do not to any great extent.

I was a little timid and I did not wish to risk *The Three Musketeers*, so I put out as a feeler another costume play, *The Mark of Zorro*.

I take no great credit to myself for foreseeing the result. It is the story, and not the period, that the General and Mrs. Public want. Then, too, we have had so many dramas of supposed domestic crises, and we have had so much fancied realism, that a new period was a good deal of a relief to everyone.

If the German films proved nothing else, they did prove in *Passion* and *Deception* that costumes do not scare audiences away from the picture theater.

When the pictures were firmly established we invited the whole world to compete in this new arena. Whether he was a writer, a painter, an actor, a builder, an electrician, a costume expert, everyone had a chance to enter. Because of the enormous success and the possibilities of this quickly growing industry we were able to offer the man who wished to join us more money than the older creative arts could give him, and to promise him the freedom and security from worry which sufficient money brings.

Since that general call for help, the process has been one of elimination; and perhaps those of us who have continued to hold our heads above water have a right to our opinion about the future of the pictures.

We are Young and Growing Up

For myself, I have no very firm convictions, and those that I have are often changed. Even the generalities that I have expressed here may not always seem basically true to me.

I do not believe that—unless someone comes along who is to be to the pictures what Shakespeare was to the drama or Beethoven to music—the pictures will change much artistically. The best of the pictures of the present will, I think, continue to hold their own with the most artistic of the pictures of the next few years.

Technical improvement will go on just as changes in lighting in the theater have continued with the advancement of electricity. The camera may one day get a wider range, and there is always room for improvement in the stereoscopic quality of the pictures.

This last, of course, will carry with it greater reality. I am not altogether in sympathy with the things that are advocated for the betterment of the pictures on the ground than they are to make them more real. The things that have been lastingly popular in the other arts have not been so because of their great realism.

The film in natural colors seems to me another fetish. Every now and then someone discovers a new process for making colored photographs, but the photograph which goes on being taken and purchased the world over is not the photograph in supposedly natural colors. We have our own medium in the films, and I see no particular reason for wanting to alter it. Sculpture is not like life. It is a suggestion, or an impression, or an interpretation of life. No one wishes to change it, nor to redden the lips of the Venus de Milo.

It is because we are young that people tell us how we might, if we are good, grow up.

*This feature originally appeared in the September 1922 issue of the **Ladies Home Journal**. Look for several more articles Fairbanks penned for this publication in the pages ahead.*

As Douglas Fairbanks Sees the Film Play of Tomorrow

New York, Oct. 13, 1922
Special Correspondence

W hen makers of motion pictures realize that theirs is an art separate from any other, and succeed in divorcing it from the drama, it will have earned the right to be classed as a great art. This is the opinion of Douglas Fairbanks, who, with his wife, Miss Mary Pickford, was recently in New York arranging for the opening, at the Lyric Theater on Oct 30, of "Douglas Fairbanks in Robin Hood," the biggest picture this player has ever made.

Mr. Fairbanks was stopping at the Ritz-Carlton, and interviewing him there proved no easy task. Not because of any difficulty with the star himself—for so full of enthusiasm is he over anything connected with his work that he is eager and willing to talk about it—but because of the constant interruptions, the incessant demands that are made upon his time by the public. The telephone in his suite rings constantly and his secretary patiently answers requests for everything from a signed photograph of either star to requests for "a chance to act in the movies."

The suite itself gives away the personality of its occupant, and reflects something of his volatile and numerous interests. In one corner are stacked high several long bows used in "Robin Hood"; arrows tipped with feathers lie carelessly on the dressing table, a sword just brought from England by Edward Knoblock, the playwright, for use in "Monsieur Beaucaire," Mr. Fairbanks' next picture, occupys (*sic*) an otherwise comfortable armchair. A model of an airplane flippantly tops an open wardrobe trunk. Mr. Fairbanks was in conference with Mr. Knoblock at the time the interview was supposed to take place, but came swinging out of the inner room with the graceful movement of a trained athlete when called by his secretary.

"In conference?" he said in answer to a question. "Well, hardly that. It sounds so pompous and, after all, that phrase has been so overdone. I have just been talking over a few things about 'Monsieur Beaucaire' with Mr. Knoblock and Mary, my wife."

Asked to talk about the future of the motion picture Mr. Fairbanks enthusiastically agreed with the recent statement by Prof. George Pierce Baker, of Harvard College, who said that the movies must cease to imitate the drama.

"That is my idea exactly," he said. "We who make motion pictures must realize that we are working with an entirely new medium of expression, and even the rules governing the drama, the sister art, cannot always be applied to us. We must forget the stage and forget stage mechanics. We must develop a new art—one that will not be an imitation. How we are going to do it I do not know. We are still feeling our way, trying to get ideas out of the air, maybe, but still we are searching and we will surely find what we are looking for.

"To begin with, the motion picture is so much more plastic an art than is the drama. Language is an inadequate thing at the best to express emotion. We ask a friend whom we love, 'Are you happy?' and he answers 'Yes,' but the word means nothing to us. We know he is by the expression of his face, the light in his eye and the joy in his smile. In other words our eye seeks the truth and finds it.

"How then, can we hope for an enduring success if we try to develop by rules that may apply to the drama with dependence on the spoken word?

"The most significant thing in the progress of the motion pictures during the past few years?—Why, there have been so many that it would be hard to enumerate them, and they are all significant. I should say, however, that when we workers in the motion picture world began to take in artists, authors, and educated people of all descriptions into our studios with us, a definite advance had been made. You may laugh at me, but I always have said that I want more newspapermen, more artists, and more school teachers working in the industry. Newspaper men, because their thinking is trained to find the fundamental thing in a mass of non-essentials; artists because they help us in matters of taste, and school teachers because they are capable of discipline. And artists need discipline.

"The most difficult thing about making a picture is to get the perfect proportion of all the ingredients. The exact amount of comedy to balance the tragedy, the proper pinch of burlesque, perhaps, and the exact amount of all the other elements that go to make up a picture. But we always dream bigger than we can accomplish. We see a vision of a picture as it might be, we feel the undercurrent that we must try to express when we make it, but the finished product is always less, some way, than our dreams. Every one hopes sometime to produce a picture that will be as fine as it was when he dreamed of it.

"I think when I make my pictures that every one could be tagged by some old adage that has been proved true through the ages. I feel, in a way, that is a test which might be applied to all pictures.

"It is a game of mine to try to find the truth that will apply to each picture I see. Because unless a picture expresses some persistent truth it is valueless as a work of art. For instance, although it may sound childish, I think that 'The Three Musketeers' might be tagged 'A rolling stone gathers no moss,' and 'Robin Hood' proves that 'When the cat's away the mice will play.'

"Before I begin to make a picture I get a feeling from it myself that I try to express on the screen, and if the audience does not leave the theater with some such feeling, then I have not succeeded in doing what I tried to do. From 'The Three Musketeers' I got the rollicking, fighting spirit of Dumas' time, and I got the beauty and bravery of the days of Robin Hood. If the audiences who see those pictures get the same feeling I will have succeeded in a way.

"As for censorship—well, we never would have had Milton or Shakespeare had the censors been operating in England at the time of these two great men. And a salacious play must be stopped at its source where it is made—before it ever reaches the censors. It should never be allowed to get as far as that."

Speaking of the fact that every man, woman and child in New York seemed to be trying to reach him and his wife on the telephone, Mr. Fairbanks laughed, and said, "When we were in England Winston Churchill and Lord Northcliffe were talking in our apartment about why the public was making such a fuss over us. Lord Northcliffe said, 'It must be because Mary and Doug have really given something, don't you think?' and Churchill said, 'Well—perhaps. But 20 years from now we will know for sure whether they were famous or not.

"It is like," finished Mr. Fairbanks whimsically, "the ping-pong champion who, years ago, when that game was the rage, won a huge silver cup. Now if he were to come into a room proudly holding the cup, and boasting that he once was the ping-pong champion of the world, people would be puzzled and contemptuous. And so 20 years from now, people may wonder who Mary and I were. It's too soon to tell anything yet in the movies, you know."

J.P.

This revealing interview with Douglas Fairbanks was originally published in the **Christian Science Monitor***, October 17, 1922. Only the initials "J.P" identify the special correspondent. Of the hundreds of printed interviews the Douglas Fairbanks Museum has in our collections, this piece in particular was chosen mainly for how it conveys Doug's unique ability to express himself verbally—and quite eloquently—without ever "lecturing." This interview, like many others, also demonstrates that Fairbanks wrote just like he talked, using the same phrasing, emphasis, and choice of words. Comparing Doug's interviews side-by-side with his own written works, there can be no doubt as to authorship—his own personal style was inimitable.*

DOUGLAS FAIRBANKS IN

ROBIN HOOD

Story by Elton Thomas
Condensed version by Lotta Woods

"For he was a good outlawe
And did pore men much god."
Old Ballad

Richard the Lion Hearted set his kingdom in order as much as in him lay and prepared to rescue the Holy Sepulchre from the hated infidel according to his vow. Before he started on his long march with the recruits gathered in England, he held tournament on the lists before his castle.

If you would reconstruct the lively scene you must read the ancient chronicler who sets forth:

"The sound of trumpets loud and clear strike
upon the ear. Pennons without number float

from the tops of spears, and shields glitter
in the sun."

And if you would see the knightly combatants in your mind's eye, refer you to
the same writer who says:

"Oh, how splendidly were they equipped.
They had on costly armor and very valuable
and many-colored garments. They rode
war-horses that champed the foaming bits
and they were girded with swords of proved
metal."

Challengers and challenged had met and clashed. The victor in one contest
was the vanquished in the next and when the contestants had narrowed down to
two, excitement was at its height.

Beneath the excitement was an undercurrent of scarce-acknowledged interest.
Few spoke of what everybody knew. The two knights who had jousted their way
to the finals were the outward and visible signs of a secret and more deadly combat going on in the midst of the gaiety and merry-making.

The Earl of Huntingdon, sitting his white charger with restless grace, was, it
was well known, King Richard's favorite knight. Sir Guy of Gisbourne stood high
in the favor of the King's sulky brother, Prince John.

The King, whether from royal arrogance or more kindly fraternal feeling, gave
no sign that he was aware of Prince John's scarcely concealed jealousy and bitterness toward him.

With jovial good-humor he offered to bet his gold chain against the Prince's
favorite falcon that Huntingdon would win the day. Prince John sullenly took
the wager and hated his royal brother the more for making it.

Betting was eager all along the line. Knights gaged their horse-furniture, maidens the baubles they wore at throat or belt and a rash boy, viewing the contest
from the top of a tree, hazarded his jerkin.

It was the custom to crown the winning knight with a chaplet of flowers and Lady Marian Fitzwalter had been chosen by the King to perform this office.

Threading her way to the throne-like gallery that had been prepared for her, she was checked by Sir Guy of Gisbourne.

"Your veil for a favor to wear on my shield," he called to her airily. "The favor of so fair a lady will add lustre to my victory."

For some secret reason the Lady Marian acutely resented Sir Guy's assumption that he would emerge winner of the tilt. She considered such a speech to her at such a time both irregular and insolent and she briefly murmured a request to be allowed to pass to her chair of state.

Sir Guy was offended, malignant, more than ever determined to win. To that end he contrived with a tricky squire to manipulate a strap to hold him to the saddle. It was cleverly enough done to be undetected by the marshals and it would advantage him greatly over his opponent.

The heralds shouted their orders. The trumpeters shrilled their blasts. The keepers of the gates threw wide the barriers. From either end of the field rode the contending knight. From north to south the black streak that was Gisbourne, from south to north the white streak that was Huntingdon. The combat was on.

They turned again at the barrier and rode back toward each other. Silence settled over the watching thousands. The clatter of lance on shield sounded like a myriad thunderpeals. The wild burst of applause that followed prolonged the clamor.

Each knight had splintered a lance. Each rode to his waiting squire to secure a fresh one. Interest quickened in every breast. A watching franklin shoved his elbow into the side of the neighbor who impeded his view. Lady Marian Fitzwalter's gaze never left the Earl of Huntingdon. King Richard twisted his truncheon until it well-nigh broke and Prince John frowned in bitter rage.

For the third time the combatants met in the center of the field. Then the courage, the force, the honest sportsmanship of the Earl of Huntingdon achieved its due and Gisbourne's trick served him not at all. Huntingdon's sure blow sent

Sir Guy hurtling to the ground, dragging horse and saddle with him, and he groveled in the dust while Huntingdon was declared winner.

The galleries were aflame with waving veils. In every corner bets were being paid and that rash youth who wagered his jerkin disclosed so little under it that he was forced to flee in confusion.

Prince John transferred his falcon to the wrist of the royal falconer and left the throne in a huff. He hurried to the pavilion of Sir Guy of Gisbourne and gave such comfort as he might to that disgruntled and vindictive knight.

What of the King? Hear again what the ancient chronicler hath writ:

> "Now was Richard's joyous coun-
> tenance conspicuous above all."

He rose to his feet and stepped to the front of his gallery. His motleyed fool, whose favorite trick it was to "play king" slipped into the great chair and flourished his bauble as if it were a sceptre.

King Richard bade the trumpeters call his people to listen to his words. Calling Huntingdon to the throne he gave him the signal mark of his favor—his two hands resting on Huntingdon's shoulders. Then he called all to witness:

> "Huntingdon hath proved his knightly mettle.
> Upon this Holy Crusade he shall be our sec-
> ond-in-command."

The lists rang with the plaudits of the crowd.

In the breasts of Prince John and Sir Guy of Gisbourne rancor and bitterness reigned.

"He rides the top wave now," Gisbourne said spitefully. "'Twill be more sport to drag him down."

The Prince looked at him thoughtfully.

"The rank of second-in-command should come to you," he told Gisbourne. "'Tis a bitter slight the King has given you. Remember it against him."

As for Huntingdon. His honors were coming thick and fast. Quoth Richard:

"Go you to the fair maid, Marian, and receive your chaplet of valor."

Huntingdon's courage oozed from his finger-tips.

"Exempt me, sire," he begged. "I am afeared of women."

But Richard was adamant. With a friendly push he started Huntingdon on his way to Lady Marian. With quaking knees, Huntingdon knelt to receive his wreath, albeit awkward and unaware of the fair maid's warm interest in her work.

Like a whirlwind of blossoms the maidens flitted from their boxes gathered about the successful knight, smothering him with congratulation, begging him to wear their favor. Richard watched the scene humorously. Lady Marian smoothed her face to a blank. Huntingdon, overborne with so much adulation, fled. A backward glance told him that the maidens still pursued him and with a wild leap he disappeared in the friendly waters of the moat.

All night long the feasting, the merry-making and the revels had gone on. In the great hall the tables were thinning. Servants bore away remnants of the feast or fetched the ewers and basins for washing the hands of the guests.

Richard sat alone at his table, leisurely watching his knights whisper words of love and farewell in ears that heard with sadness.

Prince John was showing signs of a long evening over the wine-cup. Staggering toward a passing squire, he demanded to quaff from the goblet he carried. The terrified squire explained that it was the King's goblet.

As usual the Prince's savage temper came to the surface.

"'Twill be mine to-morrow with everything else in the Kingdom, you fool," he told the squire and grasped the goblet in both his unsteady hands.

Gisbourne was still sober enough to know the folly of such intemperate speech. He whispered discreet advice to the Prince and sent the squire on his way.

Among the knights who told again their love to maidens fair Richard looked in vain for Huntingdon.

That young champion had no mind for maids. Instead he engaged in a test of strength with some of his comrades in arms. With a dagger pressed against his head he pulled a winecup from the hand of a similarly handicapped knight.

King Richard was disappointed.

"How now, my knight," he asked. "Have you no lady-love to give point to your spear and edge to your sword?"

"Nay, my liege," replied Huntingdon. "I fight for all fair ones."

"Find *one* to fight for," insisted the King.

With veils and ribbons borrowed from the ladies, Huntingdon was lashed to a pillar. The fair ones of the court, not loath to please the King, and perhaps win the fealty of a very knightly knight, passed in pageantry before him.

Richard, with that freedom of badinage permitted to royalty, pointed out a dimple, a pair of blue eyes, a curl. Huntingdon admired them all with lavish impartiality.

Lady Marian Fitzwalter watched the boisterous game with mingled emotions. Not for worlds would she have joined in this contest for favor, yet her heart beat a bit the faster as she faced the idea that Huntingdon might choose a lady from these lists. Half blindly she turned to hide herself from the sportive group.

Prince John was just tipsy enough to resent the King's diversion. He grasped at the chance to still further infuriate Gisbourne against the King.

"Why should you not have your pick of maidens?" he asked Sir Guy. "I will see to it that you do. Name your choice."

Half unconsciously Gisbourne's eyes sought Marian.

"Sits the wind in that direction?" the Prince exclaimed. His wine-bleared eyes appraised Marian owlishly.

He intercepted the departure of the unsuspecting girl and, plucking her sleeve, thrust her into the arms of Gisbourne.

Gisbourne's arms closed about her but she wrenched herself free from him and with a scornful look she fled from the hateful Prince and his more hateful companion.

On the dais, Huntingdon had taken his baiting so good-naturedly that the game palled. His wandering gaze focused on the Prince and Gisbourne and their drunken diversions. His muscles hardened. He broke his bonds and rushed from the scene. His flight was regarded as a mere continuation of his hasty departure from the lists after the tournament and the laughing maids sought quarry less shy.

Marian's headlong flight took her up the stairs to the minstrel gallery and thence to the battlements. Determined not to be balked, the Prince pursued her. And Huntingdon followed the Prince. Gisbourne would have followed also, had not the bulky presence of Huntingdon's squire blocked his way.

On the battlements, Marian turned to face the Prince. The Prince reached out his hand toward her and Huntingdon stepped between them.

Prince John was sobered instantly by the steady eye and firm wrist of Huntingdon.

"I am the Prince," he said with arrogant emphasis.

"Your Highness seems to be the only person who has forgotten it," said Huntingdon.

There was cool challenge in his tone and in his bearing. Challenge that the Prince had not the courage to accept. He turned on his heel with a malevolence that boded ill to those who crossed him.

Huntingdon watched his exit, then turned to Lady Marian.

"That man is dangerous. I fear for your safety here," he heard himself saying. "I shall leave my worthiest squire to watch over you."

Marian raised her candid eyes and softly murmured her gratitude. A multitude of queer sensations chased each other up and down Huntingdon's spine.

But for her need and his response to it—but for the sense of responsibility for her welfare that grew out of that need and that response—he might have ridden away heartfree.

But now, her gaze enchained him. He looked and looked away. He looked and looked again. He reached a tender, tentative finger and touched the veil that hid her golden curls. He whispered haltingly, yearningly:

"I—I—never knew—a maid—could be—like you—"

◆   ◆   ◆

Morning came and o'er the kneeling troops the bishop raised his hand in holy benediction. This was the Age of Faith and for the cross that gleamed upon his shoulder each knight breathed a silent vow to die if need be.

Lovers embraced and parted. "Soft eyes looked love to eyes which spake again."

The King bade his trumpeters signal the departure. He looked around for his lieutenant and called him in stentorian tones that scared the pigeons from the parapets.

On the battlements—the scene of their meeting in the early dawn—Lady Marian Fitzwalter and the Earl of Huntingdon lingered, masking the pain of parting with tender foolery.

She sketched in silhouette his profile boldly outlined on the wall by the morning sun. He fondly teased her as she drew. He placed his ring upon her slender finger and kneeled to kiss the hand that wore it.

Lifting his sword from its sheath, she struck him gently on the shoulder, dubbed him her "loyal knight and true," then kissed the hilt of that same sword with a passion so new she shyly withheld it from her lover.

The King's lusty cry of "Huntingdon!" broke into the idyllic moment. Grasping hands like two affectionate children they hastened to him to unfold the story of their love.

"My liege," said Huntingdon, "I go half-hearted on this march of thine. Half my heart I leave here in your castle."

Richard slapped him gayly on the shoulder.

"You'll fight better for wearing the maid's veil over your heart," he said warmly and lifted his hand in benison on their love.

Two bitter onlookers watched the scene and whispered furtively together.

"Richard must not return from the Holy Land," Prince John said to Gisbourne.

He added with grim menace:

"Nor Huntingdon neither."

Gisbourne bowed. His eyes rested on Marian where she lifted her shining head and bravely waved farewell to her lover.

"Huntingdon's head for Lady Marian's hand," he murmured.

Then he, too, rode away, and the great hall was empty save for three, Lady Marian, fragile and tiny in its vast spaciousness, Prince John, sinister and malevolent, and, scarcely seen in the tapestried arch far down the hall, Huntingdon's burly, faithful squire.

◆   ◆   ◆

Scarce had the dust of the Crusaders' march settled to the ground ere all England fell under the black pall of John's perfidy.

Night, and the smoky torches lighted a scene of cloaked infamy. One by one his sycophantic supporters crept forth into the dark, half shamed at the part they were to play, half-exultant over the princely favor that was to grant each a castle in return for sorry deeds.

Left alone, the Prince, looking stealthily about as if the hall might be peopled with watching foes, crept to the great chair of state where he rested, on its velvet cushion, the symbol of Richard's power, his golden crown.

With itching fingers he set it on his head, holding it lest the circlet fashioned for Richard's massive brow should slip to his very shoulder. He studied his reflection in a shiny shield, tasting in anticipation the joys to come.

Day followed day and the sufferings of the people of England grew greater. Saith the chronicler of Prince John:

> "He cared not for the wretch-
> edness of a perishing people."

To raise the money that paid the troops needed to carry out his behests, he taxed the poor beyond their meagre endurance. They could not pay and he took of their scanty belongings, perhaps a stool, a kettle, a house door.

In the princely forests if a starved peasant crept out to bring down a deer or a wild boar he was punished by the loss of his bow finger or blinded with hot metal.

Women fled from his presence with shrinking dread and many paid for their temerity with stripes on their bare backs or long imprisonment in filthy dungeons where, mayhap, they died of slow starvation or poisoning.

Good officials were ousted and the Prince's favorites took their places. Notable among these was the new High Sheriff of Nottingham.

◆   ◆   ◆

Lady Marian Fitzwalter, sewing among her women, carrying succor to the poor, hearing from every side tales of misery and suffering, blanched with horror as the full measure of Prince John's perfidy came home to her. She pondered in her heart how much one woman might do to meet the evil.

One measure she tried. Turning bravely from the scurrying women of the castle who fled the hall when Prince John and his friends were there, she intrepidly faced him as he sat among his henchmen.

The Prince was in heady spirits. The High Sheriff of Nottingham had just fetched him the agreeable news that his order to raze and burn Huntingdon's castle had been executed.

He listened to Marian's plea for the people of England with a satirical levity that was an insult in itself.

Marian's head reared haughtily.

"Prince, your oppressions will not please our King," she told him.

He flicked one of her curls insolently.

"A Prince at home outranks a King abroad," he said maliciously.

Marian's courage did not fail.

"The King shall know of this," she exclaimed and indignantly left his presence.

The threat rankled.

"That wench will bear watching," he told his henchmen.

◆   ◆   ◆

Marian's determination might have failed her had she not fled to the battlements for comfort. The silhouette—half-hidden under vines—renewed her spirit.

That night she prepared a message and sent it by Huntingdon's faithful squire.

"Follow the march of the army," she told him, and, that some word of comfort might return to still the ache of her heart, she sent along a homing pigeon.

◆   ◆   ◆

The Squire was missed. Prince John, characteristically, chose the indirect method of finding out what he wanted to know.

He quizzed Marian's tirewoman.

She proved recalcitrant.

This was a sport he thoroughly enjoyed.

Two grim, black-garbed henchmen. A scarred board. A brazier heaped with red coals. Needles heated white-hot. These were his tools.

That the tirewoman's flesh proved frailer than her loyal spirit somewhat marred his pleasure. He relished more prolonged agony. One needle boring into the sensitive flesh beneath her nail she endured, and another. But the third broke her tortured resistance. She told him the truth—that Marian had sent a message to the King through the medium of Huntingdon.

This was more than the Prince had bargained for. The spectre of Richard's reckoning was always with him. He flung his wretched, half-fainting victim from him and turned in a panic of rage and resentment on his fawning followers.

"The wench has dared to meddle!" he shrieked. "She shall die."

The words pierced the swooning senses of the tirewoman. She dragged herself unnoted from the hall and struggled up the stairway to her mistress's room.

The time gained was infinitesimal but it served. The Prince and his followers invaded Marian's room. They found only Marian's women, galvanized into sufficient courage to oppose his questioning with stubborn resistance.

A clatter of hoofs in the courtyard below—a flurried henchman bringing the news that Lady Marian was fleeing fetched a prompt order from the Prince to trail her and bring her back.

Little by little the troopers gained on the two women. They caught glimpses of them from time to time through distant aisles of trees. For a while they lost sight of them, and then, as they rounded a curve in the path, they were halted by the tirewoman. Her face was streaked with tears and ghastly with fright.

With trembling fingers she pointed to the edge of an overhanging cliff. Two horses nibbled unconcernedly at the herbage. On one of them was a twisted saddle and Lady Marian's long riding veil clung to it, torn and bedraggled, telling a tale of tragedy.

The edge of the cliff was broken. The troopers gathered and looked down. A stolid-faced peasant woman crept from her hut and listened as they questioned the tirewoman. She heard the maid's hysterical answers and followed the troopers to the embankment. It was plain that a body falling into the brawling river below would have been carried away immediately.

The leader of the troopers shrugged his shoulder. His instructions did not cover this. He looked at the moaning tirewoman. Neither was she included in his orders. He gave a hasty command to his men and they rode away.

The stolid-faced peasant woman watched the woman awhile and then her interest flagged. She went indoors and took up her drab duties.

The tirewoman looked guardedly about. After awhile she disappeared in the shadowy forest with a finger on her lip and a furtive signal to a fleeting shape among the trees.

◆   ◆   ◆

Across the fields of France the Crusading hosts were marching. Ever busy among them, comforting the weary, cheering the homesick, prodding the stragglers, went the Earl of Huntingdon.

This morning the King watched him from his open tent flap.

"Mark how he spurs them on," he told a knight standing near. "He is the very backbone of the army."

He went back into the inner tent. His jester, "playing king" as usual, slipped out of his chair and dodged a cuff he felt was due.

Scarcely had the King disappeared when Sir Guy of Gisbourne, speaking in full hearing of Huntingdon, said sneeringly:

"'Tis well-known these tricks of discipline are played to curry favor with the King. I hate a sycophant."

Huntingdon's steady eyes held Gisbourne's gaze.

"Were it not for discipline," he said quietly, "I would crack your spine."

The clash might have gone further, but it was ordained that Squire John, dusty and travel-worn from his long ride in the trail of the army, should arrive at this time.

Huntingdon greeted him, affectionate but apprehensive, and drew him aside to inquire his mission.

Marian's letter enlightened him.

"Beloved"—so she wrote—"In the King's absence his people perish. His throne totters. Prince John builds up a following paid from the public treasure. Horror reigns everywhere. I almost fear to write lest Richard should return and this Holy Crusade should fail."

More she wrote, of tender love, of loneliness bravely borne, but always she came back to the danger to England and to England's King.

Huntingdon pondered long and then spoke his thoughts to his squire.

"Richard must not be told," he said. "If there were one man in England brave enough to oppose this cur, these things would not be."

Unconscious of the spying Gisbourne, Huntingdon wrote a letter and gave it to the squire to wrap about the leg of the homing pigeon. Then, squaring his shoulders, he went to the King's tent.

Squire John finished securing the letter, released the bird, and watched its flight for a moment. Sure that it had taken its course, he went about his further duties.

Gisbourne whispered a word to his own man who left him for a moment and returned with a falconer, upon whose wrist there clung a hooded hawk.

Gisbourne gave the signal. The falconer unhooded the hawk and gave it wing. It soared high and circled round its victim. Instinct and training served the falcon. He made his strike unerringly. For the tiny white pigeon setting forth so bravely for her long flight homeward, the tragedy was soon over. Her little body fell to earth and untender hands removed the message she carried.

Gisbourne read it.

"My Marian," Huntingdon had written, "by one excuse or another I shall persuade the King to allow me to return. On the heels of this missive I shall be in England."

Gisbourne smiled a satisfied smile and set himself to watch the King's tent.

Within that tent, Huntingdon impulsively pleaded for permission to return to England. He was by nature straightforward and ingenuous. He had no tricks at his command. He could only base his plea on the King's friendship and his trust in him.

The King was inclined first to be angry—then to consider it a boyish prank. He ordered crisply that Huntingdon return to his work.

Huntingdon insisted.

Richard took pause.

All unbidden there came to him a remembrance of the morning of the departure—Lady Marian's bright face—Huntingdon's confession of love.

He rose questioningly.

"'Tis not the maid?" he asked.

Huntingdon turned away his head, refused to answer.

Then did Richard's Plantagenet temper give way.

"You!" he shouted, "turned chicken-livered about a wench! Begone. Go join your men."

He would listen no more. He propelled his lieutenant toward the door.

Hurt, bewildered, but angrily bent on saving Richard, whether or no, Huntingdon sought his squire.

"He has refused me leave," he flung out and commanded his squire to mount and accompany him.

It was the moment for which Gisbourne had waited. Seizing a crossbow from the hands of a man-at-arms he let fly the bolt. The dart pierced Huntingdon's side and as he dazedly pushed back his coif the heavy hilt of Gisbourne's dagger struck him across the head and fetched him unconscious to the ground.

Squire John, struggling in the clutches of four burly yeomen, was hauled along. Two other yeomen picked Huntingdon up and bore him to the King's tent.

Gisbourne followed. Pointing to the limp body of Huntingdon as it lay on the floor of the tent, he said, with silky emphasis,

"Sire, a deserter."

Some measure of consciousness returned to Huntingdon's tortured brain. He tried to lift himself—spoke haltingly—

"Sire, back in England—"

Unseen by the King, Gisbourne kicked the prostrate figure. Huntingdon relapsed again into insensibility.

With ready wit Gisbourne gave the King the letter that seemed to supplement Huntingdon's unfinished speech.

> "My Marian, by one excuse or another I shall
> persuade the King to allow me to return.
> On the heels of this missive I shall be in
> England."

"Sire," said Gisbourne, his insinuating tones more silky than before, "Sire, the penalty is death."

Richard looked at him witheringly.

"Have his wound bound," he commanded. "Lock him in yonder tower. Let him remain a prisoner till our return."

"But, Sire," Gisbourne spoke with pained insistence, "the penalty is death."

"My orders—obey them!" shouted the harassed King.

Gisbourne bowed low. "Your orders, Sire. Let me be sure that I understand them. He is to remain a prisoner *until you return.*"

◆　　◆　　◆

Sir Guy of Gisbourne lost no time. The unconscious Huntingdon and his belligerent squire were placed in closely barred cells in the tower.

Mindful that the King's weakness for Huntingdon might bring him to visit the prisoner before he resumed his march, he gave his orders accordingly.

"Give them food and drink until the army is well under way. Then let them rot."

He supplemented his instructions with a bag of gold and the jailer expressed his entire willingness to obey.

Hours passed. Huntingdon roused. He dragged himself to the narrow embrasure in the wall and looked through the bars to the shining road where the army of his King, marching with flying banners, was disappearing in dim perspective.

As long as he could bear it he followed their progress, then faintness again overcame him.

But one thing marred the effectiveness of Gisbourne's carefully laid plans. Two things, rather. The magnificent strength that lay in Squire John's great hands and the magnificent loyalty that lay in his great heart. For that faithful servitor brooded over his master's predicament until the shadows of night thickened the gloom in his narrow cell. Then, in sheer desperation, he twisted the bars in the little wicket of his cell door until they gave passage to his mighty arm.

The jailer, somewhat the worse for the potations Gisbourne's gold had enabled him to purchase, staggered in with the scanty rations he had tardily remembered. The squire's arm pushed through the opening he had made in the wicket. His steel-like fingers gripped the fellow's windpipe. He squeezed until the wretched fellow yielded him the keys.

The rest was easy. Tossing his victim back into the cell, the squire opened the other dungeon and carried his beloved lord to freedom.

Out under the stars, Huntingdon felt his swimming senses anchoring. His blurred vision sought the tear-furrowed face of his staunch retainer. With careful precision he formed the words:

"To England—with all haste. I have work to do."

◆   ◆   ◆

Douglas Fairbanks as the Earl of Huntingdon

Art from the 1922 program book for **Robin Hood**, with original photo caption.

And in England, Prince John abated not from his oppressions. The sting of his lash grew sharper and under it the people drooped, save here and there some sturdy soul that would not bend. For such as these the forest became a refuge and there grew up in Sherwood and Barnsdale and other great crown forests scattered bands of such outlaws, strong of heart, fleet of foot, steady of eye, potent for great deeds should a leader appear who could weld their disjoined forces.

◆   ◆   ◆

The day came when the Earl of Huntingdon was back in England. He found his castle in ruins. He saw the long lines of gibbets that told the fearful tale of Prince John's tyranny. He traced Marian's flight from the castle until the stolid peasant woman by the cliff told him in simple words of the drama she had witnessed there, the stern leader of the troopers, the sobbing tirewoman, the horse that cropped the herbage unmindful of its twisted saddle and the torn veil that clung to it, the broken earth that marked the brink.

The woman finished the tale and left him.

Then did the Earl of Huntingdon reckon his account against Prince John and kneeling before high heaven he vowed to collect it to the last jot and tittle.

◆   ◆   ◆

In Palestine Richard had achieved his first great victory. Surrounded by his cohorts, midst all the panoply of war, and in the presence of the vanquished, he tasted the sweets of his triumph. But with it came a sense of bitter loss,—that Huntingdon was not there to share it with him.

◆   ◆   ◆

A year passed and then, from the mysterious depths of the forest of Sherwood came whispers of the rise of a robber chief.

Covert tales were told of the magnitude of the band that was gathering under the leadership of one Robin Hood. Wherever two or three villagers, or tillers of the soil, or foresters foregathered they smacked their lips in appreciation of his deeds.

They told of the naked arrow of Robin Hood that spelled death to the enemies of King Richard.

They discoursed of arrows that came wrapped in a sheet of parchment blazoned with the three lions of Richard.

"It is Robin Hood's manner of saying, 'If ye be brave, come to Sherwood Forest. Richard is your King,'" they told each other and they spoke approvingly of the many who were responding to that invitation.

In many a poor home a father or brother creeping home with an armful of food or a handful of pennies murmured the name of "Robin Hood."

And "Robin Hood" gurgled the hired trooper of Prince John, stumbling into barracks with a slit throat, after inflicting base abuses on the people.

Those sycophantic officials who owed their appointments to Prince John began to discover that they were not having everything their own way. They dodged into and out of their houses fearful lest the naked arrow should convey to them its threat and warning. And finally, panic-stricken, they took the case up to Prince John.

"Something must be done," whined the High Sheriff of Nottingham. "If this goes on his army will outnumber ours. Our very mercenaries desert to his cause. His naked arrows come out of nowhere. He brings his insolence to our doorsteps, and pins the arms of King Richard on our housefronts."

The name of his brother had ever a potency to send chills down the spine of Prince John. Now it frightened him into an extravagance his mean soul would have evaded. He directed his scribe to prepare a proclamation offering a bag of fine gold for the delivery to the castle of the person of Robin Hood.

And then—out of the nowhere, as the sheriff had said—the naked arrow came hurtling and pinned the proclamation to the desk on which it was written.

For a space, fear, stark and dread, filled the souls and paralyzed the senses of the Prince and his followers. Then it goaded them to panic-stricken flight.

There was a woman in the hall. A ragged creature, haled before the Prince for gathering faggots in the royal forest. And, too, the purse-bearer remained, hugging to his terror-filled breast the bag of fine gold he had fetched from the treasure chest at the Prince's command.

To them it was given to see a lithe figure appear in the window above them—to feel the dominating presence of the man who knelt on the window-sill and leisurely surveyed the great hall.

Behind the cheerful carelessness that masked his face there lay a powerful purpose. Cool, unafraid, debonair and deadly, his every movement bespoke his ability to accomplish his will.

"Robin Hood!" exclaimed the ragged woman, then knelt at his feet, kissing his hand and repeating, as if it were a shibboleth, "Richard is our King!"

He raised her gently and set her outside his path. It was his whimsy to collect the reward offered for his capture and with an arrow from his good longbow he impaled and retrieved the bag of gold.

The castle guards, summoned from all directions by the Prince and his fleeing knights, gave him chase. He led them a pretty dance, as his fancy dictated, through hall and gallery and courtyard and battlements.

Do you recall that spot on the battlements where Lady Marian Fitzwalter, one early morn, sketched a portrait of her lover, the Earl of Huntingdon, favorite of King Richard and his high constable on the march?

Chance brought Robin Hood to this spot. His head drooped. Almost his courage deserted him, his will to persist. Then he seemed to feel a presence near him—to see a bright face—an upraised arm bearing his sword as if it were a cross to lead him onward. It was but the vision of a moment but it left him uplifted in spirit and grim with purpose.

He finished his triumphal progress from the clutches of his enemy. He marked his course in a way that multiplied the fears in the coward heart of the usurping Prince. The lions of Richard appeared on the very breasts of the guards who pursued him. When he had tired of his sport, he kept rendezvous with gay outlaws in the forest: Little John, who bore a striking resemblance to the favorite squire of the erstwhile Earl of Huntingdon, Will Scarlett, that plump churchman, Friar Tuck, Alan-a-Dale and the rest of his green clad foresters.

◆   ◆   ◆

Meanwhile, through the varied fortunes of Richard the Lion Heart, Sir Guy of Gisbourne had never lost sight of his main purpose. He clung pertinaciously to the idea implanted in his mind by Prince John when they had parted. Prince John desired the death of Richard and Sir Guy of Gisbourne desired what Prince John desired.

Richard's tent was still save for the untroubled breathing of the sleeper on the narrow camp bed. Guards had been set but they had not prevented Gisbourne from slashing the wall of the tent and making an opening that admitted him.

Guided by the sound of the breathing, he crept to the bed and drove his dagger deep into the breast of the sleeper. Before he could withdraw the blade a sound from the inner tent sent him hastily away through the slashed wall. A squire awaited him with his horse. Spurning with his foot the body of the guard he had slain he mounted and galloped away.

Within the tent, on Richard's bed, a still form lay. King Richard, come from the inner tent, bent over the bed and turned the white face toward him

Once too often had his poor jester "played king." This time it had brought him the death meant for a King, for Gisbourne's stroke had been well planted.

Richard closed the staring eyes tenderly—then pondered his plans for the morrow.

◆   ◆   ◆

In England Prince John was still feverishly gathering funds to replenish his depleted army. It was ever his favorite method to make the abbeys and priories yield him forced tribute. If their treasuries were empty his men were empowered to compel them to surrender their sacred implements of worship.

Thus it was that Robin Hood and his merry men, joyfully engaged in relieving the distress of needy villagers with gifts of food and money, were summoned by one of their lookouts to take toll from a band of the Prince's mercenaries who seemed to be in possession of rich treasures.

To overcome the mercenaries was all in the day's work for the foresters but it was not part of their program to convert church treasures to their own use. Hence, when Friar Tuck had identified the holy vessels as belonging to the Priory of St. Catherine's, they rode to the Priory to restore the property.

And slinking after them, after sending a message to the sheriff to come to his assistance, was a spying follower of the Prince.

There was in the Priory garden a nun, with a delicate, high-bred face and an air of lively interest in all about her. While Robin Hood was delivering to the Prioress the treasure they had recovered, this nun kept her eyes fixed upon him.

"It is the Earl of Huntingdon," she said, half-questioningly to Friar Tuck.

"'Tis Robin Hood," replied the good Friar.

"To the poor, mayhap," she told him, "but the Earl of Huntingdon to me since he was three years old."

She whispered a word in the Friar's ear and, surprised and shaken, he carried that word to Robin Hood.

The fair-faced nun crossed the garden and spoke gently to a maiden who sat bent over sewing.

There was a flutter of white hands—a hurried rising—two figures stumbling toward each other with outstretched arms and eyes half-blinded with tears—

Oh, blessed Priory garden! Blessed the leaves of its trees and the water trickling from its fountain! Blessed the walls that surround it and the roof that shuts it in! Blessed all that have given shelter to the fair maid, Marian, and brought her again to the arms of her true lover.

Worshipfully Robin Hood knelt at her feet and worshipfully his arms enfolded her. They had no words—only feelings too deep for words.

◆   ◆   ◆

When speech came back to them, they pieced out the past year between their words of love.

Two novices watched with bright, curious eyes this scene so unusual in their placid garden and Marian's tirewoman, excited and voluble, told them that Robin Hood was really the Earl of Huntingdon and the betrothed of her mistress, the Lady Marian Fitzwalter.

Prince John's spying sycophant overheard the tirewoman's revelation and let himself carefully down from his secret perch on the wall.

Warned by one of his men of the approach of the Sheriff of Nottingham and a band of his mercenaries, Robin Hood and his men took to their horses.

Robin Hood lingered a moment at the gate. He kissed the fair hand of his lady.

"When the lark sings in the morn," he told her, "I will send you a message."

The High Sheriff of Nottingham and the spy from the Priory wall came together to Prince John.

"Lady Marian Fitzwalter lives," they told him, "and Robin Hood is but a name assumed by the Earl of Huntingdon."

Rage and fear trembled in the voice of the coward Prince as he shouted:

"Surround the forest with all your men. Fetch Huntingdon alive. I must *see* him die. And bring the maid from the Priory. Bring her here."

His henchmen departed to do his bidding and the Prince stayed to review the miscarriage of his plans during the past year and to realize that he owed his failures to Richard's friend—his own powerful enemy.

◆   ◆   ◆

Sir Guy of Gisbourne made good time on his long journey homeward. But King Richard who followed soon after him made even better time. He might have overtaken Gisbourne had he not suddenly deflected his course. He sent his men on alone.

"I have a debt to pay," he told them. "I go alone to pay it."

When the lark sang in the morning there was already activity in Sherwood Forest. Among the caves that served as their hiding place, Robin Hood's outlaw band mended bows, sharpened arrow points and discussed their plans for the day.

Apart from the others Robin Hood mused. With the discovery that Marian lived there came an overpowering desire to bring the issue with Prince John to a head.

His band was well organized. He knew to a man the defense of the castle. He saw no reason for delaying.

Picking a blossom from a wildrose bush, he summoned Little John.

"Take this to Lady Marian," he said, "and tell her that when the sun drops over Nottingham hill, I'll come to her."

Little John rode away on his errand of love and Robin Hood threw himself wholeheartedly into a game with his men.

A breathless scout ran into camp.

"All of Nottingham's troops are surrounding the forest," he told his leader.

The announcement fell in well with Robin Hood's plans.

"To the trees with all your men," he told Friar Tuck. "Entrap these troops. I go to Nottingham with Scarlett and Alan-a-Dale. We three shall take the town."

As he spoke he rolled aside the log that concealed one of the secret exits from the lair and he and his two attendants disappeared into the tunnel.

They came out near one of the spots where troopers had picketed their horses and deemed it good strategy to commandeer horses for their own use and thus attract a section of the troops to follow them from the forest.

Friar Tuck and his merry men, dropping mysteriously from the limbs of trees among the troopers left in the forest, surprised and took them prisoners.

And at the same time, Robin Hood and his two friends, safe in Nottingham town, enlisted the townspeople on their side and trapped the soldiers who had pursued them.

Thus far, Robin Hood's plans had worked in tune with his desires.

◆   ◆   ◆

The High Sheriff of Nottingham was never one to risk his skin unnecessarily. He had wholesome respect for the prowess of Robin Hood. He sent his men to Sherwood Forest. For himself, it looked like an easier job to attack the defenseless women of a Priory and drag from that shelter a delicate maiden.

Hence when Little John arrived at the Priory of St. Catherine's he found that the High Sheriff had been there before him and carried the Lady Marian away to the castle and to the Prince.

It took him an appreciable time to discover the whereabouts of Robin Hood and meanwhile that gallant outlaw had given the downtrodden townspeople of

Nottingham a taste of freedom such as they had not known since their King had left for the Crusades.

It was of a piece with the rather grim humor of the time that they should celebrate this freedom by hanging Prince John in effigy.

◆   ◆   ◆

And while the grotesque image of the Prince swung from an improvised gibbet in Nottingham town, in the castle, Lady Marian Fitzwalter was being locked in her old room, and the key of that room was being delivered to Prince John—the man who desired above all things to make her suffer a punishment commensurate with the influence she had exerted against him.

It was the arrival of Sir Guy of Gisbourne that checked Prince John from making an immediate example of Marian.

Gisbourne brought news of magnitude and he delivered his message with dramatic effect. "Sire," he exclaimed with intense feeling, dropping to his knees and kissing the Prince's hand: "Richard is dead. Long live King John!"

Prince John was by nature suspicious. He measured Gisbourne with a wary eye and thought of Robin Hood.

"What of Huntingdon?" he inquired.

"By Richard's orders he rots in a dungeon in France," Gisbourne told him blithely.

The Prince meditated. He could well believe that the bars of a French dungeon were inadequate to hold Huntingdon and therefore his appearance in England did not discredit Gisbourne's story. Also he was eager to believe that Richard was no more.

He summoned a follower.

"Heralds to the north, to the south," he exclaimed, "England is mine."

◆   ◆   ◆

Oddly enough at that very moment a mysterious stranger invaded Sherwood Forest. Clad in black armor and walking with the stride of a man of strength and purpose, he appeared before Friar Tuck. That doughty priest was not in the least perturbed.

"I seek Robin Hood," the stranger told him and when he asked for what purpose, the answer came promptly:

"Mayhap to join him—mayhap to slay him."

Friar Tuck grasped a quarterstaff. He looked at the intruder belligerently.

"It takes a man of mettle to do either," he said, and flourished his staff.

The stranger nodded his acceptance of the implied challenge. He plucked a staff from the hand of a bystander and weighted it with the hand of an expert.

Blows were exchanged thick and fast. Each man recognized in his opponent a worthy foeman.

The forest outlaws, ranged about to see fair play, appreciated the care of the stranger to allow his armor to work him no advantage. A lusty blow was a lusty blow to them regardless of the giver.

It must be conceded however, that the outcome was a surprise to them and to Friar Tuck. That worthy man was so sure of an outcome in his favor that the blow that reached his tonsured head and sent him reeling came as a shock in every sense.

But he rallied to his duties as chief in the absence of his leader. If the stranger wanted membership in Robin Hood's band he had proved his fitness and he was frankly taken in upon that basis.

◆   ◆   ◆

In Nottingham town the swinging image of Prince John still furnished amusement to the townspeople and Robin Hood was teaching them a song his foresters loved to sing:

> "We rob the rich, relieve distressed,
> On damned John to score.
> We'll take a life if sorely pressed,
> Till Richard reign once more."

It was upon this scene that Little John burst with the news of Marian's arrest.

Leaving Will Scarlett and Alan-a-Dale to hold the town, and sending Little John to summon all his men to attack the castle, Robin Hood galloped alone to keep his rendezvous with his love.

And while Marian huddled her slight body against the little altar in her oratory, Sir Guy of Gisbourne was reminding Prince John of his promise.

"My reward, sire—Lady Marian," he said.

But the Prince's usual insolent arrogance was augmented by his sudden elevation to majesty.

"You failed to keep your bargain," he told Gisbourne. Then, superciliously, he flourished the key of Marian's room.

"I have other plans for Lady Marian," he said, and tucked the key back into his belt with a gesture of finality.

Gisbourne bowed low in simulated humility, but when the Prince turned from him to renew his potations with his servile followers, he stealthily filched the key.

◆   ◆   ◆

Robin Hood urged his horse along the forest road that led to the castle.

Little John penetrated to the lair and roused Robin Hood's troops to form for their march to the castle. With them marched the mysterious stranger, the new member of the band. With them, also, went the troops from Nottingham.

And in the castle hall, Gisbourne drew himself quietly away from the noisy party surrounding the Prince and disappeared in the narrow stairway.

Robin Hood came to the outer barrier of the castle. He delayed not to answer the sentry's challenge but galloped toward the drawbridge. The sentry blew a shrill blast. The warder of the drawbridge heard the warning and signaled. The great chains clanked. The beams creaked. The bridge started to lift.

But Robin Hood did not tarry. His jump from his saddle and his leap to catch the lifting bridge were simultaneous. Clinging to the chain he mounted with it and landed on the warder's platform. For a fleeting instant he looked behind him and caught a new peril preparing. A bowman was nocking his arrow and aiming at him. He dodged aside and the warder receiving the shaft full in his breast, tumbled to the moat far below. Robin Hood hurried on through the tower and out on the battlements.

Marian, huddled pathetically at the foot of the altar, roused at the sound of a key turning in the lock of her door. She rose to her feet. The door opened and with sleek tread and satisfied smile Sir Guy of Gisbourne entered.

Lady Marian's upflung head—the tense straightening of her slight body—her gesture of repulsion did not check the recreant knight. He came toward her, leering—vulpine.

For death, death at the hands of a vengeful Prince, Marian had prepared herself during her vigil. Death by torture perhaps.......... a death so terrible that the word of it would tear at the heart of her lover like the claws of a wild beast.

And death—death by torture—was preferable to this unwholesome, loathsome thing that was stalking her. Her mind worked with lightning quickness. She thought of her lover—so long lost, so newly found. His life would be darkened but his heart would ache with pride in her, that she could find a way to save herself from this pursuing pestilence.

She backed away toward the window, the high tower window that looked down on the round stones paving the courtyard so far beneath.

Gisbourne followed. He was very sure of himself, sure of his power—confident of his ability to conquer.

The girl's retreat to the window ledge served to entertain, to amuse him. He knew the height of the ledge on which she stood—he waited for her to sense it—to shrink—and to return to him. He continued to smile his gratified smile and to draw closer to his victim.

Robin Hood's progress along the battlements was checked. A guard with drawn sword crossed his path. He hewed him down. Another. He, too, fell under Robin Hood's onslaught. A third. Robin Hood's sword broke near the hilt but with the stump of it he battered down the man's resistance and left him helpless.

And then as his quick eye sought a method of entering the castle he saw, far above him, in the window of the high tower, the swaying figure of Marian.

He dared not ask himself what tragic explanation accounted for her presence there. Whatever it was, he would save her or go down to death with her.

He leaped from the battlement and caught the thick stem of the ivy that mantled the tower. It held. He climbed upward.

Within the room, Gisbourne took a step nearer to Marian. She repelled him with her outflung hand. He looked at her smirkingly. His sly smile seemed to say, "Why pretend? 'Tis a pretty game, but it can only end in one way. You will not batter your pretty flesh on the hard stones of the courtyard. The shelter of my arms will be much softer."

And then he gasped—his hands flew wide in horror—then lifted to cover his coward's face.

For Marian's fingers, slipping around the pillar that supported the window arch, loosened their grasp. Her eyes blazed with a martyr's purpose. Without a glance behind her to measure her fate she flung herself backward and disappeared from his gaze.

Robin Hood climbing toward Marian's window with desperate haste was instantly aware of her fall, his practised muscles set themselves. He braced himself and flung out his arm to catch her.

Again the thick stem of the ivy met the strain that was put upon it. The two figures dangled high in the air, but they dangled in safety.

Marian's senses swam. She recognized her lover. She murmured "Gisbourne" and then she sank into unconsciousness.

Robin Hood held her tightly. He looked about him. On the battlements in the courtyard below the guards were gathering. The window ledge was but a few feet above him. He climbed until he could lift himself and his unconscious burden over the ledge.

Gisbourne, still sunk in a stupor of terror, roused at the sound and stared as at an apparition.

It was not until Robin Hood had gently placed Marian on the cushions of the window seat and faced him challengingly that Gisbourne realized that his adversary was unarmed. He drew his sword and rushed to impale him.

The battle that followed was brief and Homeric.

Against the berserk rage of Huntingdon, the giant strength of Robin Hood, Gisbourne's desperate defense availed him nothing. He felt himself battered, battered as Marian might have been had her fall not been broken. He felt his grasp on life slipping—slipping. He felt his spine giving—giving—as Huntingdon bent him round a stone pillar and dragged his head and feet toward each other. He seemed to hear from some hazy distance a voice saying:

"But for discipline, I'd crack your spine."

Then—nothingness.

Huntingdon let the body of his enemy fall to the floor.

He lifted his eyes to the window seat. Marian, pale and wan-eyed, struggled to her feet and held out her arms to him. He went to her.

The guards were battering at the door.

Huntingdon and Marian clung to each other for an instant. He whispered to her.

"My men are on their way to the castle. God willing we shall take it for our King. If we fail—"

He took a dagger from his belt and gave it to her. She raised her candid eyes to his and nodded her understanding.

The door gave under the onslaught of the guards. A henchman recognized Huntingdon and departed to report to Prince John.

The guards entered—they packed the room—and yet he did not yield. If he could but withstand them until his men arrived! He fought them off with the sword he had taken from Gisbourne. They retreated—then formed for renewed attack.

Huntingdon had been listening. Listening with the keen senses that he had trained as Robin Hood. Suddenly he heard the sound he had been awaiting, the three blasts on the bugle that was the chosen signal of his band. He tossed his sword away and raised his arms in token of surrender.

And down below, a warder, hearing the blast had come to the platform that gave on the drawbridge.

The leader of the troopers from Nottingham hailed him. "We have captured Robin Hood's band," he shouted, "lower the drawbridge and admit us."

The delighted warder made haste to obey. The troops from Nottingham town looked fine and upstanding and each had a forester hooked to his elbow. This would be welcome news to Prince John.

So the bridge was lowered and the troopers and their companions marched into the courtyard and the warder had not discovered that every trooper held his head erect under compulsion of a sword pressed into his back by one of Robin Hood's faithful followers.

In the courtyard Friar Tuck, Little John and the mysterious stranger put their heads together and discussed ways and means.

Marian—having followed the guards from her room—came to a halt at a gallery window overlooking the great hall.

She saw her lover haled before the Prince. She saw him turn his back squarely upon that arrogant usurper and heard the Prince's wrathful exclamation:

"Strap him to yonder post. We'll teach him which way to face."

She saw the crossbowmen ranged to shoot and the Prince's hand raised to drop the signal for letting fly the darts.

She sobbed in agony. It was unthinkable that she should live if he were gone. She raised her dagger. Then she felt a hand pluck at her sleeve, she heard again the three blasts that were the chosen signal of the band, she saw the creeping figures of the foresters as they filtered by her toward the hall.

She dared to look again.

They had come too late!

The Prince made a down sweep with his dagger, the crossbowmen loosed their darts. They flew toward their mark.

And then—

A huge arm appeared from behind a pillar. A long shield was thrust before the figure of Robin Hood. The darts deflected harmlessly.

Every eye fastened on the device on the shield.

Someone gasped breathlessly: "The three lions of Richard!"

Prince John shrank back in his chair. The crown he had been fondling dropped from his nerveless fingers.

Robin Hood's men looked toward each other questioningly. This was the new member of their band. They watched him as he threw aside his great helmet. They saw him throw his great arm about the shoulder of their leader. They shouted irrepressibly:

"Richard reigns once more!"

Richard and Huntingdon smiled at each other—a smile of understanding.

Then each sought his own.

Huntingdon looked toward the gallery. His eyes and Marian's met. They started toward each other.

Richard stalked to the great throne chair. His scornful gaze encompassed his panic-stricken brother. He said no word but with a heave of his huge arm he swept the shaking ingrate from the throne and set him aside as easily as he would have brushed an insect from his path.

And with him he brushed aside the past. As of old his great voice boomed:

"HUNTINGDON!"

The pigeons on the parapets flapped their surprised wings, Robin Hood's lusty foresters singing on the edge of the minstrel gallery flopped backward in assumed dismay, and Richard saw in the narrow embrasure of the stairway, a sight that pleased him well.

Robin Hood, at last, was bound in chains that would not break.

About his sunbrowned neck two dainty arms were clasped. Hushed whispers of love so deafened his ears that he did not hear the King until he called a second time:

"HUNTINGDON!"

The lovers, hand-in-hand, approached their King.

"Hear all," he shouted. "This is my friend. Him for a time I doubted. I say it to my shame and here and now bespeak his love again."

A burst of wild applause greeted his speech.

Almost did Huntingdon's old shyness overcome him to be thus publicly honored by his King. But the King, gathering Huntingdon and the maid in his embrace made whispered plans for their future.

That night the great hall of the castle gleamed with the light of innumerable torches. In the King's own chapel the sacramental marriage of the Earl of Huntingdon and Lady Marian Fitzwalter had been celebrated.

Now the jovial King and his hastily gathered knights and ladies were ready for the wedding revels. They lined up in formidable array. There was the wheat to shower on the bride and the groom and the wheaten cake to break over the bride's head. There was wine to drink and there were jokes to crack. It was a frank age and had a frank humor all its own. The frolic would last far into the night.

But Marian had been long hidden in the peaceful shelter of a cloister garden. Somehow, Huntingdon felt that she was ill-fitted for a night of courtly merry-making.

He drew her through a seldom-used passage. They came out on the minstrel gallery. He waved a gay defiance to the disappointed throng of knights and ladies and foresters below and then, with his finger on his lip, he signaled his bride.

Marian threw her long train over her arm and tiptoed after him.

With soundless steps they entered the great nuptial chamber and closed the door against the world.

Through the open window the soft night air came laden with the scent of flowers. The crescent moon gilded the towers of a castle on a distant hill. The room was hushed and still.

Huntingdon knelt at Marian's feet. Her soft arms drew his head against her breast.

Outside the door the impatient King summoned them to join the revelers, but they smiled at each other, tenderly, dreamily, and answered him not at all.

The days of their parting had been long and the path that brought them together had been rough to their feet.

But now the past was but a forgotten blur, the future scarce a thing to dream about. It was enough that they had the present—peace and each other—alone—together.

ROBIN HOOD

"FOOT NOTES"

In the first of those mediaeval expeditions undertaken by the Christians of Europe for the purpose of recovering the Holy Land from the Mohammedans, Jerusalem was captured. Later, it was re-taken by the Mohammedans. Hence Richard the Lion Hearted of England (1189–1192) joined with continental rulers in the Third Crusade, an attempt to recapture the Holy City.

◆   ◆   ◆

Tournaments were prohibited under Henry II but when Richard the Lion Hearted came to England and began to organize his army for the Crusade he found his nobles clumsy in the handling of weapons and authorized tournaments for the purpose of giving them practice. "In the first year of his reign the young king caused a solemn tournament to be proclaimed for the purpose of ascertaining, by experiment, the stoutest knights in his dominion."

◆   ◆   ◆

The metrical romances of the thirteenth century describe Richard as one who loved to go about as a "knight adventurous" and for that purpose had several disguises prepared, one of black armor, one of red and one of white.

◆   ◆   ◆

The art of falconry or hawking goes back to the remote past. It had become a common sport in England as early as 875. Warlords of the Middle Ages never left their courts without a cage of hawks to be flown at game birds whenever opportunity offered.

◆   ◆   ◆

The use of homing pigeons to carry messages is as ancient as the time of Solomon. They were used by the Crusading armies from the time of the First Crusade.

◆   ◆   ◆

The use of torture was one of the clauses in the bill of indictment against John. As it was "a thing unknown to the common law of England" its practice was an act of usurpation. A common method of torture was to heat iron needles on the end of wooden handles and thrust them under the nails of the victim.

◆   ◆   ◆

In the Third Crusade the different armies were distinguishable by the color of their crosses. The English wore white crosses.

◆   ◆   ◆

From 1180 to 1250 was the period of chain mail. During this period the pot-helm for head-defense came into use.

◆   ◆   ◆

Surcoats—the loose robes worn over the armor—came in with the Crusades. They afforded protection from the hot sun of the desert.

◆   ◆   ◆

The crossbow, or arbalest, was the popular weapon in Richard's time. It was strung by the archer placing the end of the grooved portion on the ground and bending the bow by the force of both hands, hooking the cord, straightening up, and placing the bolt or quarrel in the groove.

The bolt or quarrel was a dart much shorter than the arrow of the long bow, but it was heavier.

The longbow, at this period, was the weapon of the foresters. It was about five feet long and its shaft or arrow was a cloth-yard, a trifle longer than our modern yard, in length.

◆   ◆   ◆

Robin Hood was born at Locksley, in the county of Nottingham in the reign of King Henry Second and about the year 1160. His extraction was noble and his true name Robert Fitzooth, which vulgar pronunciation easily corrupted into Robin Hood. He is frequently styled and commonly reputed to have been the Earl of Huntingdon.

RITSON.

◆   ◆   ◆

The quarterstaff is an old English weapon formed of a stout pole about 6 1/2 feet in length. It was held by the middle with one hand and the other hand shifted from one quarter of the staff to another, giving it a rapid motion that brought the ends on the adversary at unexpected points.

◆   ◆   ◆

Pocket or hand mirrors were indispensable articles of the toilet much used by the ladies in the twelfth century. The mirrors were made of polished metal.

*From the pen of Fairbanks (under his usual pseudonym, Elton Thomas) comes this telling of the old Robin Hood tale, as originally published in the 1922 program book-let for **Douglas Fairbanks In Robin Hood**. These programs were sold at screenings of the film, and were lavishly produced, including color cover art, cast list, and a condensed version of the photoplay illustrated with scene stills from the film. Because the text style is Olde English, many of the words used here have long since been dropped from our language. We decided to also include the original "footnotes" section of the program, where these words are defined for modern readers.*

Health Plus Enthusiasm

One of the best things in this little world is enthusiasm. All children have it, but when they grow up they often lose it, and that's one of the world's tragedies. To be successful you must be happy; to be happy you must be enthusiastic; to be enthusiastic you must be healthy and to be healthy you must keep mind and body active.

Whatever you undertake, whether it be grinding knives or building railroads, there will be plenty of competition. Learn the value of competition by competing with yourself. Make today's mark better than yesterday's, whether it be in deportment or dialectics.

This system of ours-the universe-is founded on motion. Everything in the world is motion-is made of motion. Motion reduced to elementals means activity, and accelerated activity is just another name for pep.

All men walk, but the man who walks fast is the one most apt to be noticed. Keep active, be enthusiastic, keep moving in mind and body. Activity is a synonym for health, and with health plus enthusiasm, wealth is just around the corner.

Douglas Fairbanks
(Signature)

Article published in a 1924 book entitled **The Truth About The Movies***.*

YOUTH POINTS THE WAY

BY

DOUGLAS FAIRBANKS

WITH A PREFACE BY

JAMES E. WEST
CHIEF SCOUT EXECUTIVE
BOY SCOUTS OF AMERICA

INTRODUCTION

D ouglas Fairbanks is one of our national characters. Of the people best known in this country he would probably be among the first six; of the most popular Americans known in foreign countries he is likely to be among the first three. Indeed, his is a reputation that has penetrated into strange places in far-away corners of the world where America is known simply as a distant country, and everything about it is a sealed book read only in the universal language of the screen.

The moving picture, which is something comparatively new, has already made vast changes in our organized life, and, without it, popularity such as Douglas Fairbanks enjoys would not be possible. The screen enlarges the field that once belonged to the traveling storyteller, but the secret of "Doug's" success was known to the first troubadour who spun a story for the entertainment of a gaping audience. He appeals to the eternal boy in us, the stunt-loving, swashbuckling, romantic boy in us, and screen language is as easily understood in America as it is in Turkey or among the Malays of Borneo, where the sub-title is spoken by a man who stands by the screen.

What forgotten dreams of our youth, drilled out of us by years of "grown-up" endeavors, are called out by D'Artagnan and the Three Musketeers, by Robin Hood, by the Thief of Bagdad and the Arabian Nights Entertainments? The leaping, somersaulting, climbing "Doug" is infectious. I am no longer in my mad youth, but coming out after seeing "Robin Hood," the stunt-centers in me were a-itch, and it required all the restraining influences of the lighted streets, the people passing to and fro, and the other tokens of a sane and orderly world to keep me from at least scaling a wall.

If Douglas Fairbanks can talk to the mature in language as intimate—and I use the word as connoting something that lies deep in us—think with what appeal he speaks to boys, to those youngsters of ours from whom the energy floods, as over a dam, seeking an outlet! The Douglas Fairbanks of the screen talks to them in a voice as authentic as their own, and the appeal is as healthy as it is interesting.

It is because of this that I am somewhat proud of having induced Douglas Fairbanks to write *Youth Points the Way* for *Boy's Life*, the magazine published by the Boy Scouts of America, of which I am editor-in-chief. This work was not only extremely popular, but, judging from the evidence we have had, was found by boys all over the country of practical helpfulness to them. *Youth Points the Way* has two great virtues: it is readable, and carries Douglas Fairbanks' personality. It would not require a very acute critic to discover the author if it had been issued anonymously.

The pages are full of his personality, but they are more than that: they give you a key not only to the boy in the man, but the man in the boy, the man who is doing so much to adapt the classic and preserve its charm through the moving picture. It is a success for which he deserves every praise.

In this book he makes no attempt to preach. Instead he talks in a friendly fellow-to-fellow way about such things as success, keeping fit, tolerance, on making a start, on advancing, on the inspiration of a sunrise. He illustrates them from his own experience in a way which gives his words more force than any other method could succeed in doing—for the virtue of words is only as they interpret the one who uses them.

It is a straightforward, manly message of a fighter who finds joy in overcoming obstacles rather than in the accomplishment; of one who finds a keen delight in physical well-being; of stunts on the rings and horizontal bars of a gymnasium; of racing his horses up a hill to watch the sunrise, of adventuring youth that took his first sight-seeing trip on a cattle boat; of a purposeful worker building on the best there is in him.

I have been happy to cooperate in developing plans whereby this material can be made available to a larger number of boys and I earnestly recommend this little book to parents and friends of boys as well as to boys themselves as not only worthwhile but extremely interesting.

James E. West
Chief Scout Executive
Boy Scouts of America

Youth Points the Way (1924) *by Douglas Fairbanks, was originally published in association with the Boy Scouts of America. We have reproduced this rare book in its entirety on the following pages.*

Youth Points The Way

◆

CHAPTER I

ENTHUSIASM AND OBSTACLES

O nce upon a time many years ago (this is not a fairy tale) a man came to call upon me when I was busy at the telephone. When I had finished telephoning, he called my attention to some words which I had scrawled absent-mindedly upon a pad while the conscious part of my mind had been occupied with talking and listening. You will find that most people have this same habit of making marks of some kind on a piece of paper, provided one is handy, when they are telephoning. Sometimes these marks are undecipherable. Sometimes they resolve themselves into strange designs like enlarged fingerprints. I knew one man who always composed bars of music while he telephoned, reflecting, perhaps, some haunting melody that was dancing about in the back part of his mind.

The word, which I had written over and over again until it sprawled over the entire page, was SUCCESS. Now this struck my visitor as such an odd characteristic that he told other people about it and it got into the newspapers. The result was that many people seemed to think that I must be a sort of authority on success, since even my subconscious mind was always dwelling on it, and whenever I am asked to speak or write about anything, in the majority of cases it is on the subject of success. Just as if I had discovered some magic secret about it which would act as a talisman for other people if I handed it over to them! I wish I had, for it would have made life much easier for me. But I am afraid there is no such magic secret.

If there is such a thing, I am sure it is more in the possession of youth than maturity. And sometimes the odd thought occurs to me that instead of having age instruct youth on how to succeed, it ought to be the other way about and middle age should be humbly asking youth for the secret, for it is one that seems to be lost and forgotten as the years go by. If you don't understand me now, you will as I go on, for I am going to tell you as well as I can what I think is the great underlying principle of success.

Let us see what the ordinary rules of success are: clean and regular living, steady application and industry, a consecration of all our energies to our main purpose and the sacrifice of less important things that conflict with it—above all, hard work and perseverance. This or something like it you must have heard or read a hundred times. Now this is all right. I do not believe that real success has often been achieved without regard for these rules. One of the illusions not only of youth but of maturity is that there is some way of cheating these rules and discovering prosperity and happiness by some pleasant short cut, thereby dodging all the drudgery and hard work to which other people have stupidly committed themselves. But there isn't.

As I say, these instructions are very fine and all that, but I do not believe they go far enough. For the truth is that, although you will not discover success if you do not follow them, you are not by any means sure to discover it if you do. This seems to argue that they lack something. I believe they lack the greatest thing of all. The reason why this thing is so seldom mentioned among the items of advice on success is that it is hard to put into words. It is like many feelings that mean so much to you when they are stirring in the mind and so little when you try to express them to other people.

Let us put it in this way. You may have all the machinery of success before you, but unless you have sufficient motive power behind it, it won't run. It needs electricity—or, since electricity is seldom applied to human nature, let us say, for lack of a better word, "enthusiasm." Without this you will have a piece of very fine but quite lifeless machinery with nothing to turn the wheels.

I don't mean the kind of enthusiasm that cheers loudly at football games. I don't mean the kind of enthusiasm that makes New Year's resolutions. I mean the kind that keeps New Year's resolutions when they are once made. And you must admit there is a great difference. It is that unconquerable spirit of enterprise that laughs at reverses, knowing that they are part of the game, takes obstacles as something to whet the appetite for further endeavor, and fights for what it wants for the pure joy of fighting. It is the great desire that nothing can defeat. If you have this, you can put all the rules for success in the wastebasket and forget them, for they will take care of themselves.

Perhaps now you will understand what I meant when I said that youth was more in possession of the magic secret of success than age. For the spirit of enthusiasm is the special property of youth. Older people often find it deserting them and they are forever trying to recapture it, for you seldom appreciate the real value of a thing until it shows signs of escaping from you. Your problem will be to retain this spirit of enthusiasm as you grow older. And you will not find it always an easy thing to do.

Since whatever success I have attained has been due to my efforts to retain my enthusiasm, I will tell you briefly how I have tried to manage it. I have done it first of all by keeping my circulation and digestion in good order. Fresh air and regular daily exercise are absolute necessities. They are the only sure medicine for driving away the doubts and fears that are the greatest enemies of accomplishment. The moment you begin to entertain any doubts of your ability to do a thing is the moment when your failure begins. And these doubts usually come from a sluggish circulation or an improper care of the body.

If I am about to try to jump over some obstacle, whether it is a table or some mental difficulty in producing a picture, I first try to get a clear mental picture of myself successfully accomplishing it. I get a clear vision of the thing already done, and then doing it, if it is within my power, is comparatively simple. I refuse to admit to myself the possibility that I cannot do it. I suppose that thinking in pictures of this sort is partly the result of my work on the screen where everything is a matter of images. But whatever the cause, I have found it a very helpful habit.

Speaking of obstacles, upon which enthusiasm often trips and falls, I tried to train myself in a new way of looking at them. I felt that, since the world was so full of them, it would be better to cultivate a taste for them. There were certain kinds of food, I knew, which one does not like naturally and for which one has to acquire a taste. I decided to see if I could not acquire a taste for obstacles in the same way. When there were no natural obstacles in my path, I used to create them, just to get used to going over them. If the direct path was too simple, I took a roundabout one which made me jump over and tear through things. I did the same thing mentally. When I had nothing particularly on my mind, I used to say to myself: "What would I do if at this very moment I were asked to make a five minute speech on trade unions?" If some one was with me, I would take one side of the question and he the other and we would argue it out as if we were having a public debate, usually with the result of proving that neither of us knew very much about the question. But it is great mental exercise, and, when mental hazards come in the course of your work, you have cultivated such a familiarity with them and such a taste for them that you go at them with positive relish. Personally I like obstacles. Instead of dampening enthusiasm, they quicken it. I still practice all these experiments with physical and mental obstacles. It has become not only a habit but also a very pleasant pastime. And it keeps the body and mind in great condition.

Of course, no one can maintain enthusiasm very long over any purpose that is not a worthy one. It is hard to think, for instance, of an enthusiastic gambler or an enthusiastic pawnbroker—that is to say, in the sense in which I am using the word. I do not believe that enthusiasm will ever accompany for any length of time any purely selfish endeavor. There comes a sure day when you are struck by doubts whether what you are doing is after all worth the effort, whether the world is in the slightest degree better for what you have done. And, as I have said before, doubts and fears are the two things that enthusiasm cannot survive.

If I did not believe that, in my own work, in addition to making a personal profit, I was in some measure adding to the satisfaction of other people, I fear that my joy in doing it would long ago have died. But to me there will always be a tremendous enthusiasm for all forms of artistic expression. If I can feel the chivalrous spirit of the Middle Ages, if the magic of those days sends a glow through me, that in itself is a very pleasant feeling. But if I can to some degree transfer that feeling to the screen and thence to other minds, there is a triumphant mounting of the spirits that is perhaps the very greatest sensation of all.

One can never be quite sure that his own ideas will fit other people. Perhaps you will discover some better way of holding on to your enthusiasms. But try to hold on to them. For if you do, the world is yours.

This article originally appeared in **Boys Life** *magazine, November 1923.* **Boys Life** *was the official magazine of the Boy Scouts of America, and Fairbanks frequently contributed articles to this publication, aimed primarily at young readers. This piece was also included in a book published by cooperation with the Boy Scouts in 1923 titled* **Youth Points The Way***, a collection of the many columns he penned for* **Boys Life** *Magazine. The series continues on the following pages.*

Youth Points The Way

◆

CHAPTER II

THE ONLY MEDICINE
I EVER TAKE

I f, after having set down what I consider to be the underlying principle of success, I now warn you that success, particularly if easily won, is a very dangerous quality which only a strong constitution can survive, it may strike you that I am contradictory. Still, I shall be no more contradictory than life itself, which often seems to resolve itself into a strange and baffling game of striving for a certain object and then wondering when you have captured it what you are going to do with it. Human nature is so constituted that most of us can meet failure with fortitude, can even extract from it a tonic or stimulus for fresh effort, for the one thing that never dies in human hearts is hope. The really dangerous moment in the career of an individual or a nation is the first flush of success.

I think you will understand exactly what I mean if you recall how you felt at the end of a long period of mental training for an examination or physical training for some kind of athletic competition. When the event was over and you had accomplished what you had set out for, you felt, if I am not mistaken, a sudden let-down of the spirits, a burning out of the enthusiasm which had kept you going at high speed. Your purpose accomplished, your first inclination was to relax and take it easy—to bask in the pleasant contemplation of a task well done. This mood of contentment is natural and proper enough if it does not continue too long, but if you do not soon discover that what you have accomplished, no matter how long and arduously you have struggled for it, is only a trifle in the big scheme of things and that other greater things lie ahead, you will become a victim of the most dangerous of all maladies, the chief enemy of progress—contentment. Discontent with the conditions of life, and the earnest struggle to improve them, discontent with one's self and the desire to rebuild one's self in a better and stronger mold—this kind of discontent and the desire to remove its causes has made the world advance until it is a pretty good place to live in. To me, cheaply purchased contentment is the great evil of mankind. It leads to inaction, to flabbiness of mind and body, to self-indulgence and decay. Motion, forward motion, is the ruling principle of life. When we cease to move, to struggle, to reach out for something yet unaccomplished, we are ceasing to live.

This same kind of danger—that of contentment and its vices—which attacks the individual often attacks a nation. Success, or civilization, which in the case of a nation is the same thing, killed ancient Rome. She was ruined by too much civilization. The sinews of the nation became soft and flabby from too much contentment, too much ease and luxury, and decay set in. I sometimes fear that we are facing a similar plight. We have risen rapidly to such a high degree of civilization that we are in grave danger of sitting back comfortably in soft-cushioned chairs and taking things easy, of allowing our muscles to grow soft and flabby, of yielding to that crime against life itself—inaction. We have too many contraptions for comfort, too many inventions which cater to luxury, too many labor-saving devices, too many easy ways of getting things done. Civilization has brought us automobiles, elevators, French chefs; everything is so arranged that we can extract the maximum of pleasure with the minimum of effort. We won our civilization by battling with the forces of nature, by fighting for our food and a safe place in which to sleep, by developing powers of resistance and endurance and building up new faculties, by a sturdy reaching out for things that were beyond us. The way to lose this civilization is by complacently enjoying it, by sitting in soft chairs and having things brought to us.

My antidote for that dangerous contentment which comes to nations and individuals after a period of accomplishment is a very simple one but is, or has been in my case, very effective. It is nothing more nor less than hard physical exercise. I will make a confession to you. Several times in recent years, after completing a picture I have almost yielded to that demoralizing sense of satisfaction that I have spoken of. I have been in great danger of becoming contented and ceasing to strive further. The picture has "gone over" better than I had expected; I have felt that my ambition of becoming an important producer has been realized. I have seen before me pleasant avenues of idleness leading far into the future, pleasure jaunts around the world taking me wherever the fancy beckoned—a soft, easy, luxurious existence from which the inconvenience and annoyances of work were completely banished.

Fortunately at these times I have usually caught sight of some of the exercising paraphernalia that I keep on some unoccupied part of the studio grounds and have devoted an hour or so to work on a horizontal bar, to swinging myself over as great a height as I could manage by means of a ring attached to a long suspended rope which offers endless possibilities for new stunts, or to any other kind of activity that the spirit of the moment prompted. The effect of an hour or two of this is like magic. The blood tingles in your veins again. The thoughts of a little while ago seem like the twisted ideas of a maniac. It is like letting a breeze blow through the mind. There is no longer any exaggerated notion of the value of what you have already done—only a realization of how pitifully small any achievement has been in comparison with what it might have been—only a great pulsing desire to go forward instead of looking backward and to surpass anything you have done before. I challenge any one with a high idea of his own achievements, to walk briskly to a hilltop at night, to spend ten minutes looking at the stars, and then to return home with the same idea of his own importance.

It may seem that I have used a considerable amount of space in establishing the very urgent need of regular exercise in these days of comparative ease and luxury. But from most instructions on the subject you get the impression that people should exercise in order to acquire enormous biceps and become encrusted with muscles like a gorilla. I have tried to show you a more sensible reason, for few of us, I think, have any ambition to become physical giants. The great thing that exercise can do is to fix a proper balance between the body and mind, to give us a healthy, active outlook on life so that neither our petty failures will discourage us too much nor our petty triumphs give us too much cause for satisfaction and contentment. I see it as the great antidote for the softening and demoralizing effect of too much civilization. It will help you to realize that the fruits and rewards of labor are not nearly so enjoyable as the labor itself and that the only permanent satisfaction comes from continued activity.

The kind of exercise you take is of minor importance. The main requirement is that it shall be regular and done in a spirit of enjoyment. Perhaps the word "medicine" that I have used in the title of this article is an unfortunate one, since it suggests something disagreeable taken under compulsion. The only medicine I use is some kind of liniment for cuts and bruises. I do not believe that exercise taken in a spirit of indifference does a particle of good. If you can't get a spirit of fun in it try some other form of exercise which appeals to you.

Generally speaking, exercise of any kind becomes enjoyable when you introduce the element of competition. This does not mean that you must confine yourselves to tennis, baseball or other games. If there is no opponent handy to compete with, you can learn to compete with yourself. If it took you fifteen minutes to walk to school or to work yesterday, see if you can do it in fourteen today. Throw your head back, walk erectly, breathe deep, and you will find that although it may not be the most exciting kind of exercise, there is considerable fun in it.

I cannot give you a list of the kinds of exercise that have kept me in fine physical condition, because they have constantly changed to adapt themselves to my surroundings. When I am in the country I ride horseback every day and swim if there is water handy. But if horseback riding and swimming were denied me, it would not make the slightest difference. There are a hundred other things that I like just as well. Since most of my time is spent at the studio, I have to confine myself largely to the kind of exercise that I can crowd into the short intervals between working hours. I have rigged up a number of devices that permit me to combine hard exercise with the fun of competition. The most successful of these is one that I have mentioned. It consists of a ring attached to a long rope, suspended from a stout cross-bar. It is not unlike the swinging ring that you will find in every gymnasium. At one end of the pendulum swing of this ring I have placed jumping standards. Catching the ring on a run away from the standards, the idea is, on the backward swing of the rope, to see how great a height you can clear by letting go of the ring at the end of the swing and shooting over the bar on the standards. There are usually plenty of competitors in this sport, but if there aren't any, it makes no difference. If I cleared twelve feet yesterday and can't make it today, I know that there is something wrong with me. In this fashion I compete with myself. I do all the stunts I can think of on parallel bars which are part of my outdoor gymnasium and try to invent new ones. The more imagination you get into exercise, the more fun you have and the more good it does you. The game I play most at present is a relative of tennis and a descendant of the old English game of battledore and shuttlecock. This is the fastest and hardest exercise I have ever taken. Some of my friends have christened this game "Doug," but by any other name it would be as fast.

But if all these devices and games with which I like to surround myself were thrown into the Pacific Ocean, I wouldn't care a snap. There are always steps and platforms which challenge me to jump them, there are always people to wrestle with, and projections from which I can chin myself. In exercise, like almost everything else in life, it is not the outward form but the spirit behind that counts. If you have this spirit, you will not confine your exercise to any set form or any number of minutes or hours a day. I suppose that ten minutes of perfunctory exercising in the morning is better than nothing, but personally I am prejudiced against that kind of thing. It seems to lack that spirit I speak of. I would just as soon confine my thinking to a certain number of minutes a day, or my religion to a portion of Sunday morning.

So let me tell you that if you think that you are living under conditions or in surroundings that make proper exercising impossible, there are no such conditions or such surroundings. Not if you have the spirit and the desire. My work is as exacting as that of most people, but I find time for exercise each day because I know it is an absolute necessity. When I am living in a New York hotel, although the conditions are not very favorable, I get the same amount of exercise. Even when I am traveling across the continent I devise some means of exercise, although it is a poor substitute for out-of-door games. When a Pullman porter finds me chinning myself on the upper berth, he may think I am crazy, but it is a very harmless form of insanity.

My own methods must be successful as far as I am concerned, for at the age of forty I can do any physical feat that I could do at twenty, but I cannot prescribe them for you. You will have to invent your own system. The one thing I can confidently advise you to do is to beg, borrow or steal the equivalent of two hours' hard exercise a day. If you do this, you will rarely need any other medicine to keep your body strong and resistant against illness and your mind clear and efficient. It is the only way I know of to beat the effects of too much civilization. Resist everything that tends to make you soft and satisfied. If your food comes too easily, make a game of eating. Take your soup from the mantel and chase your pie across the back yard. I do not need to explain that I do not mean this literally. What I *do* mean is *keep in motion* and do not accept the benefits of civilization too easily. Work, fight, play for everything. If you will do this, you will need no other medicine.

*Originally published in the December 1923 issue of **Boys Life** Magazine, later reissued in book format as **Youth Points the Way**, printed by the Boy Scouts of America.*

Youth Points The Way

◆

CHAPTER III

Sunrise and Other Things

When I spoke of the pitfalls of contentment and the dangers of too much civilization and urged you, when the path is too smooth and life too easy, to create obstacles for yourselves, to make a game out of living, to pursue your food so that you may eat it with greater relish and better digestion, I was not joking. Or if I were, I am to be excused, for it is a joke which I often play upon myself. On a Sunday morning before the sun is up and the hills of Beverly, where I live, are still sleeping under a blanket of mist and darkness, I chase my breakfast to the top of a mountain and manage to overtake it just as the first fingers of dawn are touching the hilltops.

Early rising, I know, is a pastime which most people will admit at once is a great thing for others. I once invited to my home a man who kept me up until two o'clock at night with a powerful argument in favor of early rising and then slept until eleven o'clock the next morning. The most profound conclusion I can arrive at on this subject is that early rising is a great thing for those who like it.

It depends, I suppose, on the part of the day you like best. Each has its special mood and charm. If you take the verdict of poets and song writers, twilight, with its sentiment and melancholy, easily wins first place in the affections of mankind. Midnight, by wrapping a veil around things, makes life magical and mysterious. It is a time when imagination and emotion no longer held in leash by the common-place facts of daytime, run away with us. But one thing is certain. You will have to choose; you cannot enjoy the pleasures of both midnight and sunrise. For me, the dawn—the beginning of a new day, with the air keen and fresh, and the sun sending the vapors of night and the cares and troubles of yesterday scurrying into the distance.

I presume that this preference for the dawn is explained by the fact that I like beginnings better than endings and promise better than fulfilment. I find a greater mystery in birth than in death. I like looking forward better than backward and would rather anticipate what is to come than review what has already gone before.

Sunrise provides a great acid test for the thoughts that come to you late at night. Take out the idea that took possession of you the night before and hold it up between you and the rising sun. If it still seems reasonable you can be pretty sure that it is a sound one. But in many cases, I am afraid, it will strike you as fantastic and impracticable and will disappear like a sprite with the first streak of dawn. The ideas that come to you at sunrise may not have quite the same imaginative quality as those that are born in the silence and shadows of evening, but as a rule they will stand up better and live longer.

But enough of this philosophy. It is time to get up. It is four o'clock on a Sunday morning in southern California and if we are to see the sun rise, we must be stirring. It is still dark with just a pale glimmer of light streaking the East. A solitary coyote, one of a band which steals down nightly from the mountains to prowl about the house, is barking a protest against the coming dawn, but save for this sound and the first notes of a mocking bird tuning up for the day's performance, there is dead silence. It is something of an effort to propel one's self out of bed, for it is warm and comfortable and California nights even in the summer are damp and chilly. But it is worth the struggle.

There are two things which seem to be almost impossible. One is to take a cold bath every morning without bragging about it, and the other is to get up early in the morning without an irresistible impulse to wake other people up and tell them what they are missing. I am consumed with a vast pity for my unfortunate guests who are with me for the week-end. Poor folk, they are lying stupidly in bed, when they might be outdoors, enjoying the freshness of early morning. I lose no time in going to their rooms and waking them up. Some of them seem to think that I have conferred a doubtful favor by arousing them but they get up none the less. It is one of the penalties they have to pay for visiting me.

In a few minutes we have horses saddled and someone has been sent ahead to our destination with provisions for breakfast. It is now almost clear daylight and a brisk breeze is tearing the veil of mist from hill and canyon. Back in the city of Los Angeles a few lights are still palely burning and night seems to linger there, but the hilltops ahead of us are already catching the glow of dawn. We must hurry if we are to beat the sunrise to the top of the mountain.

Our path is so densely buried beneath brush and thicket that we would have difficulty in clinging to it if it were not for our sure-footed western ponies which need no guidance. If it were not for our chaps, the whipping of branch and twig, as we dash upward, would be extremely painful. Even as it is, they sting and hurt a little. The ridge which the path follows is a narrow one and on either side there are deep canyons. A misstep would be dangerous. But without some danger, there is no flavor to adventure. There is a primitive wilderness ahead, and the only reminder of civilization is when we look back at the city still slumbering at our feet. To the west the Pacific Ocean is dimly visible, gray and mysterious in the neutral light of early morning. And one can discern the long island of Catalina, which tourists like to visit, in the distance.

There is a terrific scurrying in the underbrush as we stir up some wild animal in hiding. Maybe it is a coyote, maybe a wildcat, maybe a mountain lion. As long as we are guessing we might as well make the guess a good one. This gives two of us an idea. We dash ahead of the others and lie in waiting for them behind a dense thicket. As they pass us we rush upon them with a yell. And they, after a moment of panic, pretend, of course, that they knew who it was all the time and weren't startled at all. It's all fun, all adventure, all high spirits—a natural reaction and relief at breaking away from the cramping effect of cities, of too much conventionality and too much civilization.

We have reached the spur, which was our objective, in just half an hour. We have beaten the sun by a scant five minutes, for the East is now kindling with a tremendous glow. The man we sent ahead has not been wasting time. Already a fire is burning in an improvised stove made of hastily assembled stones and enough assorted food is cooking to ration a small army. One pleasant thing about pursuing your food is that you don't need the advice of a dietitian. After a hot pursuit, you are in a condition to devour cobblestones and digest them easily. We have ham and eggs, jam, coffee, hot cakes and maple syrup, which if taken at home in the quantities we now consume would completely unfit us for the day. We are a strange and motley looking gathering, as the sun breaks over the rim of the world and lights up the oddities of our costumes. Most of my guests do not come prepared for this sort of jaunt and I have had to outfit them as best I could. Chaps drawn on over Oriental pajama suits and purple smoking jackets give a comic opera touch to our expedition. One of my guests carries a long scratch across his countenance where a rebellious twig slapped him. But everybody is hungry and happy. And everybody exclaims as usual over that daily miracle—the rising of the sun—just as if it were a personal discovery. I like this. To me, the sunlight slanting over the fair country of southern California with its infinite variety, its hills, its rugged canyons and its peaceful ocean demands some sort of vocal demonstration. It may not be dignified. It may not be a high form of artistic appreciation. But when I see the sun bound up over the California hills, I shout. I can't help it.

The morning, as I have said, is a good time to test out the thoughts of yesterday. After you have climbed a mountain and eaten a hearty breakfast, it is pleasant to settle back for a while and take things easy; to watch the fire go out, and see the landscape kindle with the light and warmth of a new day. Our particular location makes a pleasant background for thinking. Civilization is behind us and wilderness ahead. In one direction we could lose ourselves in the mountains, but in the other a big city sprawls at our feet and we have the satisfaction of knowing that in a few minutes we can recapture all the comforts and refinements of modern life. It is possible to balance one against the other and taste the pleasures of each. To the north steadily mounting foothills lead to the Santa Monica mountains. To the south lies Hollywood with its bright Spanish roofs, and its level boulevards leading to the ocean.

In the far distance there are strange looking conglomerations of architecture, ancient, medieval and modern, which might puzzle the casual observer until he remembers that this is Hollywood and that the odd edifices he sees are only motion picture "sets," serving as backgrounds for picture plays representing various periods in history. Perhaps the most fantastic of all is our own studio where the medieval castle of "Robin Hood," still standing, rubs shoulders with the spires and minarets of the ancient city of Bagdad, newly erected for our present production, "The Thief of Bagdad."

This brings me to the thoughts of yesterday. Last night, in a pessimistic moment, it seemed to me that the motion picture industry was perhaps a weak and feeble sort of pastime which was hardly worth the effort that went into it. These gloomy moments come to all of us. But to-day, as I sit in the morning sunlight, everything seems different. I am confident that whatever its weaknesses and present shortcomings may be, it is the greatest medium for expression the world has ever known, and that it will ride sooner or later to a high destiny. It reaches more people than the combined art, history and literature of all time. And for thousands of people it provides the only touch of color and romance that creeps into their lives.

Those of us who are engaged in this form of entertainment should be conscious of a great obligation, for it is in our power to shape and direct its future. Indirectly this same obligation is shared by the public, of which the youth of this country is the most important part. There has never been any kind of art which is equally responsive to the demands of the audience. If you don't get the kind of picture you want you must blame yourselves a little. For every producer is struggling to give you exactly what you want, and if you make this want emphatically enough known, in the end you will get it. The trouble is that although the box office serves as a kind of barometer of public approval, there has never been any very emphatic or well-voiced expression of opinion which will set the stamp of approval on what is good and condemn what is bad.

So it may be in your power more than it is in mine to direct the future of the motion picture art. If, for instance, the Boy Scout organization should critically give its approval to a picture which it finds meritorious and publicly demand more pictures of that sort, and if it would be equally candid in condemning a picture which it found weak, bad or not, in accordance with clean American ideas, I think you would find that producers would not take this criticism lightly.

But thinking is a luxury which one may not continue too long on an expedition of this sort. Such rambling thoughts as have come to us give way before the necessity for action. The breakfast things must be taken care of and the fire completely extinguished, for forest fires are too common occurrences in this locality. Once started, they sweep over the hills for miles, charring the entire landscape and endangering lives and homes.

We have had enough rest, enough meditation for a while. What we want now is action, motion, speed. We are in the saddle again, a little stiff from sitting so long but eager to take the trail home. Downward we plunge through the thicket, bracing ourselves—so steep is the descent—so that we will not slide over the heads of our horses. In a few minutes we are in the depth of the valley where the sun has not penetrated and it is still almost as black as midnight. In the clothes which protected us from the chill of early morning we are now hot, sticky and uncomfortable. The same inspiration occurs to us all simultaneously—the swimming pool! We race for it, just as we have raced for the sun earlier in the morning.

We come out of the pool, greatly refreshed and invigorated, glad that we are alive and amazed to find that it is still only six o'clock and that only two hours have elapsed since we arose. But if you try, you can crowd a lot of fun into two hours.

*Originally published in **Boys Life** Magazine, January 1924. Also included in the Boy Scouts of America book **Youth Points the Way**. See following page for next chapter in sequence.*

Fairbanks was never happier than when he was riding the open range with his cowboy friends.

Youth Points The Way

✦

CHAPTER IV

ON GETTING A START IN LIFE

"So you see," concluded the pompous gentleman who had been reviewing his past for the delectation of a younger audience and whose achievements loomed much larger in his own mind than in anybody else's—"So you see how I got my start in life."

"Yes," remarked a facetious listener, "I see what gave you your start in life but what was it that stopped you?"

This is not quoted as an example of rare humor, but because it represents an attitude of protest and rebellion which is growing in people's minds against the flood of advice, sermons on success, and easy lessons in greatness which is swamping the world to-day. We are living in a time of quack remedies, short cuts and magic formulas. If something is wrong with your health, instead of removing the cause, just take Mr. So-and-So's new treatment and you will be yourself, or somebody better, in short order. If economic or industrial or political conditions are in a bad tangle, Mr. What's-His-Name has a cure-all which will prevent anything from a labor strike to a European war. By reading a single number of almost any current magazine you will find how without particular talent or long period of labor you can become a ruling figure in the world of finance, art or science—a wizard in any line of work you choose to take up. Your salary will increase by the most astonishing leaps and bounds.

Now this, of course, is the most arrant nonsense, as any one knows. We are suffering from an epidemic of too much advice, too many instructions on how to achieve distinction of one sort or another. We are so saturated with expert information on how to do things that we incline to overlook the fact that the principal thing is to do them, and the only way to do them is by the hardest and most grueling labor—the kind that leaves you so exhausted you will have little energy to absorb quack notions handed to you on a silver platter by people who think they have discovered quick and easy routes to greatness.

So if I were to advise you who are trying to get the right start in life, I would advise you to stop listening to advice and paying attention to other people's rules, including my own. All I can hope to do in these little essays is to stimulate your appetite for accomplishment. You will have to do the rest. I cannot give you any ready-made curriculum on how to conduct your lives successfully. And neither—I think—can anybody else. I do not mean to say that you can not absorb helpful hints and inspiration by studying the lives of men of accomplishment. But do not attempt to pattern yourselves too rigidly on someone else's model. His way of living may suit him to perfection but it may be the worst thing in the world for you. I used to know a fine oarsman, a champion single sculler, who won race after race against the keenest competition and used to arrive at the boat landing, just before the race, smoking a long black cigar. Imagine how ridiculous it would have been if this man had seriously prescribed his own habits for others and had said, "The way to win boat races is to smoke a cigar before every race." And you have read no doubt many times in the newspapers of men who live to be a hundred years old and who state, as if there were some connection between the two facts, that they have always helped themselves liberally to Scotch whisky. I mention these exaggerated cases to emphasize the absurdity of trying to apply the notions and habits of other people to yourself.

If you will study yourselves carefully, you can make your own rules and administer your own advice. You will know almost instinctively what is good for *you*. Some one whom you admire may tell you very convincingly that the time to do one's best work is at night. But if you can work best in the early part of the day—as most of us can—don't be influenced by what he says. Follow your own impulses. Just because a man who is accomplishing wonders goes without eating until evening, don't jump to the conclusion that this is the thing for you to do. For in nine cases out of ten it isn't. Try things out and discover under what conditions you can get along best. Then make your own rules.

I would not bother too much about how other people have got their start in life. It's better to be a self-starter, and begin in your own way. You may find that many of our great men spent their early youth in log cabins, read by candle-light, split rails or painted barns to help out the family exchequer. But there is no more relation between these humble beginnings and later success than there is between boat racing and cigar smoking. They simply show that these men had a power to conquer adverse circumstance and to move ahead in spite of a bad start. Many of our presidents have come from Ohio, many of our most talented writers from Indiana. But no one but a lunatic would seriously recommend to young men with political aspirations that they immediately change their residence to Ohio, or to young men with ambitions to become great writers that they move to Indiana, any more than one would advise you to leave a comfortable home and intern yourselves in a log cabin as a fitting preparation for future greatness.

It seems that many of our leading financiers left home in early youth and hit the big city without a cent in their pockets. This is another of the old familiar traditions as to how to start out in life. But I would hesitate to recommend it. If you hit the town in this reckless fashion, it is quite likely to hit back.

All I am trying to say is that these pleasant old traditions make diverting reading but hardly furnish an infallible guide to future greatness. It will take a more profound person than I am to establish the relation of cause and effect between these early beginnings and later success of life. The best you can do is to adapt yourselves to your own circumstances whatever they may be, and make the most of them. If they seem to cramp and handicap you the battle against them will develop strength, courage, and the habit of surmounting difficulties—qualities which will be of immense value to you through life.

If the college is within your reach, by all means avail yourselves of a college course and do not accept the silly notion that four years of abstract academic training will unfit you for the practical problems of life. The more your mind is trained in studying science, art, philosophy, the history and customs and languages of the past, the better it will be prepared to grapple with the problems of the present, which with a little variation are only the old ones repeated. If on the other hand, circumstances make college impossible, you will find many consolations; among them that some of the best educated men never went to college and that many of the leaders in the world of business to-day had almost no schooling at all. Teaching yourself, which is what these men had to do, requires much more patience and harder work than absorbing education from experts, but sometimes it is more effective. To be absolutely impartial in this matter of condemning other people's rules of living and theories of success as applied to you, I would like to include my own. They have worked out very well for me, but I can think of no greater folly than of foisting them upon other people.

For example, I believe that I got my first real impetus in life by borrowing a thousand dollars. I decided that I wanted to see the world. So I borrowed this money and toured Europe. My struggle to repay this obligation gave me a momentum which continued after the money was paid. It gave me the habit of continuous activity, of extending myself to the utmost. The ordinary human being will do exactly what he has to do and not very much more. I had to pay back that thousand dollars and to do it I had to work as I never worked before. Incidentally on this trip abroad I met a producer who afterwards signed me up for a long-term contract on the stage.

But I hardly need to tell you how preposterous it would be for me to advise you to start out in life by borrowing money. It happened to work in my case. My own theory is that the more obligations a man has the harder he will work. A man exerts himself most when he is in a hole and has to fight his way out. The more the odds are against him the harder he will struggle to equalize them.

But this might be a very dangerous philosophy for you to follow, and if I were you I would throw it into the same discard with other people's theories in general and build my own philosophy and my own rules of living, borrowing the precepts of others only when I was sure they fitted me.

No man is quite sincere who accounts for his start in life or his later success without taking into consideration the element of luck. It has become popular to advise youth that nothing in the world counts but one's own efforts and the determination to succeed. But to be quite frank about it, this is not the whole truth. There is such a thing as luck and we might as well admit it. Otherwise how do you account for the fact that Jones and Smith both started out with equal advantages, with nearly equal ability, with the same determination to succeed and that Jones is a multimillionaire, holding an important executive position in one of the biggest industries in the country, and Smith a small-salaried man holding a subordinate place. Apparently Smith has spared no effort in his struggle for success, but something went wrong; but with Jones, something quite beyond his own calculations and control lifted him to a position way beyond his wildest expectations. Or take the case of Brown and Green. Brown was interested in real estate and had his eye on a piece of property in Hollywood belonging to Green. On the day when Green was to sell his property at a low figure to Brown, he was the victim of an automobile accident and was in the hospital for several months. When he came out he found that his property had increased a hundred per cent in value and that he had made many thousand of dollars by accidentally holding on to it. Certainly Brown was not to blame for Green's accident. If it hadn't happened, Brown would have made the money instead of Green. This was good luck for Green and bad luck for Brown.

But there are two things to bear in mind about luck. One is that, since it is entirely beyond our control, there is no use in worrying about it. The other is that after all it is fairly evenly divided and you will get plenty of both kinds. Opportunity, which is another name for luck, will come to you sooner or later.

You can bank on that. If you are ready for it—that is to say if you have trained yourself in mental alertness and physical fitness so that you can make full use of it—you will have all the ingredients of success. But opportunity, without the proper preparation, without the ability to seize it, turns out to be a hollow and useless thing. It passes swiftly, leaving only a pitiful realization of what might have been. Honest and persistent endeavor toward the realization of some worthy purpose, a faith that acts as a shock absorber to all the jolts along the rough road of life, an enthusiasm that laughs at adversity, and a regulation of one's life so that body and mind are at their best—these are the fundamentals. Turn your back upon them and you will be like a man in a foot race who starts to run in the wrong direction. The most colossal luck in the world cannot help you.

*This chapter of **Youth Points the Way** originally appeared in the February 1924 issue of **Boys Life** Magazine. The next chapter in sequence follows.*

Youth Points The Way

◆

CHAPTER V

THE OTHER FELLOW'S POINT OF VIEW

Having tried to explain what age may learn from youth, it now seems only fair to turn the tables and show, if I can, what youth may learn from age. To you who are embarked upon the tempestuous adventure of youth, with the blood boiling in your veins and ambition calling to you, this thing that you may learn from age may seem a pale and feeble quality compared with the more ostentatious prizes that life has to offer. This meek and un-imposing quality will put no more money in your pockets. I doubt whether it will have any bearing on what the world calls "success." But I will guarantee that whether or not the thing I speak of will commend itself instantly to you, the method of procuring it, which I will outline later, will have your eager approval. Not to make a conundrum out of it, the quality I have in mind is tolerance.

I do not believe, as I have said before, in any of the quack remedies, in any of the swift and easy routes to success and happiness which are so current in the world to-day. I have no passion for reforming the world. I know no method of so altering human nature and draining off its weaknesses that men will begin at once to return borrowed umbrellas. But I do believe that the more we learn and practice the virtue of tolerance, the better place the world will be to live in.

Since words mean different things to different people, let me see if I can explain what tolerance means to me. Then if it seems to you a desirable quality, I will show you a most agreeable way of acquiring it. We are all gazing upon a more or less familiar world with different eyes,—almost as if we were wearing spectacles with different colored lenses. What seems highly important to you strikes somebody else as trivial and silly; what interests and excites you bores and

174

annoys another; what seems right to you seems entirely wrong to some one else and *vice versa.* The hardest thing for us to understand is people whose ideas and tastes differ from our own. We have a secret feeling that there is something wrong with them. They may not be positively insane but they are at least trembling on the border of insanity. If your favorite study is mathematics and your favorite outdoor sport is baseball, you will be inclined to view with suspicion some one whose tastes run to Latin poetry, and golf. And if you have a practical mind leaning toward business, you will look with pity upon your acquaintance who is stuffing his mind with useless ideas about literature and the fine arts. Your neighbor is a shiftless fellow who never keeps his lawn properly mowed and lets weeds overrun his garden. Do you know what he thinks about you? He wonders if it wouldn't be a good thing if you spent less time in trimming your grounds and more time in trimming your mind which he thinks is so overrun with weeds that you can't use it properly.

If I were to state in one sentence what tolerance means to me, I should say that it was the rare gift of getting the other man's point of view. It means a sufficient acknowledgment of our own deficiencies so that we hesitate to judge other people too harshly. It means an understanding which allows for some other point of view than our own,—a soft, charitable bent of the mind which has come to understand that the frailties of human nature are a common inheritance from which none of us are exempt and that the chief difference between us and those we condemn is that they make a different kind of mistake. The quality of tolerance admits that other people have the same right to arrange their lives, to pursue their ambitions and choose their pleasures that we have. If we are annoyed by their manner of living and their habits of thought, we can be quite sure that there are several people who would like to see us shot at sunrise for ours.

Tolerance is unfortunately so much more uncommon than intolerance that in trying to find examples of the former I find my mind flooded with instances of the latter. I think of the soldier who complained that every one else in the company was out of step with him. In any one of our political campaigns you will see intolerance swaggering out into the field, armed with its usual weapons of abuse and denunciation. You will find one ardent partisan condemning his opponent as an idiot, a scoundrel and a man of loose principles who would willingly betray his country simply because he holds a different opinion on the League of Nations, or government ownership or some other issue upon which it is conceivable that people might honestly disagree. This vilification of people who do not agree with us, this violent absorption in our own point of view and reluctance to admit the possibility of any other, furnish a very good example of the exact opposite of what I mean by tolerance. It is the commonest mental malady I know of and, like many others, attacks youth most severely. As one grows older, some fortunate mellowing influence sets in. The suspicion arises in your mind that in some things at least you may be wrong and others right. You find yourself studying other people's views and reconnoitering on the other side of the question with a certain pleasure. And it dawns on you suddenly that you must have some better reason for holding any belief than the fact that you have always held it before. You become gradually intolerant of yourself and tolerant of others, which is a very good sign. So, just as enthusiasm makes a gay and rollicking companion for youth, tolerance makes a comforting counselor for later years.

The prescription which I offer as a cure for this widespread disease of intolerance is, as I promised you, so agreeable and easy to take that I think you will be inclined to follow it whether you have the malady or not. It consists simply in travel. Do not misunderstand me. I do not intend that you should immediately start out on a tour of Central Africa. But you can at least make frequent journeys away from your immediate environment. Without been conscious of it you are slowly becoming a slave to that environment; your eyes day after day are filled with the same images, your minds with the same ideas, your social world with the same people. Viewing things constantly from the same angle, narrows the vision, shuts up the mind and kills the imagination. If I lived continuously in Hollywood, in the atmosphere of motion picture production, I might quite conceivably come to the conclusion that this was the one important business of the world, that the camera gave the only proper interpretation of life, and that nothing else mattered.

You are living, let us say, in Springfield (an imaginary Springfield in any state). Take a little trip to Hillsboro about ten miles away. If I am not mistaken, you are strongly of the opinion that everything about Springfield is superior to Hillsboro. The people in your town have more sense, are more progressive citizens and better fellows in every way than these misguided people who for some obscure reason have chosen to live in a place like Hillsboro. Walk, if you can, to Hillsboro, and on the way let the sun and wind get into your system and take some of the kinks and prejudices out of your mind. You will be surprised to find that these benighted people who live in Hillsboro average up pretty well, and, except for one ridiculous notion, are just as useful members of society as the citizens of your own home town. This notion is that they are a trifle higher in the scale of life than your unfortunate townsmen who are condemned to live in a place like Springfield.

Everywhere you go you will find this exaggerated loyalty to a particular locality, which we call provincialism and which is a form of intolerance, since it has little use for other places and other customs. I was sitting one winter night in a New York hotel with a native New Yorker whose mental horizon did not go beyond Manhattan Island and who thought that civilization had never penetrated west of the Hudson River. It suddenly occurred to me that both he and I had been living too long in the shadow of elevated railways, skyscrapers and metropolitan hotels. We needed new images in our minds, wider horizons, a fresh point of view. Having an adventurous spirit, he promised to accompany me wherever I went. Three days later we stepped off the train at Boulder, Colorado, and started across the Great Divide on horseback. A fierce blizzard was raging and we were warned against making the trip at that time. But we went ahead, got lost at nightfall in a deep ravine and were almost frozen to death when we were finally found by the ranger who had set out after us. But it was worth it, for we had lost our stale outlook on life and received a fresh point of view. I felt amply rewarded when, several months later, back in New York I overheard my companion addressing a group of friends as follows: "This cramped and narrow life in New York may be all right for you boys if you like it, but give me the wide spaces out west where you can breathe deep and think your own thoughts. Let me tell you about the night I spent crossing the Great Divide...."

If you can manage it, it is well to start your travels early in life while the mind is still impressionable. I took my first trip abroad on a cattle ship, with fifty dollars in my pocket. I was gone three months and saw a great deal of Europe. Although I have taken the trip many times since, this first one, with its struggles and its hardships and the daily necessity of earning enough to eat and sleep, was by far the most enjoyable. I worked with street gangs, unloaded cobblestones from barges and formed amazing contacts with all sorts of people. By absorbing or at least examining their point of view I corrected and broadened my own. I found that a London cab driver's philosophy of life was fully as good as my own and that a Belgian peasant could talk more intelligently on the politics of the world than I could.

But the discovery that amazed me the most was that beneath the differences of language and custom, the foreigner was remarkably like us. The English workingman, for instance, was confronted with precisely the same problems as our own workingman. In his tastes, his desires, the whole routine of his life with its petty satisfactions and its petty annoyances, the Frenchman was in no way different from us. This, of course, seemed surprising to me at first, for the very word "foreigner" suggests some one who is strange, remote and different from us. But I found that his chief eccentricity consisted in being born in a different country. This country that he was born in was, according to his views, the best country in the world, but I hardly knew how to blame him for that, since that is precisely the feeling that we have about our own country. If you are talking with an Englishman, you will be surprised to learn that he honestly considers a country better off under a king and a parliament than under a president and a congress. And, if you take the trouble to study his government carefully, you will be even more surprised to discover that in some respects he is right. Even if your loyalty to your own institutions holds you back from such a conclusion, the fair-minded examination of his point of view is a very healthy and broadening exercise for the mind.

In other words you will be gradually acquiring that intensely desirable quality of tolerance. For knowledge and tolerance usually travel together. The more you learn, the more you will realize the very small compass of the human intelligence and the more prepared you will be to admit that in the large field of knowledge which you have not explored there may lie more truths than in the small parcel of information you have collected.

It will be inconvenient, I know, for most of you to pull up stakes and set forth immediately for foreign places. But I would consider it a pleasant obligation upon myself to do this whenever opportunity presents itself. In the meantime, there are shorter journeys open to every one. There are walking trips and riding trips and excursions by water. In general I would plan these in such a way that they would take me to surroundings and conditions of life as different as possible from those to which I was accustomed. You have no idea how eagerly the mind will respond to the change, how readily it will discharge stale and tiresome images for fresh ones and exchange old ideas for new ones. And there is one kind of travel you can take without moving a step. This is an excursion into other people's minds, either by reading or in conversation. I would particularly cultivate people who disagreed with me, for in getting the other fellow's point of view, you will broaden and strengthen your own.

*This chapter of **Youth Points the Way** was originally published as an advice column in the March 1924 issue of **Boys Life** Magazine.*

Youth Points The Way

◆

CHAPTER VI

KEEP ON MOVING

No doubt you have felt a certain sense of indignation, of protest against the infringement upon the personal liberty to which you consider yourself entitled, if, when standing upon a busy street corner in a big city, a policeman has commanded you to "keep on moving," or when making your way in leisurely fashion from a subway or elevated train, the conductor has urged you to "step lively!"

And yet these custodians are voicing a much higher dictate, a much more universal command, than any man-made regulations for law and order. Unconsciously they are expressing the ruling principle of nature, of life itself. This law of motion began long before the advent of man and will run as long as the sands of time. It is a law which nature never breaks and man can break only with disaster to himself. In the beginning of things some impulse, which most of us believe to be a divine one, set the universe in motion. Nebulous or fine granular matter began whirling through space with a terrific momentum, later—after countless ages—to solidify, to form clusters of stars, solar systems; in short, what we call the universe. This initial motion has never subsided. There is no luminary in the heavens that is not traveling in some direction at a rate of speed compared with which the fleetest aeroplane crawls at a snail's pace through the air. If this earth upon which we are so comfortably riding at a rate of sixteen miles a second—and which seems so solid and immovable—should in some inexplicable way lose the momentum which carries it around the sun, it would plunge like an arrow into the hot caverns of the sun and all its civilization and all its grandeur would come to a tragic end. If you will study astronomy, a most entertaining exercise for the mind and imagination, you will find that I have not exaggerated.

Now this principle of motion governs not only suns and planets and everything else in nature, but human beings as well. When they remain in motion life flows smoothly and pleasantly without untoward incident, but when they cease to move, when they cease to be vigorously active and progressive, the same kind of tragedy on a smaller scale overtakes them as the imaginary disaster which I described as happening to the earth. It is not so spectacular or appalling, but it is just as sure. If you stand still you make an excellent target for all the ills and misfortunes to which human nature is prey, but while you are moving you are harder to hit and you dodge most of them. You will find that a large percentage of all human calamities—ill health, poverty, accidents, crime and vice—descend upon people who have ceased to move, whose vitality and power of resistance are no longer strengthened and stimulated by activity. Some of these misfortunes attack you, to be sure, even if you are in motion, but they hit you only glancing blows which may temporarily retard, but do not cripple you.

When I speak of motion as applied to human beings I mean some useful kind of activity, the continual struggle along the path of achievement toward some appointed goal, the normal human impulse to project ourselves forward in the direction of some ideal. Whether we ever reach this objective is of comparatively little importance, so long as every ounce of energy goes into the struggle. When we learn that it is the fight that counts more than what we are fighting to acquire, that there is more pleasure and happiness to be found in working for a thing than there is in getting it, more enjoyment in keen pursuit than there is in the reward that lies at the end of the trail, we have learned a most valuable lesson. Study the people you know. Who are the healthy ones, the happy ones? Those who have chosen to withdraw from the turmoil and adventure of active life and to sit back in soft-cushioned luxury? Or the other sort—those who are still working for something that lies beyond, those who are still in motion? I do not need to tell you that happiness lies all on the side of the latter. I believe that man's capacity for happiness can never exceed his appetite for work, his desire to keep on moving. I would rather be what the world calls a failure and be making vigorous motions to get along than the kind of success who has come to a stand-still, who took his first achievement as a signal to stop work forever. It is this kind of success, with its demoralizing ease and indolence, its arrested functioning of the faculties, that ruins men more often than the kind of failure which I first mentioned. Defeat often hardens the muscles and strengthens the will, while victory, especially if it is easily won, tends to make one smug, complacent, soft and inactive. I shall never wish to retire from active life until I am ready to retire from life altogether.

There are two periods in life when one is most likely to become a victim of arrested motion, of aimless drifting. One comes after a certain measure of achievement, when a man has acquired a fair degree of prosperity and decides to take things easy and enjoy some of the fruits of his labor. The other comes at an earlier stage, which I will take up later. First watch the misguided man who determines to retire from active life and enjoy himself. If he doesn't go to pieces it will be a miracle. Gradually the fine zest in living which he felt when he was active deserts him. The enjoyment which he seeks becomes a phantom. The days hang heavy on his hands and he views the prospect of other days to come without enthusiasm. There comes a sluggishness of mind and body, neither of which thrives on inactivity. He finds himself floating about in an uninteresting vacuum, aimless, motionless and discontented. Having no real problems to occupy his mind he invents imaginary ones which are much harder to solve than real ones. He becomes morbid and pessimistic, immersed in a profound dissatisfaction with himself and life. Compare this figure of suspended animation and gloomy outlook with the same figure who attacked life before with such a fine frenzy, who welcomed trouble so that he might develop the strength to conquer and relished obstacles because they incited him to higher effort, and you have a tragic comparison. Often, to make matters worse, he is stricken with some illness which would never have touched him so long as he kept in motion. It is a pity, I often think, that some benevolent custodian of his welfare, some policeman of the spirit, some conductor of our larger transportation through life, cannot tap him on the shoulder and say "Keep on moving!" or "Step lively!"

The other period of which I spoke is when one falls under the temptation of idleness in early youth. Instead of being a retirement from work, as in the other case, this is a hesitancy about getting started. There seem to be so many avenues of accomplishment and so much time as one looks ahead in which to do things, that one hesitates to do anything at all. And it is a curious illusion that as soon as we embark on one road of accomplishment, all the other roads seem infinitely more alluring. Some one else's job always seems a little more satisfactory than our own. To the writer, putting colors on canvas seems a much easier and more inviting occupation than his own, and to the business man, the profession of medicine with its short office hours and high fees seems such a sinecure that it is like taking money under false pretenses. But while youth is contemplating the opportunities that glitter ahead of him, wasting his time in false starts, and yielding to the lure of a thousand bypaths that do not lead anywhere, he is forming a dangerous habit. Hesitation about choosing a career is natural enough, but when continued so long that it becomes a habit it is likely to be fatal. You have all met the type of person who is always about to accomplish something in a few days or weeks or months. But somehow present conditions always seem to be adverse—the present moment always the wrong one to start. He expects that in some mysterious way circumstances in the future will take a sudden swing in his favor and that he will then be able to get at that important piece of work that lies ahead. One of the oldest anecdotes I can recall is the one about the man who looked continually forward to repairing a hole in the roof of his house, but when it was raining he couldn't do it, and when it was pleasant weather, it didn't matter. People of the sort I have described do not realize that their chief enemy is not circumstances conspiring against them, adverse conditions or lack of opportunity, but the fatal habit of inaction which kills all initiative and drains the will of all its power of accomplishment. If I were starting life over again, I am not at all sure what I would do, but I would do something quickly, so that I might at least form the habit of activity rather than the habit of hesitation and idleness.

I am not sure that my life is a pattern that other people would care to follow. Perhaps I go to an extreme in the matter of motion. I do not like idleness because it makes me discontented. I try to fill every waking hour in the day with some stimulating sort of activity, either of body or mind. Most people will advise you to check your work and your worries when you leave your office at the close of the day. But if I am interested in what I am doing I cannot dismiss it quite so peremptorily. It comes to my mind during the evening and my best ideas often come to me in the morning when I wake up.

Whenever I become thoroughly fatigued, what I want is not rest but a change of activity. If the mind is exhausted it is a good time to exercise the body. The refreshment is much greater than sitting in a chair and thinking of how tired you are. For doing nothing is one of the most exhausting occupations in the world, and even as a respite for hard labor it is not to be recommended. It is better to turn to something entirely different but equally active. In this way you do not lose the exhilarating sense of motion. You do not slow down. You simply use a different set of faculties. Slowing down is really a bad practice because it takes so much more steam to get under way again.

I do not mean to convey the impression that one should spend every hour in the day in feverishly seeking violent forms of activity, or that when he is not exerting his mind to the utmost, he should be straining the muscles of his body. There are plenty of recreations which keep the mind pleasantly active without violent effort. Interesting conversation is exercise for the emotions, a part of us that we do not cultivate any too carefully these days. Seeing good plays and motion pictures is a mild form of intellectual and emotional exercise—not a very robust form of activity perhaps, but still it is something. I have spoken so fully of the great benefits of physical exercise in other articles that it is not necessary to repeat them here.

There are, in short, so many interesting forms of activity, of pleasant and stimulating motion of body and mind that there is never any excuse for prolonged idleness. Sometimes we confuse leisure with idleness. Now leisure is a very fine thing. I wish I had more of it. It gives one an opportunity to indulge in more varied kinds of activity.

If you have never tried to account for what you do with the twenty-four hours in each day, you will be amazed to find how much leisure you really have, even if your time seems to be fully occupied. If you spend eight hours in sleep, eight hours in work and two hours in eating which, I suppose, is the average routine of American life, you still have left six mysterious hours of leisure. I say "mysterious" because they are usually hard to account for. They usually slip by without our knowing exactly what we do with them. The way in which you employ this long period of leisure every day will have a tremendous bearing upon your health, your happiness and your character. If you spend this time in sheer idleness, you will be cheating yourself out of great profit and satisfaction. For in these six hours a day, if you systematize them, you can work wonders. You can keep yourself in such fine physical condition that the mere condition of being alive is a great joy. You can pursue any hobby or avocation that you like. You can become an expert on any subject under the sun. And you will come back to your daily routine with greater refreshment and enthusiasm than if you spent this leisure in idling and "killing time." "Killing time" is, by the way, a most extraordinary expression, for time is the one thing you can't kill. It moves relentlessly and inevitably on and to get the most out of life you must move with it.

As I am writing this, I am looking forward to a long period of leisure myself. I have just completed "The Thief of Bagdad," which has taken a year of the most concentrated and uninterrupted work. I shall go to New York and probably to Europe. If this were to be a vacation from all activity, I should contemplate it with the greatest distaste and foreboding. But there is a vast amount of reading I want to do, there will be stimulating contacts with people and other parts of the world and I shall be reaching out for an idea for another picture.

THE END

*1924 was the equinox of Douglas Fairbanks' career, both on and off the screen. 1924 not only saw the release of his cinematic masterpiece, **The Thief of Bagdad**, but was also by far the most active year of his creative output as a writer. In addition to publishing the book **Youth Points the Way** (concluded above), Doug also penned a series of lengthy feature stories for the **Ladies Home Journal** and brief articles for other publications that year. In addition, he co-authored the story treatment for **The Thief of Bagdad**, seen on the following pages as it appeared upon initial publication in the 1924 program book for the film. How he managed to find time to write in the midst of producing a film of such magnitude, as well as running the business affairs of both his own studio and United Artists, is utterly mind-boggling.*

Original Program Book for

"The Thief of Bagdad"

(1924)

✦

Prefatory—

T HERE is a touch of the fantastic even in the reason I made "The Thief of Bagdad"—for it is a reason impelled by the unseen. It is a tribute to the fineness that I believe underlies the workaday philosophy of men; a recognition of the inner forces that belie the sordidness of Life.

There can be no doubt that the human soul's reaching for finer, higher, more ethereal things is intuitive and first manifests itself in a child's love of fairy tales and fantasy.

The dreams, longings and roseate ambitions of childhood are relegated to the background of Life by the struggle of existence, but stifling them doesn't kill them. They persist throughout the years. There are moments when we all "dream dreams."

Imagery is inherent in the human breast. The brave deeds, the longing for better things, the striving for finer thoughts, the mental pictures of obstacles overcome and successes won are nearer to our real selves than our daily grind of earthly struggle.

"The Thief of Bagdad" is the story of the things we dream about; a tale of what happens when we go out from ourselves to conquer Worlds of Fancy. We set out to win our Heart's Desire; we confuse our enemies; we demean ourselves bravely; our success is complete; our reward is Happiness.

I believe that this is the story of every man's inner self and that every man will thus see it.

That's the reason I made "The Thief of Bagdad."

Douglas Fairbanks
(Signature)

The THIEF OF BAGDAD

◆

An Arabian Nights Fantasy

As played by DOUGLAS FAIRBANKS
Written for the Screen by ELTON THOMAS
Retold in Story form by LOTTA WOODS

AGAINST the velvet blackness of the desert sky, the low-hanging stars gleam in brilliant points of light. Below, picked out by their light, is a lonely group. A Holy Man drones over and over again the lesson he is teaching to a little, brown-skinned, naked boy. The child listens, his eyes fixed on the stars, until it seems to him that the very stars themselves spell out in star clusters the words of the lesson: "Happiness Must Be Earned."

Bagdad, Magic City of the East, lay dreaming in the sunshine of a thousand years ago and, from far-off kingdoms, three Princes turned their greedy eyes thereto.

For thus the word had gone forth: A moon hence may suitors come from all the East to seek in marriage the hand of Bagdad's royal Princess.

The word came to the Kingdom of the Mongols and to India and to Persia and to the Princes thereof, and these Princes, wholly resolved to win the Princess, departed each from his own kingdom.

Now, on this same day, Ahmed, a thief of Bagdad, pursued his nimble-fingered way and, as fruit of his dishonest calling, there came to his hand a magic rope.

Escaping from the owner of the rope, Ahmed made use of its magic powers to climb to a nearby window and found himself within the walls of a mosque. Never before in all his life had he set foot in a mosque.

Within, a Holy Man expounded his doctrine.

Ahmed listened. For a moment he was confounded by this, his first contact with Good, but he recovered himself and flouted the Holy Man with rude gesturing, loudly shouting the tenets of his own creed:

"I see what I want—and I take it. Paradise is a fool's dream and Allah is a myth."

Then, unchecked by the Holy Man, he flung himself from the mosque and came in time to his own evil den where he lived with one other, a Bird of Evil who fawned upon him to share his loot.

"Behold this rope," said Ahmed. "It is a magic rope. With it we can scale the highest walls."

A moon waxed and waned.

Through Bagdad's gates a train of laden porters came. They bore rare trappings for the Palace and viands to feast the suitors who, on the morrow, would come to sue for the hand of the Princess.

Ahmed, the thief, and Bird of Evil, creeping from their den, beheld this wealth pass by and joined them to the end of the train hoping thereby to win an entrance to the Palace.

Repulsed, they whispered cunningly together and marked the high wall of the Palace with the sign of Ahmed.

"To-night," they said, "with the magic rope."

That night Ahmed and Bird of Evil came to the foot of the Palace wall and Bird of Evil waited below while Ahmed, by the aid of the magic rope, surmounted the wall and made entry to the Palace. Once inside, he moved stealthily about until he came into a treasure room.

There, as he burrowed in a chest of jewels, his hand was stayed by the tinkle of soft music. Forgetting his rope, he followed the sound. It led him to a room where—but just left by her slaves—the Princess lay asleep under a canopy of silken gauze.

He looked—went away—came back and looked again. Vainly he tried to drag himself back to the treasure chest. Finally he found himself close to the couch of the sleeping Princess, crouched there, listening to her soft breathing. Discarding indifferently the string of priceless pearls he had brought from the treasure room, he picked up one of the tiny slippers that still bore the warm impress of the Princess' foot. He examined it with curious interest.

Then, a strange new thrill. The Princess moved in her sleep and her slender white hand fell athwart the rough brown fist of the thief. Gently he moved to disengage it. The Princess was roused. She tossed aside her silken coverlet and it fell across his huddled form, hiding him from discovery through all the hubbub of alarm that followed.

Only one person—a Mongol slave girl—glimpsed him and she was silenced by the threat of his dagger. So he escaped, without his magic rope, whose loss troubled him not at all, and bearing with him the little silken slipper, his only booty save the memory of the Princess' loveliness.

Next day the Princess came with her slave girls to a high pavilion which overlooked the courtyard of the Palace. It was the Princess' birthday and suitors were coming from all the East. The robbery of the night before was forgotten in the excitement of this new interest.

The fluttering Princess bade a slave girl to read her fortune in the sand tables whose sands had been fetched from Mecca itself.

Blown gently by the breath of the sand reader, the sands shaped a rose.

The Slave of the Sand Board expounded the meaning thereof.

"Whoso of thy suitors first toucheth the rose-tree in the Palace courtyard, he will be thy husband," she said.

The Mongol slave girl, noting the deep interest of the Princess evinced in this prophecy, slipped furtively away.

The Princess mused over her fortune.

All that morning had Ahmed, the thief, brooded over the little silken slipper of the Princess, neglecting to follow his usual calling. Like a lodestone the slipper had drawn him to the Palace and, high up in a perch of leaves and vines that overlooked the pavilion of the Princess, he secretly watched the lovely maiden of his dreams.

Bird of Evil, trailing him, found him in his hidden refuge. He read in the thief's brooding eyes the secret of his heart. With sly hints and innuendoes he pointed out to Ahmed that even a Princess might be stolen if one were master of craft and knew the secrets of subtle drugs that drowsed.

Cupidity shone again in the eyes of the thief and he and his companion climbed down from their perch bent on finding a way into the Palace.

The throb of a huge drum gave warning to the Princess that suitors were at the Palace gates, and, from her high vantage point, she watched them as they came. Scarce did she breathe as each drew near the rose-tree.

There came the glowering Indian Prince—purse-proud and haughty.

Praise Allah, he touched not the rose-tree.

The Persian, fat and gross and sleepy, followed after.

He too, failed to touch the rose-tree, and the Princess breathed freely again.

Now came the Mongol—cold and impassive. The Princess, frozen with dread, watched his progress with painful interest.

Close on the heels of the Mongol Prince came another.

He was announced as "Ahmed, Prince of the Isles, of the Seas, and of the Seven Palaces." In contrast to the luxury and state of the others, he came with one attendant, a pigmy fellow in clothes many times too large for him.

But the garments of Ahmed lacked naught of splendor for they had been pilfered from the richest bazaars of Bagdad.

The Mongol Prince watched this new arrival with suspicion, but his attention was diverted by the voice of the Mongol slave girl addressing him in his own tongue.

From behind a lattice she whispered to him furtively that the superstitions of the Princess were centered on the rose-tree.

To the Princess, the coming of the Prince of the Seas seemed a reprieve. She watched his progress in simple state and her eyes shone and she prayed within her heart that he might be the first to touch the rose-tree.

Then her face blenched with horror. She shrank against the parapet, trembling and unnerved.

The Mongol Prince was walking with grave deliberation toward the rose-bush. He was reaching forth his hand to pluck a rose.

Strange is the way of destiny!

A bee, disturbed in its meal, flew from the rose and menaced the out-stretched hand of the Mongol Prince. Brushing it aside with his fan, he set its course directly toward Ahmed. Its sharp sting pierced the sensitive ear of Ahmed's spirited horse. The animal sprang unexpectedly from the ground and tossed its unprepared rider straight into the heart of the rose-tree.

Ahmed, none the worse for his experience, descended from the bush bearing in his hand a rose he had plucked in his flight.

So quickly was the whole incident over that none save two had witnessed it, the Mongol Prince and the peeping Princess. The angered and suspicious Mongol went his way into the Palace but the Princess clasped her hands to her beating heart in an ecstasy of joy.

In the pageantry of the Prince's entrance into the Palace, the Prince of the Seas slipped unnoticed into the garden of the Princess' pavilion. He drenched the rose with the drug of drowsiness and, unseen by the Palace attendants, he climbed to the pavilion.

The maiden in love is always a sweet compound of modesty and boldness. The Princess saw in Ahmed, "The Prince of the Seas," the suitor chosen for her by Allah and the rose he offered her seemed a precious omen.

With shy delight she showed him the rose shaped in the sands and, as she explained its mystic meaning, her soft white fingers fell once more athwart his rough brown hand.

Once more he knew that sweet wild thrill.

Breathless with the urge of it, he pressed a kiss upon her hand and, in a moment, they were in each other's arms, conscious of naught save the exquisite fervor of their love.

Ahmed scarce knew with what dissembling he regained possession of the drenched rose and made his departure from the pavilion. He was aware only of an overpowering desire to flee from a place where he did not belong—from a sensation for which he was unfit.

He looked about dazedly for an opportunity to escape from the garden but he was engulfed in the machinery of state and borne along to the throne room.

Here, according to the age-long custom of the House and the will of her high-born father, the Princess was to indicate her choice among her suitors.

Ahmed was scarce recovered from his daze when the ring of choice was pressed upon his finger by the chief eunuch.

Overcome with the shame of his imposition, Ahmed detached himself from the Caliph's train and stood alone in the great hall from whence the others had gone to the feast room.

As he stood there pondering how he might reach the Princess, the Mongol slave girl passed him with a stare of recognition.

So it was that while Ahmed was finding his way to the garden bent on confessing his shame, the Mongol slave searched out the Counselor of the Mongol Prince and told him that the Prince of the Seas was no Prince, but a common thief.

The Counselor reported to his master and the Mongol Prince denounced Ahmed to the Caliph and nobles of Bagdad.

The Princess heard her lover's confession with bewildered amazement—but, through it all, she read the story of his love and his repentance and, at the last, she bade him to keep her ring and her love, the while she begged him to flee from the merciless wrath of her father.

But Ahmed would not flee. He was in a mood to expiate his crime and, resisting not, he was dragged before the Caliph.

Because he was a thief he was flogged until he swooned. Because of the trick he had performed against his ruler, he was condemned to be torn asunder by the great ape.

Warned of the punishment to be meted out to him, the Princess bribed the guards to spare his life and, bruised and battered as he was, he was yet set in safety into the dark shadows of the streets.

The Caliph would have compelled the Princess to choose among the real Princes who remained. Urged by the Slave of the Sand Board to forget not the prophecy of the sands, she temporized. She begged her father to leave the matter to chance. "Send them away," she pled. "Let them return at the seventh moon bearing rare treasure. Who brings the rarest, I will wed."

So it was left and so Bird of Evil explained it to Ahmed the next morning. For, when the tigers that were set at night to guard the Palace gates were led away to their daytime quarters, Bird of Evil crawled through their tunnels to the streets and found Ahmed near the Palace wall where he had brooded the night away.

"They will return at the seventh moon," he said. "If you would have the Princess, return with me through these tunnels."

But Ahmed would have none of him, and when Bird of Evil nagged him through the streets, he took refuge in the same mosque where but yesterday he had flouted the Holy Man.

To the Holy Man he bared his bruised soul and the Holy Man convinced him that on the bedrock of humility he might build a new life.

While Ahmed drank in the teachings of the Holy Man, the Mongol Prince instructed his Counselor to remain in Bagdad, disguised from the recognition of the guards.

"From time to time I will send you men in the guise of porters," he said. "Build me an army within the walls."

And the Princess, turning to the tables of sand for comfort, found that the rose persisted. So she nourished a tiny hope for the future.

The Holy Man brought Ahmed to the gates of the city and set him on the path of his adventures, saying:

"At the end of this way is a silver chest that doth contain the greatest magic. Go forth to seek it. Be brave. Control thy destiny."

Taking from his finger the ring of choice, Ahmed split it into two rings with a stroke of the sword the Holy Man had given him.

"Give this to her who hath already my heart," he told the Holy Man, and went forth alone to test his soul.

At a caravansary in the desert, a day's journey from Bagdad, the three Princes took leave of each other, promising to meet there again at the end of the sixth moon.

The Mongol Prince, with suave courtesy, wished the other good fortune, second only to his own. And ere their trains were well started toward their own countries, he set spies to follow each.

But Ahmed:

He traveled far from Bagdad and came at length to the defile that led to the Mountains of Dread Adventure.

"I seek a magic chest," he told the Hermit there.

The Hermit regarded him speculatively.

"Many have gone this way," he said, "but none returned."

Then he described what dangers dire and manifold, what fires and floods, what ravening beasts and birds, what spirits of earth and sea infested the way.

Yet was Ahmed's resolve firm.

So did the Hermit give him a talisman.

"And thy courage fail not," he said, "thou mayest live to reach the Cavern of Enchanted Trees. Touch with this talisman the midmost tree."

And Ahmed fared onward.

Within the Kingdom where he bade and forbade, the Mongol Prince awaited the reports of his spies.

So came a runner telling him that, while the Persian Prince had slumbered in his litter, his chief attendant had purchased for him in the bazaars of Shiraz a rug of such magical properties that it would carry one through the air withersoever it was directed. And the fat and torpid Persian Prince was convinced that this rug was the greatest rarity in the world.

Came another runner telling that a driven slave had clambered to the lofty head of a forgotten idol near Kandahar and plucked from its eye-socket a crystal of such magical properties that in it one could see whatsoever he desired to see. And the arrogant and purse-proud Indian Prince for whom this crystal was secured was convinced that it was the greatest rarity in the world.

Then the Mongol Prince smiled a crafty smile and conferred with his court magician, a man of foul favor. And after he had thus conferred, he sailed to the Island of Wak where the court magician wrested from its sacred shrine an apple of such magical properties that it would cure any sickness, no matter how grievous. So, convinced that his treasure was the greatest rarity in the world, the Mongol Prince smiled anew his crafty smile and commanded a runner that he made haste to Bagdad and gave order that at the end of the sixth moon the Princess be given a deadly poison.

This was the case of the three Princes, but as regards Ahmed:

After many days and nights he came to the Valley of Fire. A surging wall of flame barred his advance. He plunged through this to find another and another. Then his unaccustomed flesh shrank, his undisciplined soul rebelled, but the ring of choice upon his finger became a cool band of courage and he persevered, coming at length to a cooling stream of sweet waters.

So, praising Allah for his cleansing fires, he fared onward.

Coming nigh unto the Cavern of Enchanted Trees he would have entered therein but for a prodigious dragon that came snarling and bellowing from between two beetling crags. So he fought the dragon until it perished and he won past it into the Cavern of Enchanted Trees. The midmost tree, when he touched it with the Hermit's talisman, creaked and stretched and spoke to him, directing him where he might come upon the Midnight Sea.

So he left that place and fared onward many days and when he had come upon the Midnight Sea, the Old Man thereof sent him many fathoms below the surface of the sea in search of a star-shaped key.

When he had found the star-shaped key, Ahmed felt himself clasped in the hairy arms of a vile and monstrous sea-spider. Which when he had killed, he would have returned to the surface of the sea, but that his ears were ravished with sweet sounds and certain daughters of the sea would have tempted him to stay with them and be the king of their fairy caverns. But, resisting temptation, he came again to the Old Man of the Sea who told him that his star-shaped key would unlock the stable of the winged horses.

"Take the white horse that nibbleth at thy right hand," he said, "for he alone knoweth the way to the Citadel of the Moon."

So, even as the Old Man of the Sea had said, Ahmed climbed to the cloud-borne abode of the winged horses and took from thence the white horse that nibbled at his right hand.

And the winged horse traveled with him far up the pathway of the sky and, after many days, he came to the base of the flight of a thousand steps that led to the far Citadel of the Moon. Up to this silvern shrine Ahmed fared alone. And there, wrapped about in a cloak of invisibility, was a silver chest that fitted itself to the palm of his hand.

His heart overflowed with gratitude to Allah. He felt within himself the power to do good, to make amends for all his grievous past.

At the caravansary in the desert the three Princes met according as they had planned. Each displayed his rare treasure and each believed his own the rarest.

In the breast of the Mongol Prince was hidden the knowledge that by now the Princess would have succumbed to the poison he had ordered.

With his customary suavity he suggested that the Indian Prince put his crystal to use and discover whether the Princess had waited as she pledged.

The crystal disclosed the desperate illness of the Princess—showed her surrounded by physicians helpless to give aidance and agonized over by her royal father.

Mindful that the Caliph had promised the throne of Bagdad to the fortunate suitor who won his daughter, the Persian and the Indian were impatient to go to her assistance. The Persian offered his rug to convey them and the Mongol pointed out that the apple might save her life if they arrived in time.

On the magic carpet the three Princes flew across the wastelands to Bagdad and appeared without warning in the sleeping-chamber of the Princess. With every appearance of sympathetic solicitude, the Mongol Prince made his way to the bedside of the dying maiden and by the magic of the healing that was inherent in the golden apple, he restored her to glowing health.

Far away at the flat rock within the defile in the Mountains of Dread Adventure, the flying horse alighted so that Ahmed might dismount. Then it flew away to its stable above the clouds.

The Hermit of the defile came to meet Ahmed. He saw the silver chest and gravely salaamed to the man who bore it.

"Only its rightful heritor can carry that magic chest," he said. "Thou hast won the power to do good than which there is no greater happiness."

He gestured toward the box in explanation of its uses. Ahmed, listening, pondered in his heart the secrets of the silver chest. Then he scattered from it some of the seeds it contained and saw before him a horse to his needs and a garb suited to the quest before him.

So he mounted and rode away toward Bagdad, wondering if now he might fairly compete for the hand of the Princess.

To the Princess came the knowledge that health had been restored to her. She begged her father to explain how this had come about.

Each in his turn the princely suitors claimed the credit of her cure.

"I," said the Mongol Prince, "with my golden apple, I saved your life."

"Not so," said the Indian Prince, "I—by discovering your plight in my magic crystal—I saved your life."

"They claim too much," said the Persian Prince. "I—with my rug—I saved your life."

And, while they argued among themselves, the little Slave of the Sand Board crept to the Princess' side and looked into the magic crystal.

She whispered to her mistress: "He cometh. He cometh. Gain time." She held the crystal up for the Princess to see.

The Princess gazed into the crystal and pressed her hands to her lips to stifle a cry of joy. For what she saw was Ahmed riding boldly, his head upflung, and he held high above his head the magic silver chest.

The Princess reflected for a moment and then summoned her father.

"Who can decide which of these gifts is rarest?" she said. "Without the crystal they would not have known, without the carpet they could not have come, without the apple they could not have saved me. Each had been useless without the other two."

Perhaps the Mongol Prince might have argued the matter but at this moment his Counselor, advised of events by the Mongol maid, came into the room.

Behind his fan he whispered to the Prince: "You have twenty thousand troops within the walls," and, soothed by this assurance, the Mongol Prince, with his customary soft composure spoke of taking quiet thought on the matter through the night.

Through the night twenty thousand Mongol troops threw off their disguises and took possession of Bagdad.

The Caliph and Persian and Indian were thrown into a cell and told that morning held death for them in vats of boiling oil.

Guards were sent to put away the attendants of the Princess and keep watch over her during the night.

When morning came, the Mongol Prince was comfortably ensconced on the throne of Bagdad. He ordered the Princess fetched before him.

Benumbed by the events of the night she came. Once more the cup of joy had been dashed from her lips. The hope roused by the sight of her beloved in the crystal was drowned in her despair. Unprotesting—she heard the Mongol Prince bid her prepare for marriage to him and silent—numbed—she was led away.

Ahmed, pulling up at a well on the desert to make his ablutions and pray the dawn prayer, learned from frightened refugees that the Mongols had taken Bagdad. He mounted his horse and galloped to the gates of the city.

"Open wide the gates of Bagdad!" he ordered, and when the Mongol guard in the gate tower voiced a contemptuous refusal, he opened his magic chest and scattered seeds broadcast.

The Mongols on the battlemented walls watched in fascinated dismay.

Below them there appeared out of nothingness a group of shining soldiers.

The guards bent lower to watch.

Ahmed's hand flashed in sowing motion—once—twice—thrice—and the Mongols lost count.

And with every motion of that sowing hand, there appeared on the plain below unnumbered hosts of silver clad warriors.

Stark panic seized the Mongol soldiers. With one accord they fled from the wall, shouting warnings to their fellows within the town.

Out from their houses came the townspeople and into the town thronged the great army.

Like a stream of white lava it poured through the town, covering all the streets with its wide expanse.

Before its steady oncoming, the horrid black shapes that were the Mongol army melted into nothingness.

Warned of the coming of the gleaming multitude, the Counselor rushed panic-stricken to the Mongol Prince to tell what he had learned.

"Set my guards at the Palace gates," his Prince ordered and hastened from the throne room.

But, ere he had fled far, came a runner, kneeling to say:

"Great Khan, every way of escape is blocked."

Then did the Mongol Prince bare his neck and order the runner to sever his head from his body.

The runner raised his sword, but the Mongol slave girl checked its fall.

"The flying carpet," she reminded, "and the Princess."

Again the smile of craft envisaged the Mongol Prince. He hurried away nor knew that the little Slave of the Lute, listening behind the arras, had caught the words and crept from the room.

To the sleeping-chamber of the Princess, where the rug was under guard, the Mongol Prince betook himself.

He ordered the spreading of the rug, and then—with a look of cunning and desire—his gaze encompassed the Princess. He strode toward her.

And while the Princess fled from his pursuit, the little Slave of the Lute plowed her way through the crowded streets and bore to Ahmed the word of the peril of the Princess.

Ahmed could not wait for his army. With orders to a lieutenant to rescue all who were still under the yoke of the Mongols and to follow him to the Palace, he sped away.

It facilitated his speed to don the cloak of invisibility and a silver whirlwind swept through the Place, knocking aside soldiers, furniture, whatever impeded.

The Mongol Prince had harried the Princess until she swooned.

His Counselor had joined them and, together, they placed the unconscious Princess on the rug and made the magic signs to lift it in flight.

They braced themselves for the uplift and then—they saw nothing and heard nothing—but they felt the impact of a lithe, muscular body and they measured their lengths on the floor.

Then they gasped in amaze as invisible hands lifted the Princess and carried her up the bridge that led from the room. Bent on possessing her, the Mongols followed.

Ahmed, dropping his cloak, revived the fainting Princess. His soldiers handed the Mongol Prince and his Counselor over to the untender mercies of the Palace eunuchs. And then, as the reunited lovers would have clasped each other in arms of love, came an influx of grateful friends.

The Caliph, gladly bestowing his daughter upon their rescuer, was profuse in his expressions of satisfaction.

The Persian, the Indian, the dignitaries of the court, all must say over and over again their phrases of fervent gratitude.

It was too much.

Ahmed bethought him again of his magic cloak. He threw it round the Princess and himself. Scarce would it cover them both and the astonished court caught the twinkle of feet going away from them. They followed.

Straight to the magic rug tripped the twinkling feet. Ahmed dropped the cloak and again the lovers were disclosed. Waving farewells to the grateful court, they floated out of the Palace, over the heads of the doting populace, out into the desert night and up toward the stars that spelled in star clusters: "Happiness Must Be Earned."

To alleviate any potential confusion as to who actually wrote the lion's share of this photoplay, it should be noted that in the original production credits, Lotta Woods is only listed as a scenario "editor." The author of the work is given as Elton Thomas, a pseudonym Fairbanks often used, comprised of his two middle names. Also note that he chose to copyright the work under his personal name, not in the business name of the Douglas Fairbanks Pictures Corporation.

Ahmed (Douglas Fairbanks) and the Princess (Julanne Johnston) flying over the turrets of Bagdad on a magic carpet. To achieve this effect onscreen, Fairbanks suspended the rug with piano wires.

Why Big Pictures

✦

Better Stories—Better Acting—Better Sets

By Douglas Fairbanks

A belief that mere bigness pays is one of the heritages of the films from the show business. It was taken over bodily by the motion pictures along with various superstitions, customs and fixed ideas about the tastes of the public. We use carloads of lumber and tons of plaster, and employ almost countless workmen in building our biggest sets; and yet often they are used only in flashes. The proportion is, I believe, about one to twenty; that is to say, for every twenty feet of film used in depicting big scenes we have about four hundred feet of more intimate material where most of the time only a simple room or part of a room is necessary. This, though of more solid construction, is similar to stage scenery.

Yet I believe that most of the big building is necessary. Indeed I venture to predict that a thousand years from now anyone who wishes to give on whatever may represent the screen of that day a picture of New York life in 1924, whether of society or of the slums, or both, will begin with a view, even if it is only a flash, of the lower Manhattan of today with its towering structures. The creative artist of 2924 will feel that any picture of the life of the great city of ten centuries before must necessarily give at least a hint of the narrow streets turned into *canons* by the cliff-like skyscrapers and of the antlike existence of the millions of people, antlike by comparison with the soaring buildings they have piled up. So in order to re-create the New York of 1924 for the screen enthusiasts of 2924, it will be necessary to do a great deal of big building.

The New Yorkers of today, whether they live on Long Island or in Westchester and fancy they are in the country, are subject to the pulse beats and life vibrations that make for what looks at a distance like an antlike existence. The huge city, stretching out its far-reaching tentacles, orders the lives of people and makes them hurry, just as it dominates and overshadows them. Therefore it seems to me that the supposed drama which is to be released in 2924 on Broadway or wherever the first-run houses of that day are, will begin by a "long shot" of high buildings.

Such a long shot of an opening scene in town or country is needed when beginning to depict the life of another age. To approach it gradually is to invest it with an impressiveness which engenders respect and perhaps some awe. If great statesmen, financiers and rulers, or even our own bankers, were readily accessible, and all we had to do was to knock on the door and enter after a hearty "Come in," we would have less respect for their greatness. We get our impressions from the outer offices, from the persons we must talk to first. If we came suddenly upon a football scrimmage, saw nothing but the play at that second, and did not know what teams were playing and which side was ahead, it would not be particularly interesting.

Obviously this applies to efforts to give the flavor of life to another age, to spectacles and to big pictures generally. Indeed it seems to me that here is to be found an answer to a question which I have been asked again and again: Why all this building of elaborate sets which makes your costs so great and necessarily entail so much waste?

Long before I was in the motion pictures, the costs were kept down by avoiding building and by hurrying photography. There is a story of those days of a company operating in the East. They stole scenes whenever possible. They would go into a suburb and, without ringing the doorbell, make use of a porch or garden. On one occasion they tore up a fence for the purpose of a comedy, and when the outraged housewife rushed out to protest, the combination director and cameraman handed her some tickets for the theater—really a store—where the picture was to be shown. There was then no long interval between the taking of a picture and the release. The complicated business of selling a picture to the exhibitors had not yet begun.

But the parsimony of those days no longer pays. There is no question anymore but that if your sets are big and in a conspicuous place, they will afford good advertising in themselves. During three summer months nine thousand three hundred and eighty-four people—men, women and children—from all parts of the country and representing almost every class, business and profession, were admitted through one gate at our studio. Naturally such visitors are impressed with the sets, and they go away with something of general interest to themselves and the people back home to talk about.

This same idea is present to a certain extent when big sets are displayed on the screen. They make for an impression that is carried away, and word-of-mouth advertising is of the greatest value to supplement the advertising the producer does in exploiting his production. This was always true in the theater. Big productions were for a time enormously successful. The reason for their disappearance today is not only due to the fact that spectacles can be so much better done through the medium of the screen, but that the profits were constantly diminishing through increased cost of making, larger salaries for actors necessary in these days and the vastly higher rates for the transportation of big companies.

In my own career there was nothing deliberate about getting into big productions. Both in the theater and in my early days in the films I relied a good deal upon personality. It was logical and necessary. I was playing a sort of young man about town, who was essentially the same in each play, and stories of films were fitted to that end. I became fed up with the sort of thing I was doing, and I was afraid the public would become so too. In the theater certain performances will bear constant repetition. Joseph Jefferson could go on playing Rip Van Winkle; it was peculiarly his own. He could mellow and grow in the role. There were always new audiences of young people.

Our screen plays, because of their simultaneous release, exhaust the first flush of success very quickly. A picture is good for years, but not at the same pace of returns. *The Birth of a Nation* is still making money, but it no longer needs D.W. Griffith's services. He was free, once the picture was released, to turn his attentions to other work.

Because of this independence from our finished work, it is not peculiarly our own. Once it has been committed to celluloid, it is an open book to anyone who wants to copy it.

Never a Stunt for the Stunt's Sake

IN MY early film plays I often had the same director for several pictures. The product was in a measure standardized and it was an advantage. I have found it best now to gather round me a group of specialists. Some of the same men, however, will continue to fit into more than one picture; but I regard each picture as an independent and complete whole, and build an organization for it.

When I write of imitation in the films, which has its counterpart in the theater, for one comedian has often been accused of stealing the work, the stunts and even lines of another, I do so without bitterness. We must be content with the satisfaction of having been the first to do something. If we cannot use things that we have invented because they have been too much copied, we have to think up others. We are kept from growing stale. This makes for progress.

I saw in the response of the public to *Manhattan Madness* that I could get away from sameness, but perhaps the turning point was *The Mark of Zorro*. This was a costume picture at a time when there was a belief that costume pictures in the movies, like Shakespere in the theater, spelled ruin. The latter contention is disproved every time someone gives a good Shakespere performance; and costumes in the movies are now the accepted rather than the rare performance. The public will respond to anything that is sincere and to which you really give something. They want to see you use some of your tissue. They want to see energy expended for their benefit.

I have said again and again that I have never in the pictures performed a stunt for the stunt's sake. Such athletic things as I have done on the screen were done to get over my interpretation, my idea of youth. The pictures did not make an athlete of me. I had done all these things on the stage in earlier plays; and long before that I had done them competitively and naturally, just as any boy does who wants to be in games. The other day I was sitting in one of the projection rooms of the studio looking at a reel in rather rough continuity—meaning that it had not been edited and titled, as it will be when released, but that it had been put in some sort of order—with John Barrymore, who had just come on from the East to act in *Beau Brummel* at another studio. I confess that I was more than pleased with his enthusiasm over what he saw of my new picture; for even though one feels he is right, there are discouraging days in the making of a big picture.

Trying for the Better Things

AT BEST I think that we seldom get over on the screen more than fifty percent of what we feel. An idea is always greater at its source; at least there is more enthusiasm. But that fifty per cent may be good enough to bowl audiences over, because they have not given the subject the thought that we have and in their eyes our effort may seem more nearly perfect. Barrymore told me that he thought that *The Thief of Bagdad* might be accepted as a challenge to the contention of some critics that "there is no art in the movies." Then he hesitated and said: "No, they might call this an art picture if someone else had done it or if it were made abroad by a Russian or somebody like that; but they think you're a jumper."

A great many of the persons who criticize a picture adversely from the preview—a Hollywood term for the showing of a film before the public has a chance to see it—till the negative of that picture is destroyed do so, I think, from a misunderstanding of what we are trying to do. We cannot do what literature does. We could not supplant, even if it were desirable, the theater. Often in the filming of a well-liked book, violence is done. That it is done willfully, as some modern authors seem to think, I do not believe. Everyone has always felt that he could build a house better than an architect, or edit a newspaper better than it is done. In recent years the making of a film must be added to these natural accomplishments of every man; but the results, when inexperienced people have made films, have nearly always been disastrous.

Those of us who have tried and learned what is known today as film-making do not believe that we are turning out great and permanent works of art. We should be acclaimed by our own standards. We make many mistakes, and the screen is an easy target to hit. These mistakes do not seem to me important. What everyone who is seriously interested in the business is trying to do is to get at the possibilities of the screen. There is something bigger and better going to come out of the films than anyone has yet found. We are all digging away for that, and meantime we are affording entertainment to millions of persons the world over.

The criticism that is leveled oftenest at the picture is that we pretend to be pantomime, but that we employ numerous titles or captions to make our meaning clear. Only recently I saw a statement of Israel Zangwill's in a newspaper to this effect. Granting that the caption is an interruption and that it is often used when not necessary, it is a convention of the films and we are entitled to it. In the making of a work of art we use and should use whatever is needed. One or two pictures may have been made without titles, and they are practically forgotten. It was a strain and an effort. We are using fewer captions today than we did. In one of my early pictures, a six-reel one called *When The Clouds Roll By*, there were two hundred and fifty-two titles. In my new picture in twelve or thirteen reels, there are only about one hundred titles.

The big production has grown upon me. If when I did *Zorro* I had been told that I was to do the *Musketeers*, *Robin Hood* and *The Thief of Bagdad* in succession, I would have been actually and genuinely scared. If they had been before me, with ready-made stories calling for great sets and the expenditure of much time, money and energy, I do not believe that I could have whipped the proposition. My big pictures have rolled along, gathering like a snowball. I think that I should be afraid to tackle a picture that was a ready-made big order.

For the *Musketeers* we did have a ready-made story, but we only took part of the book. I would like to do the whole over now; for when I saw it the last time I was not satisfied, and I am glad that I was not. For *Robin Hood* and *The Thief of Bagdad* we had nothing real to go by, except in the one case a loved character and the knowledge of the period he lived in and certain deeds and exploits which incidentally I had done again and again in modern guise. For *Bagdad* we had the *Arabian Nights*. The original scenarios of both these pictures, which were weeks in the making, I have before me as I write. They are merely diagrams, and neither covers a full sheet of paper.

And here we come to an essential difference between picture construction and that for the theater. We attack a phase rather than a well-built whole. We may get a balanced result immediately, but our first concern is flavor and the atmosphere of our period. Plot and story are vital to us, but we ought to be able to get them.

It is this necessity for finding our own material that makes it next to impossible for the outsider in this day to sell an original story or idea to the picture companies. The other day I read in a newspaper the exhaustive report of the Writers' Club of Hollywood: Of forty-two thousand and twenty plots and stories received from amateurs, only four were accepted, which is an average of not quite one in ten thousand. My advice has always been that the people who want to write scenarios should enter the business in any capacity they can get in, and learn the screen and its requirements before they attempt to write for it. A poet may be born, but a scenario writer grows.

Though I have recently done only period or costume pictures, my mind is not definitely made up to exclude altogether the modern story. I went into the costume picture, as I have written, to get away from personality, which I fancied might become too conventionalized. Then, too, it is more of a gesture to do the costume picture. It is an adventure, something like a child wanting to know what is on top of the other hill. Certain periods have always interested me, and these I have tried to do. Certain others I would never undertake. They are equally important, and have their romance and grandeur; only I myself do not feel them. Colonial America seems to me austere, forbidding and in general something of a moth-ball period. Though my interest is centered today in re-creating on the screen other times, if I could get the right type of present-day American story I would do it gladly. I should want something more, however, than a mere plot out of the day. It would have to exemplify the spirit of the country and have a theme.

So that I might select my material rather than adapt it from existing stories, I decided to limit my work and make only one picture a year. This gives us time to look around before we go ahead. I think this is a great advantage, though there is sometimes safety in a number of productions.

When I undertook to do a picture with the *Arabian Nights* as a setting, I did so because I not only was interested myself but because I thought it would appeal to the kids, and the kid in us all. Only a little more than two weeks before he died, Dr. Charles P. Steinmetz, of the General Electric Company, was here at the studio. He asked a thousand questions. He was most interested in what we were doing and why we did various things. No visitor I have ever talked to has been quicker to see the causes of certain things. He was particularly interested in the reasons I have given for doing *The Thief of Bagdad*. "Yes," he agreed, "that youthful angle is the last thing we let go of."

LHJ EDITOR'S NOTE—The next article, *Films for the Fifty Million*, by Douglas Fairbanks, will appear in an early issue.

---

*In the spring of 1924, Fairbanks contributed a series of lengthy feature articles to the **Ladies Home Journal** that explained his dedication to producing big budget films as works of fine art. The above piece, **Why Big Pictures**, was the first of the series, appearing in the March 1924 issue of **LHJ**. We bring you the entire series of articles in the pages ahead, in order of original publication.*

Films for the Fifty Million

By

Douglas Fairbanks

T WENTY MILLION people in this country see certain films. Fifty million people have seen a film. I want—and I suppose everyone who starts work on a big production wants—to turn out a picture which will, in the talk of the show business, "pull them all in"—the fifty million. In this desire I find an explanation for going on making pictures. My friends, my advisers, and occasionally even visitors at the studio ask me: "Why do you go on? You have had some share of success. Why work twelve to fourteen hours a day most of the year? And why risk more than a million dollars on a thing so variable and so unknown as the whim of the public?"

In addition to the fascinating, possible, but perhaps remote chance of making something that will entertain fifty million persons, I find work in the pictures absorbing and interesting. It exhausts my vitality as the theater never did; in fact, I didn't know what to do with my days when I was playing eight times a week in the theater. I find now that I can go home at night and sleep, even if the auditors, efficiency men, bookkeepers and others, whose business it is to record the mounting costs of a big production, cannot. This being thoroughly tired physically, together with the satisfaction of creating and making something and the opportunity we have here to be in the open air most of the time, with the daily vigorous play which we indulge in late in the afternoon, seems to me sufficient reason for the hard work of making films. And if the money risked on a picture totals more than a million, as in *The Thief of Bagdad*, and that without figuring a salary or even living expenses for me, the returns on a big picture, if it is done sincerely, are fine, as they should be where the gamble is so great. In other words, I like the pictures. I am afraid that any further questioning as to why I continue would be futile.

Philosophy May Find its Way to the Screen

A ND this brings to my mind a stray thought: Before very long philosophy and certain abstract subjects, such as futility, will find their way onto the screen. I do not mean that this will be in the form of painful soul-searching or dull and pedantic philosophy, but the vital and pictorial deductions from the sum total of human wisdom, experience and existence. If Charles Chaplin has done nothing else in his picture, *A Woman of Paris*, he has demonstrated that there is a subtler use of the screen than had before been attempted. He has proved that everyday life, touched by imagination and not ruled by exaggeration, can be made compelling upon the screen, even without an elaborate and controverted plot.

With all my enthusiasm for the films—and those of us in the business see many more reels than even the most hardened film fan—I have seen many a picture that I could sleep through. If a picture is well done I enjoy it, but my mind is, I fear, often concerned with the problems that confronted the producer. It is only when I see some of the joyous comedies—the work of Lloyd, Keaton and Chaplin—that I ever am exactly like the paying public. Then I am not concerned with technicalities or how things were accomplished.

Technicalities

T HERE are a good many things which are really not very technical, but which seem to puzzle the outsider—things which we encounter daily in the course of making a picture. The very variety of these makes for the general interest of our work. First of all, there is the camera itself. Now there is nothing complicated about the working of the moving picture camera. It is, roughly, the same as any other. It is a black box and a lens. There is one difference, and that is that the film is traveling all the time, once the crank is turned, from the unused magazine to the exposed magazine. That portion of the film, however, which is directly behind the lens is intermittently stopped and started, so that at the time the shutter is opened to admit the light this bit of film—an inch wide and three-quarters of an inch high—is held stationary. As the shutter closes after the exposure, this is pulled down and new film put in place for the next exposure.

The camera set-ups, or varying angles from which the pictures are taken, are more complicated. They give freedom to the screen, and often novelty. In the early days, once the camera was put, it stayed. Characters crossed the screen right to left and walked in front of the camera. This enabled early producers to work quickly, for the ordinary camera set-up will take at least a half hour today, and often, before the handle of the camera is turned, the platforms must be built.

Last fall we used a steel camera stand for a few seconds only. It enabled us to get some wonderful mob effects—if I may say so, I think the best I have ever seen. The camera was stationed on a platform swung from a ninety-foot, stiff-leg derrick made of steel. The camera was eighty feet above the ground or about the height of the average eight-story building. The derrick weighed sixteen tons and was operated by an electric hoist. We could move the camera on its platform across the scene. In order to take the next scenes, which were shot from another but stationary platform, it was necessary to move the derrick one hundred and fifty feet. This, in spite of rehearsals which had been held for several days, took twenty-seven minutes.

The actual footage which we got from this steel camera stand will go just like that on the screen. It will be over in thirty seconds. In the finished product, without figuring any overhead, that shot just for the construction of the derrick and the crowd of extras cost thirty thousand dollars, or one thousand dollars a second. Crowds of people will not make a picture, and the mere spending of dollars will not either. The money we spend is entirely subservient to the results we get. I'd hate to have it said of *The Thief of Bagdad* that it cost well over a million dollars and every dollar showed.

How Sets are Built

WHEN sets are built, the geography of them is considered, but more properly the camera angles. Every set is tested and planned to give a number of effective places from which it may be photographed. For my present picture more than two hundred drawings were made. As these were approved, models a little more carefully done than for the theater were made, and then the actual work of building was begun. These sets vary in height. If on our stages, they are arbitrarily under twenty-six feet, for that is the limit of our stages; but out in the open they may be any height. Obviously there is no advantage in too tall a set, for it will dwarf the people. For the camera to take them in and preclude that buildings will not seem to be toppling over, it must be moved so far away.

Sometimes we build sets larger than necessary, for it is cheaper to use lumber in the standard sizes than to saw it as for a house which is to be permanent. All of our sets are so placed that some of them will be effective for early morning shooting, some for noon hours and some for the afternoon. This necessitates that the day's work be carefully planned out beforehand, as the one thing which we cannot afford to waste is daylight.

A special problem that faced us for *The Thief of Bagdad* was my desire that a dream city should not look too well anchored on its foundations. It is easy enough to make a thing fantastic and unreal, but I wanted it to seem light in addition. By using a somewhat weird design, by painting trees and branches black even where we had real ones, by the use of light backgrounds instead of the customary dark ones which are thought to bring out the figures more clearly, by confining our colors to gray, gold, silver, black and white for everything except the actual costumes, we obtained an unusual effect; but sets built on the ground will look as if they were.

To get away from this solidity, we painted our buildings darker at the top than at bottom. This seemed to make them less solid and heavy at the bottom. We also built upon a highly polished black floor that had reflections. The vertical line of a house meets the horizontal line of the ground and ends there. Our polished floor reflects the building lines and lifts our city. And this black floor caused considerable extra work. There was endless brushing and polishing week after week. It caused visitors a great deal of worry, but of course they could not see the effects we were getting on the film.

We have another city here on our twenty-acre lot that is real and to me of continued interest, and that is our community of workers. From the time actual work started last March till *The Thief of Bagdad* was ready for release, I suppose it is not exaggerating to say that thirty thousand different people worked upon the picture. This of course includes the people who worked outside the studio on costumes and during the period of exploitation just before release. Some of those who came to the studio were here only a day, and in this extra work there may have been repeaters. We have no way of knowing, for a great many of those that make up these crowds come from bureaus and agencies. We give them a check or card with a number as they enter. This enables them to get their costume, and has a space to mark the return of it. Unless both are filled in by us the check cannot be cashed. This card also entitles them to their lunch.

All Trades to Make a Picture

THE day we used the steel derrick, we had several thousand extras. They were divided into companies of about two hundred men, each having an assistant director who shepherded them. These companies were lettered, and from five-thirty in the morning till midafternoon they were led about, except during the actual photographing, by a placard which bore the letter of their company. This sounds reasonably simple, but as these companies were made up of many nationalities and of every class, there came a time past noon when tempers began to go and conditions were a little trying. But on the whole it was a good mob, and considering the waits, the long hours, and the difficulties of handling mobs at any time, all went smoothly. To get make-up on several thousand people is in itself no trifling matter.

We had for many weeks a pay roll which varied from four hundred to six hundred—people of all trades. Within our gates we could make almost anything. The old carriages used in Mary's picture, *Rosita*, were made on the premises; and though the costumes of the principals are made outside for us, we often make simple things, like uniforms and clothes for mobs, in our own wardrobe. There is practically no prop that we cannot make in our property room. In the theater the property man used to go out to get what was needed. He rented or bought it, if necessary. We make most of the things we use.

When the studio is running we have plasterers, carpenters, scene painters, ordinary painters, costume workers, model makers, electricians, wire men, property men, blacksmiths, horseshoers, an animal trainer, and what are known in the business as "grips." They do the rough carpentering on a set after it is built. They tack up backing to conceal lights, and similar things. We have engineers, architects and draftsmen. We have costume designers; musicians to play during the taking of scenes; and a composer who works at the studio on the original music which will accompany the film when it is exhibited.

But when we needed some glass blowers to make an under-sea scene of glass, we had to send East for them, as there were no glass blowers in the region. This is one of the few occasions that I recall where it was necessary to send outside to get the men we wanted. On short notice we can find here workers of all sorts and people of all nationalities.

The much-advertised climate and the fabulous stories of money to be made in the movies have brought many people to our gates. They are still coming. Numbers of course will be disappointed, and will suffer much hardship till they get placed. This is especially true of those who want to act in the pictures. There never was room for everyone who came here with that idea, any more than there was gold for everyone in '49. Many of these people feel that all they need is to get into one picture and their merit, skill or beauty will be recognized by the producers and public. The pictures are not closed to talent and ability. Any industry that was not constantly recruiting would stagnate, but it is well for picture aspirants to question seriously before they get out here whether they have the ability that will be useful. Many who came out here to act are now in what a skeptical Eastern friend of mine calls Southern California's other business—selling real estate.

Always Something New

WHEN I decided to do a film with the *Arabian Nights* as a background, I wanted to have all the trappings, so to speak—flying rugs, cloaks of invisibility and everything. We made a diagram or chart of the trick and tricky shots that would be necessary. It was found that we really needed a technical staff to do these stunts. Most of these men have worked on comic films, where trick shots are frequently used. The things we had to work out were an illusion or basket trick, a flying horse, a slave turned black by poison and brought back to life again, an army created from seeds thrown on the ground, a ring cut in two in the air by a sword, a cloak of invisibility, a whirlwind, a magic rope that hangs from nowhere and which is climbed by the thief, jars which crumble and break away, sands which shift and take shape, a valley of monsters, and many other similar things. All of this took much experimenting and called into play, besides the inventiveness of the technical staff, the work of many artisans.

The things pointed out in this article are enough, I think, to show you why I find the making of pictures more absorbing and interesting than I found work in the theater, doing the same part over night after night if the play was a success, or being out of work and waiting for a job if it wasn't. Then, too, when you find hundreds of people with different interests and different trades and specialties working together for the making of one whole thing, there is naturally a fine spirit that makes the place jolly and provides much good-natured and wholesome fun and many practical jests.

Some of our play is less spontaneous, and we stick at it. The badminton players work very hard in the late afternoons. We have kept at this game longer than any other that we have ever taken up. It is something like but not quite like tennis, and it really is not badminton at all. Our scoring, however, is that of tennis. We play with a specially made racket, and the shuttlecock or puck used makes a very fast game; for, unlike the tennis ball, it may not touch the ground. We usually beat the visitors, and my director, Raoul Walsh, and I have beaten some of the best tennis players at this game. I said that it was not quite like tennis.

This article originally appeared in the April 1924 issue of the **Ladies Home Journal**, *part of a series of pieces Fairbanks wrote for this publication. The third installment follows (see next page).*

A Huge Responsibility

◆

Ninety Percent of the World's Motion Pictures are American Made

By Douglas Fairbanks

I t is an old story—that one of the universal language of the American films. We have heard it again and again; and to those of us in the business there are constant reminders that we are present in remote corners of the earth which we can never hope to visit. We get this not only through countless letters, but every time we meet a delegation of foreigners. At such a time there is never any of the reserve and restraint that characterize the usual meeting of two persons of different nationalities. The greeting is wholehearted and genuine.

And there is no question that the impression made by the films is greater and deeper than that of any other circulating medium. Sometimes this takes a humorous turn. One of our representatives in the East brought a story back with him on a visit to the studio that a Chinaman who had suddenly grown rich ordered his house furnished, not with the best of the very wonderful art of his own country which would have been in keeping with his surroundings, but with American-made furniture which he had seen in the films. I myself have seen, in the market place of a little town on the edge of the Sahara, Arab children who never heard of Napoleon shout with delight as they tried to imitate the walk of Charlie Chaplin.

That this influence might be used to serious purpose there is no doubt. There never was such a chance for inspired propaganda. Winston Churchill told me two years ago at a dinner party in London that he thought in two generations India could be conquered with the films. By this he meant that the civilization of India could be brought up to the European level, if a number of theaters were operated systematically in various important parts of the country and directed to the sole end of serving just the right mental food.

The danger of course is that, once there is a concentrated effort to harness such a power, too much will be attempted at once, and the result will be dull and educational in the informative, dry sense and not inspirational. It has never seemed to me that the educational use of the films lay in the unfolding of history devoid of romance, in their capacity to set forth the progress and discoveries of science or to record mere news happenings. We can with the films through human stories teach the fundamentals of life which are essentially the same the world over. And the pure drama of life correctly presented has the greatest educational value.

Bringing Nations Together

When remote peoples see how little difference there is between us, for instance, and themselves, they will come closer to understanding and to tolerance than through any medium of books and schools and, I am courageous enough to think, churches. To make one nation understood by another, and to dispel the idea of differences which create only suspicion—these results are far more progressive and important than the thin, superficial thing that we call civilization. It is only a name and a point of view, anyway. It means different things under different circumstances.

From the human standpoint the American films have been understood and accepted. In the beginning we made films solely for America. We had no thought that such stories as the one I made from the stage play, *Arizona*, would be popular in India. It seemed strange to us, but we were quite content as new territory for our product was constantly being opened. That the appeal of some of these films was basically sound and true was the reason for their success everywhere. There came a time when the mere novelty of pictures in motion wore off in the remote places as well as in what we call the key cities of this country. An interesting instance of the truth of this basic appeal of telling a story through pictures was brought home to me recently. I saw a Japanese film made from a popular Japanese novel, and I was surprised to find that it would not only be readily understood outside of Japan, but that it was really not so very different from what we do here either in subject matter or treatment.

And America Leads

Almost every country is today making films. It is too important an agency of education to be disregarded. Only the other day a member of Parliament made a speech declaring that ninety per cent of the films exhibited in England and throughout the British Empire were American. He deplored this because it was influencing, educating and impressing the youth from an American viewpoint. Statistics prepared by our Federal Board of Trade show that the average age of the moving-picture audience is only twenty-three, and therefore those audiences are young enough to be influenced and impressed by what they see depicted on the screen. Small wonder then that foreign governments should be concerned about the American control of the films. Early teaching is the hardest to undo or change.

There is no real reason for our domination of the screen, except that the start and the impetus that we have will make it difficult to overtake us. The situation is, however, slightly more complicated than that, and it may be that we are the logical country to carry on this industry. In the early days, as long as the mere novelty of the medium was an attraction, foreign companies, particularly French and Italian ones, did well here with their films, which were for a time perhaps better than the American pictures. But so quick was the response to the films in this amusement loving country, with its hundreds of big cities, that it seemed better business to adapt and suit the material to the American audiences.

For one reason or another, there are some pictures which do not appeal to all countries or even to all parts of this. A few pictures have gone well in the large towns here and have failed to draw in the rural communities. I believe that with the exception of some of the comedies—which are especially popular because they are usually short and can be adapted into bills with longer subjects, and because there is a demand for humor that is hard to supply—no feature film had had more than nine thousand five hundred contracts. This number is, of course, very high, for though there are about eighteen thousand picture theaters in this country and some five to seven thousand schools, lecture halls and other places which occasionally use pictures, many of these are in direct competition. If a picture is booked by one theater or chain of theaters it necessarily means that it will not be shown by a rival organization.

In England there are today less than three thousand theaters and halls which use pictures. This difference in numbers is true of the Continental countries as well, and therefore the foreign producer begins at a disadvantage if his material is at all local in its appeal. Since he cannot hope for the returns that the American producer would receive if he were to make a picture for home consumption only, he is not justified in spending the same amount of money. But I do not believe that the producer need bother about the locality of his story or the subject matter if it is human and has a genuine appeal to the emotions.

A Business Contrast

B ut actually, both in productions and in the theaters where they are exhibited, foreign countries are about six or seven years behind America. There has not been the money to spend, either on the part of the producer or of the public. The theaters are smaller and less comfortable and often badly ventilated, as they once were here. But what is more important is that the people have not got the habit of going to them. The running of the films, particularly the projection of them—a matter that could be remedied easily—is not up to the standard in the smaller places. The projection machines seem to chew up the film rapidly, and we retire copies much more frequently abroad than we do here. Nor is the same attention given to the music and the setting. Altogether the whole business is on a less dignified plane and lags behind; but this condition is, I think, only temporary.

Here we have quite the reverse—handsome buildings, symphony orchestras, singers, lights, prologues or introductions and every possible aid to the dressing up of the presentation. A great many persons think there is too much of this sort of thing. It is true that we are forced to hurdle a lot that is irrelevant, if it is the picture that we go to see. Music, lights and so-called atmospheric prologues do not necessarily enhance the value of a good picture, nor do they "make" a bad one. The exhibitor has brought people to his theater. Early film followers had to seek out the film theaters where their favorites were being exhibited. Today there is no such difficulty, for the theaters as well as the producers advertise, and theaters are solicitous for the comfort of the public. Perhaps the exhibitor is right, and the long, pretentious showing of films is what the people want. He is our channel to the public, and his is a more direct contact. When an exhibitor has tried to make pictures, he has usually failed, and perhaps the producer would go just as far wrong if he attempted to run the theaters; but I am not sure that I am altogether in favor of the usual exhibition of pictures in this country.

Though our knowledge of the public taste comes to us only indirectly and usually in the form of comment and suggestion about pictures already made which cannot be altered, I believe that it is obviously the producers who are meeting the public's demands, if they are met at all. We are the instigators and the enthusiasts. We must know what the public wants, even though we cannot ever overhear their comments as they file out of a theater, either pleased or bored. No one can place his fingers on the pulse of the people and decide to a nicety what is wanted. The most successful people in any work are, I suppose, those who are closest to normal. In creative work you cannot do what someone else wants. You must do what you want, and hope that it is what the public wants. It depends upon you whether you have more enthusiasm for the dramatization of mother love or the placing of a telegraph pole. Either can be made interesting pictorially, but, in addition to your enthusiasm for either, you must have patience. A bully feeling about something is not enough. There have been, both in the theater and on the screen, many plays that were right in feeling, but were crude because the persons who had the original ideas did not have the patience to work them out to their logical end.

Being an actor in films and a producer of them, I argue from the actor's and the producer's viewpoint; but what use are the million-dollar theaters, the orchestras and all the equipment if the films are not right? I have no quarrel with the exhibitors; but I think that at times they are lacking in vision. They, like some producers, want to make money while the going is good. Several exhibitors have told me that they did not like the policy I have adhered to recently—that is, of making only one picture a year. Make four or five, they have argued; you have the reputation and the start, and we can all clean up.

The Pictures Must Be Right

Now I want to give the best I can, and I could not give that if I were to make four or five pictures a year. Nor do I believe that present-day conditions are right for the making of many pictures. The costs are high, and it is only in the careful work that any progress is being made. Why go on giving the public the same old pictures simply because there is a name to capitalize upon and a trademark which has been established?

With a big production there are usually two steps in getting it to the public. The first of these is what we term road showing; and the second, the regular and more profitable method of gradual release to the houses devoted regularly to the exhibition of films. In road showing the producer rents a theater in New York and other large centers and runs his film as a regular theatrical attraction, having but two performances a day and charging regular prices or the scale of the theater for legitimate plays. We cannot move into one of the large picture theaters and stay as long as we want, and consequently the picture is on its way before a great many people have a chance to see it. In a week's run or even two weeks' at one of the big theaters, there is very little time for word-of-mouth advertising, so valuable in all theatricals, to have any effect. Such preliminary showings are not necessarily meant to make money and often are carried on at a loss. The number of films that have made any considerable money in this way can be counted on the fingers of one hand.

D.W. Griffith used this method most successfully with *Way Down East*, as I did with *Robin Hood*, not only in this country but in England and France. At one time I had ten theaters under my own management. Before the film went to general release I knew just what I had. A picture which has been tested in this way should be worth more to the exhibitors than one that has not been tried before the public and had this preliminary advertising in the two-dollar houses.

Seriously, all pictures are not worth the same amount of money to anybody. They cost a varying amount of time and money to make, and for one reason or another they have a greater or lesser drawing power. I have lost money on productions in the past, and if I made a picture today that did not draw I would hope to be a good loser. I should rather break even on something that I thought was fine than make money on a picture that seemed to me to be a cheat.

We cannot get ahead either as individuals or as an industry by doing the same old thing. A letter I received the other day from a boy, who has had a small picture machine for several years, seems to me to contain a general comment on the film industry. He wanted to know if I didn't have some old film that would be thrown away. He gives shows to the boys in his neighborhood for five and ten cents, but the films are always the same and the audiences have not been too pleased recently. As he rightly adds: "You can't do anything with that."

Where Standardization Fails

T he chief reason that so many pictures seem alike to the public is because there has been an attempt to control and to standardize the output of the whole industry. Large-scale production is necessary, and perhaps even desirable to a certain extent, but creative work cannot altogether be controlled, standardized or commercialized.

Good pictures are often made in an incredibly short time, particularly in a large plant where the facilities for everything are at hand; but no trail blazing is done in this way. Recently a picture at a large studio, for which five weeks had been allowed, was made in thirteen days! I have not seen it, but I will venture to say that in that time, however satisfying the result may be as the "killer" of an afternoon or evening, it will not be the most original or most sincere piece of work.

Through certain consolidations and amalgamations attempts have been made to control the whole business. These groups do not necessarily leave out of their consideration the independent producer altogether, but they wish the independent producer to sell his product to them at their own terms. And of course there is an ever-ready threat, if he doesn't do so. I believe that the independent producer, who is really a pioneer in that he is the only man who has time to discover things, should be untrammeled in his work, and not hampered in getting it to the public.

There are throughout the country, in every town of any size, cheap restaurants that serve good average food. They are usually run like chain stores, and the food served in all of them, whether they are under one management or not, is essentially the same. This is quite all right, and from the point of view of the public most desirable; but if the owners of these restaurants were able to get together and to control all chefs so that no food was offered to the public except of that sort offered in these restaurants, it would not be very satisfactory from a gastronomic point of view—and the public would be sure to rebel soon.

And yet, this is exactly what has been attempted in the picture business. The industry is off to too good a start for consolidations of companies, chains of theaters and attempted dictation of the producer's policy to retard lastingly or to kill the business; but such groupings, which tend to discourage independent production, postpone the growth and logical development of the business. It may only be for ten years, which is not long in the history of an industry that, in my opinion, has come to stay; but that ten years will be long enough to make sure that certain of us, who are now spending our time, energy and money—made in the films—will not be in the work when such a period of postponement is over. Perhaps in this I am selfish.

Just as I think that the business is too big to be held back long by attempts to overcommercialize it, so do I feel that it is too big to be lastingly hurt by other interference. A great many persons in the business—and many out of it—feel that censorship is all wrong. I do not. I think it good, but not the way it is done. It seems rather ridiculous that persons who spend nine-tenths of their time doing something else, and who have no special training for the job of censorship should be allowed to undo and spoil the work of many months.

The Censorship Problem

I have always believed that censorship should be worked out upon a system of signals or guides to the public. Now, when a film is passed, you know nothing about it, except that the censors in your state, if there is censorship, have found it harmless, or, according to their ideas, have made it harmless. This does not protect the mother who, because of its name, takes her children to see a film version of Ibsen's *A Doll's House*. A system of flags or other general warning that would show into what general class a film belonged would be far more helpful.

We protect our coasts with lighthouses, and at bathing beaches a signal is put up to indicate dangerous bathing. This may seem fantastic, but I think that in it there is the basis of an idea that would prove of service to the public. I like to be warned myself about plays. When I get back to New York, after about a year's absence, I cannot see everything; and I like to have friends whose judgment I trust tell me the general nature of the play, so that I may not waste my time. Certain things are suited for special audiences, and certain plays which are quite worthy and entertain a great many people do not appeal to me.

Because a film has once been censored or allowed to "get past" does not mean that it is suited for all audiences. Otherwise, the motion-picture theater, which is the only really democratic theater in the history of the world—and I mean democratic in the sense that it takes everybody in—would become a mere children's theater. We embrace the people who go to Coney Island and other amusement parks, the people who would prefer Greek drama or other classics, the persons who like good orchestras, and the people who just want entertainment.

The problems of the films—because they are conspicuous—will always be much agitated. I am convinced, however, that things will right themselves. There is just as much interest today in good pictures as there ever was; in fact, there is more. The big productions play longer in one theater and to better business than they ever did before. In one theater here in Hollywood *Robin Hood* played twenty-three weeks and *The Covered Wagon* thirty-five. Thus, in over a year that one theater had but two pictures. There never was a better time for good pictures; and certain small pictures, which are made with very little capital and every item spent closely watched, have made very handsome profits. It is a bad time for those pretentious pictures which cost from two to three hundred thousand dollars to do and are really nothing but the same old story, done in the same old way.

No, I am not worried about the future of the sincere attempts to make pictures. They will go right on playing to fine audiences and receipts. The very figures of these may not be so astounding as formerly, but that will not be due to the fact that they are smaller, but because the public has so often in the past been astounded by the figures of this industry. Yes, we will go right on from here.

This article originally appeared in the **Ladies Home Journal** *for May 1924 as part of a series of feature stories Fairbanks wrote for LHJ that year. The majority of these articles deal with the growing movie industry from a producer's point of view, and offer a fascinating glimpse inside the mind of Douglas Fairbanks as he explains his unique individual approach to making the biggest productions of his entire career.*

*It is also interesting to note the section about censorship in this article, where he suggests that a standard ratings system for the movies should be developed. This was 44 years before the advent of the MPAA-instituted system of rating films (such as **G**, **PG**, **PG-13**, **R**, etc.), and once again demonstrates the remarkable vision Fairbanks had for the industry's future, introducing ideas that were then several decades ahead of their time.*

What Is Love?

HAT is love? I've been trying to find out for years. Whatever it is, it's wonderful.

—**Photoplay** Magazine, February 1925.

The silver screen's first Zorro: When Douglas Fairbanks read a short story called **The Curse of Capistrano** by writer Johnston McCulley in 1920, he immediately bought the rights and "Zorro" was born. The photograph above is from **Don Q., Son of Zorro**—his 1925 sequel to **The Mark of Zorro**—in which Fairbanks plays dual roles of father and son.

How Douglas Fairbanks
Produces His Pictures

✦

First Like a Philosopher He Ponders the Idea
and Then Like a General He Plans And
Executes the Film Play

T he amount of careful and intricate work done by Douglas Fairbanks himself on one of his productions, aside from acting in them, is perhaps not
known to many persons. One or two pictures a season is the output of
the Douglas Fairbanks Picture Corporation, which enterprise is just Fairbanks
himself. He transacts its business, dictates its outlay and receives its income: he
manages its production and he is the featured player.

One of his managers in explaining how Mr. Fairbanks goes about his work,
says:

"Take a picture and you will concede that it is something which does not just
happen. Mr. Fairbanks thought of 'The Three Musketeers' years before he had
money or courage to make it. But when he was ready he jumped right in and produced it. He had notions about 'The Thief of Bagdad' before he turned out
'Robin Hood,' and intended to appear in a certain pirate picture, but held off in
order to make 'The Thief of Bagdad'. Then 'Don Q' entered his mind. Now he is
ready to produce the pirate story about which he is intensely enthusiastic.

"Once Fairbanks is impressed by an idea or a theme he puts somebody to
work on it. First he talks to intimate friends so as to hear what they think about
it, and when he decides to make the picture he calls in a writer, usually an outside
scenario expert, to prepare a treatment, a work of from 3,000 to 12,000 words. It
is not precisely a 'detailed synopsis' but a review of the points of appeal, the dominating motives and a sketch of the plot. This practically ends the scenarist's
work. Fairbanks goes over this perspective of the production and does things to

229

it. He gleans thoughts from his brother, Robert Fairbanks, on the subject matter, and consults with his scenario editress, Mrs. Lotta Woods: the director he engages as soon as the story is ready for analysis, and his production manager. As this treatment is reduced or expanded, through conferences, the production department prepares to erect sets, selected from sketches submitted by the art department, and costumes are requisitioned from plates drawn by designers. By this time the production manager can estimate the probable cost of the picture. He knows pretty accurately the final cost when he is told who the principal players are to be.

"You might ask how this production manager knows. Well, by that time there will be a blueprint of the 'Set Plot' which indicates what sets are to be used, by which players and approximately how long. Next to the cost of the sets themselves the period of employment is the big factor in cost.

The "Shooting" Begins

"Sets, costumes and players being ready, shooting scenes begin. Here is where the average professional gets a jolt. Remember there is no scenario. All the camera shots are made according to another blueprint which we term the 'Shooting Schedule.'

"As a matter of fact the big work on a Fairbanks picture is done strictly from blueprints two square yards in area. These blueprints are posted where Fairbanks and the director can readily see them. The 'Set Plot' and the 'Shooting Schedule' are the bibles, respectively, of the production manager and the director, and both of these men are responsible to Fairbanks.

"The 'Set Plot' has very little on it. It is only a tabulation of sets, by name, horizontally and of principal players vertically. Crossmarks carried out opposite each player's name under the sets show in which sets the player will appear during the production. The only other division is of the list of sets into exterior and interior. All the production manager has to know is which set Fairbanks is to use on any day, and he will know what players to summon for that day.

Blueprints as Guide

"The 'Shooting Schedule' is prepared almost simultaneously with the 'Set Plot.' It tells the story of the picture in about 2,000 words and is devoted only to essential action. The usual continuity, or script, with its reams of closely typewritten verbiage and the scenario writer's effort to write down a full description of several hundred scenes and imaginary camera positions are not there. Fairbanks, sometimes with difficulty, suppresses a desire to cheer when he realizes that he has only a hundred or so cues with which to torment himself. The blueprint is plain as a pikestaff. It tells in a word where, how, who and when. It omits telling why. That has already been taken care of in the accepted 'treatment.'

"The blueprint of the shooting schedule is also a tabulation. It is built up in column after column under two headings only, 'Set and Action.' Take the schedule for 'Don Q, Son of Zorro.' The set may be 'Interior Ruined Castle' or it may be 'Archduke's Servant Corridor.' What to do in 'Interior Ruined Castle' or in 'Archduke's Servant Corridor' is as easy as finding a telephone number. Under 'Action', right opposite the name of the set, one may read: 'Lola tells Cesar about Robledo and leaves with Rose for Dolores.' Then the director proceeds to 'shoot' Lola telling Cesar about Robledo and then leaving with Rose for Dolores. They may have shot her arriving with Rose at Dolores several weeks before, but there is no doubt that the director knows all he needs to know about the present scene. He takes it from several angles, the next evening looks at the result on the screen, and if Fairbanks 'O.K's' them, the stroke of a red pencil strikes out this scene from the 'Shooting Schedule.' When the blueprint is all red marks the camera work is finished.

Saves Worry

"Fairbanks believes this system of filming his stories is adding years to his life. He has been condensing the script part of his productions for years, looking to efficiency and advancement. On 'Robin Hood' he had a schedule that was on the way toward his present system. The system carried out the story on shipping tags pinned to a board, but he has now developed it into the even more tabloid blueprint form.

"The belief may exist that by working from such a sketchy outline Fairbanks may 'overshoot,' but, on the contrary, it proves very economical in film as well as in time. It is because every action listed is only a high light that useless footage is easily omitted. It gives the same reaction as working at a clean desk as contrasted with working with an untidy one.

"Fairbanks also is stimulated in the way of ideas by using his story in outline while producing it, as he feels then he has more license to add inspired touches as he goes along. The whole plot being before his eyes, he can make any changes conform with what has been 'shot' and what is to follow, while under old methods he might become hopelessly entangled in a mass of obscure details."

*Originally published in the **New York Times**, June 7, 1925. This piece is somewhat mysterious, as the reader will notice it carries no byline and is not attributed directly to Mr. Fairbanks. Although one source is directly quoted throughout, this source is never named as being anyone other than a production manager. Since Fairbanks' longtime production manager was his brother Robert, who is named in this story, it is a safe bet that the source quoted here is not Robert Fairbanks. Rather, we believe this piece to have been dictated (most likely to a secretary) by Douglas Fairbanks himself, and in comparison to his other written works, it matches up correctly in his use of words and punctuation style. It was not unusual for Doug to pen publicity material for his own films anonymously, or under a pseudonym.*

"Doug" Psychoanalyzes the Grin

T he secret of making moviegoers laugh was asked of Douglas Fairbanks recently. His face assumed a quizzical expression and then followed the contagious Fairbanks smile.

"There is no secret about making people laugh," he replied. "It's just done, that's all. Try it yourself. Try to tell a humorous story. See how many laughs you get. Perhaps you will make it too long in the first telling, and your hearers will show signs of impatience. Such signs are fatal to the success of your story. String it out, and when you finally reach the point, your little audience probably forces a laugh to get rid of you.

"Now try another way. Boil your story down. Make it as brief as possible. Bring out the point in the last two or three words. Then notice the difference. You will get genuine laughs. All of which is going back to the old saying that brevity is the soul of wit."

"But what about making screen audiences laugh?" Mr Fairbanks was asked. The questioner had in mind that "Don Q" his latest picture, now in its last week at the Globe Theatre, is considered the most humorous of any of the Fairbanks productions.

"We're coming to the screen audiences," he replied. "Your screen audience does not differ from two or three friends to whom you tell a humorous story. What's in a laugh, anyhow? An inward feeling of exhilaration, followed by an outward expression of mirth. We have many troubles, imaginary and otherwise, in marching through life, and if something occurs that makes us forget these troubles we grow happy, we smile.

"Disappointments are expected. Joys are unexpected. So when you set out to make people laugh you must give them the unexpected. Throwing custard pies in the early days of motion pictures was giving audiences the unexpected. At the same time it was appealing to that phase of humor which finds fun in the misery of others.

"Genuine humor is genuine fun, and if we are going to have a laugh at the expense of some one else, that some one should be the villain. Take 'Don Q' for instance. Don Fabrique is a crafty, fat man wearing glasses, who stands ready to

233

plot against anybody to advance his own interests. He perpetrates endless scurvy tricks, smiles alone at his own shrewdness and the audience despises him. Everybody wants to see something happen to this unscrupulous schemer. They would like to see him thrown off a cliff or fed to lions or something like that.

"But we don't want to take Don Fabrique too seriously. So the first thing that happens to him when Don Q, in disguise, enters the quarters where Fabrique is ruling as Governor General is that the fat man drops his glasses and Don Q purposely steps on them. Here is the unexpected, a trivial incident, you may say. Yet, being the unexpected, it brings laughter. The audience wanted something worse to take place, but this little act of breaking a pair of glasses is understood by children as well as grownups, because it is one of those little serio-comics of ordinary life.

"Making moviegoers laugh is the art of placing events in their own lives before them, with now and then some fantastic twist they never have seen, but perhaps have thought of. How often have you wanted to pull the nose of a snob at a social gathering? Of course, you would not dare do it. But if you see it done on the screen, you see what you have been yearning to do yourself, and you laugh at the very absurdity of it.

"I've told you there is no definite secret of laugh-making that I know of. If there is one, then study Mark Twain, Bill Nye and James Whitcomb Riley and apply their methods to motion pictures."

*This interview was originally published in the **New York Times**, August 2, 1925.*

Original Program Book for

"The Black Pirate"

(1926)

✦

Prefatory—

I T IS MY belief that the motion picture camera should not merely record. It should see through a selective impressionistic eye. It should capture moods as an impressionistic painting does.

In the human mind there is always a flickering revolt against the stifling actualities of life and a desire to escape from them. The screen offers an outlet for this spirit of rebellion. It gives actuality to our dreams—our moments of adventuring into the highroads of romance.

THE BLACK PIRATE is a romance of the sea and it has been our aspiration to catch and reflect the real spirit of seafaring, with all its colors and its odors, its swinging, crooning, shrieking rhythm.

Douglas Fairbanks
(Signature)

THE

BLACK PIRATE

◆

A Page From

THE

HISTORY and LIVES

Of the Most Bloodthirsty

PIRATES

Who Ever Infested the Southern Seas.

As Played by Douglas Fairbanks

Screen Story by Elton Thomas

Retold in Short Story form by Lotta Woods

EXTRACTS FROM "THE JOURNAL OF SANDY MACTAVISH," IN WHICH IS SET FORTH COMPLETELY ALL THE CIRCUMSTANCES IN THE CASE OF "THE BLACK PIRATE."

FOREWORD

I*, SANDY MACTAVISH, have elsewhere related how it came to pass that I, who aforetime lost an arm in the service of THE KING'S MOST EXCELLENT MAJESTY, did come by curious misadventure, to member-ship in a Company of the most bloodthirsty pirates who ever infested the SOUTHERN SEAS.*

I have told how IT WAS THE CUSTOM OF THESE PIRATES TO SUB-DUE THEIR PREY, LOOT THE SHIP, BIND THEIR CAPTIVES AND BLOW THEM UP. For the CAPTAIN held no traffic with modern and polite rules and was wont to say that DEAD MEN AND DEAD SHIPS TELL NO TALES and that a vessel reported to be "lost at sea" left no trail to lead to the hangman's dock.

I have also set down in another place the salient characteristics of those who were in the forefront of our Company—telling how the CAPTAIN'S fancy was for rings, of which he could never amass enough. He loved to strip them from the fingers of his victims and he would slit a craw to secure a ring that had been swallowed for safe-keeping.

Of MICHEL, the second mate, I have told how his taste was for swords and cutlasses and he never lost an opportunity to acquire a new one nor ever failed to try its point in the flesh of its former owner.

Elsewhere, also, I have written of the POWDER MONKEY. From serving out powder to the men at the guns he had come to delight in the feel of a pow-der keg under his arm and to find lure in trailing powder around cringing bodies.

And of him we called BABOON because of his brutish muzzle and his sul-len unruliness, I have told somewhat.

HOPFOOT, like me, had served in the KING'S wars and came into this Company by the same curious misadventure. Left to himself, he would choose always the middle course and his way of settling a dispute was to leave it to chance. "Draw lots for it," he would say, "and the short strand wins." So that he came to be known among the Company as OLD SHORT STRAND HOP-FOOT.

As for the rest of the Company, as I have said before, they were just so many reprobates together, each emboldening the other to greater spirit.

So I have described us all up to the day that there joined the Company the one who came to be known as THE BLACK PIRATE and now I shall set down a complete account of his case as I myself saw it or learned of it from others.

◆   ◆   ◆

CHAPTER I—SOLE SURVIVORS

ABOUT a day's sailing from the colonial town of Santa Juana there is a dot in the ocean—a nameless island. It is mostly sea-sand, a few stunted palms and a still lagoon, and it is crossed near its middle by thin lines of hills.

But our *Captain*, who had learned from me a certain thing about it, found it vastly suited to his purpose, and, on a day, our black craft crept forth from the shelter of this island to attack a merchantman—a ship bound for the *Old Country* after a circuit of the colonies and whose last place of call had been *Santa Juana*.

The merchantman was unprepared and a few shots raking her fore and aft put her at our mercy. Whereupon followed in due course the plundering, the durance of victims and the destruction.

Not all of our victims perished. A dark-clad swimmer struggled toward the island, supporting, as he swam, the inert figure of a white-haired old man.

These two—*Sole Survivors* of the havoc—reached the island. The old man feebly took from his finger a blazoned ring and pressed it in the young man's hand. Then he fell back, a lifeless corpse.

So the young man carried the dead body across the first line of hills and in the valley beyond he hollowed out a grave for it and buried it.

Only then did he take thought of his own desperate condition, *marooned* on a desert island more than a hundred miles from the mainland. So, sitting near the grave, with his head in his arms, he pondered his situation.

CHAPTER II—DIVIDING THE LOOT

WHILE this was taking place on the island our black pirate craft was the scene of activity such as ever followed the plundering of a ship.

The chests and caskets and bales and sacks, the finery of which our victims had been despoiled, were heaped up in plain sight and if anyone saw aught that he desired for his own adornment he could bid for it against his fellows and the monies thus gained would go also into the fund which was to be divided at the end of our piratical adventuring.

This bargaining over a cargo of plunder was a device of our *Captain*, and, of the turbulence it created, he made a hider for his own purposes.

So, while the commoner fellows of our Company wrangled among themselves over the sum that should go into the common fund to pay for a coat or a jerkin, our *Captain* was setting aside the richest portion of the treasure to go into a *Secret Hiding Place* on the island. As I have before told, it was the knowledge of this *Secret Hiding Place*, that gained me my life and that of *Hopfoot*.

To show the way thereunto we were required to accompany the *Captain* on his secret trip to the island.

Under cover of the din caused by the bartering, we pulled away from our ship and came to the island, knowing not that beyond the first line of hills the survivor from the merchantman took note of our coming and laid his plans to fit the case.

CHAPTER III—BURIED TREASURE

T O FIND the key to the *Secret Hiding Place* I had the map that had come to me so strangely.

The *Secret Hiding Place* was cleverly contrived. Beneath the water-line of the lagoon was a shelf of rock that furnished a stepping stone for entrance to a cave that, on the outer surface appeared to be merely a sand-covered dune. The inner portion had been closed with a door of rough timber.

Jonathan Mopp and *Abel Mullins* took the chest of treasure and, ducking under the rocky edge of the lagoon, disappeared from sight. Except for the *Captain* and *Michel*, who kept aloof, we stood on the border of the lagoon watching for them, when they re-appeared.

Over the brow of it came a stranger. Black tatters of garments clung to his figure.

In the tropical sun wet garments dry speedily and there was nothing about his appearance to tell us how long he had been marooned there.

He came toward us boldly and swiftly.

Mopp made a threatening movement toward him and the stranger lifted his hand and spoke.

"I would join your Company," he said peaceably.

There was something about him that tickled the fancy of me.

"Would ye, now?" I asked him. "And what are your qualifications?"

He considered the matter for a space and then said in that peaceable and pleasant way of his:

"Who is your best fighter?"

Queer as the question was, there was only one answer to it.

With one accord we looked at our *Captain*. There was no debating his supremacy over the rest of us in the fighting line.

We stepped back so that the *Captain* stood alone on the little knoll where he had remained while we were secreting the treasure.

The stranger walked evenly past us to the knoll, looked the *Captain* full in the face and deliberately slapped him with the flat of his hand.

The surprised and outraged *Captain* gave a bellow and drew his sword.

The stranger hopped nimbly backward and with a deft movement picked up one of the swords that *Mullins* and *Mopp* had put off when they went into the water.

The *Captain* pulled his dagger and moved forward to attack.

The stranger hopped about lightly for a moment, getting the feel of his blades. The *Captain* made bull-like lunges toward him.

Then with great lightness and precision, the stranger chevied his opponent from one position to another until he backed him to the border of the lagoon.

Another step backward and the *Captain* was in the lagoon, while the stranger, with punctilious ceremony, waited for his recovery.

The *Captain* was like to burst a blood-vessel. He scrambled to the bank and made a powerful thrust that backed the stranger toward the line of our men.

The stranger twisted about until he stood against a rampart of rock. There he invited an onrush, which the *Captain* made, mightily, only to break his blade by impact against the stone.

With his maddening punctilio the stranger waited until another sword had been furnished.

Then he took the offensive again.

They came so close to each other that they clinched and, with a trick of movement that held the *Captain's* sword arm powerless, the stranger pressed upon his left arm until he was forced to drop his dagger.

This left the *Captain* with only his sword, so the stranger discarded his dagger, burying it by the hilt in sand which lay back of the log toward which their fight was taking them.

It was this log and the dagger, that were the finish of the *Captain*.

For we saw the *Captain* pressed ever back by the relentless sword of the stranger. He came at length to the log, over which he tripped. Falling backward, he struck the upward pointing dagger, which pierced him to his death.

Our *Captain* dead, we forgot him and gathered about the victor. We passed judgment on his prowess.

But Michel stood aloof and spoke not. By which token I knew that he was pondering how he could make this circumstance rebound to his advantage.

So, thinking to win him to some expression of opinion, I drew the stranger toward him.

"Take note of him," I said to Michel.

Michel looked him over carelessly.

"There's more to our trade than sword tricks," he said indifferently.

The stranger looked Michel squarely in the eye.

"'Tis your trade to take ships?" he said. Michel nodded.

"The next ship you pick for prey," the stranger said, drawing a knot tighter as he spoke, "I'll wager I can take it single-handed."

CHAPTER IV—JUSTICE

While the others descanted on the stranger's boast—if that it was to be called—and laid their bets for or against it, I did a wee of hasty prowling.

I found a new-made grave in the hollow between two hills and at its head a rough piece of driftwood freshly carved. A scrap of broken hinge that lay beside it had been used for a tool, and these are the words that had been carved:

MY FATHER
I solemnly vow
To bring thy
Murderers
TO JUSTICE

So from the outset I knew the stranger's purpose and set myself to follow his lead wherever I might do so, for I, too, owed a debt to this Company of Pirates, though I had lacked the resolution to pay it.

CHAPTER V—THE BLACK PIRATE

ONE morning, when a clumsy deep-sea galleon lumbered along the sea-lane toward *Santa Juana*, we pulled into a cove we knew of to wait for its passing and prove or disprove the mettle of *The Black Pirate*.

Now what we saw, as we stood along the rail or climbed into the rigging of our ship to watch, was a droll enough sight.

The Galleon, with her sails bellying in the wind, held to her course.

The Black Pirate guided a small fishing boat, straight across her bow, saluting the foc's'le watch as he did so, and cheerfully offering him a fish.

The watch returned his salute and he disappeared below the bulging hull.

The contrast between the huge bulk of the galleon and the fragile shell of the fishing boat put the stamp of the ridiculous on the claims *The Black Pirate* had made for himself.

When *The Black Pirate's* cockleshell of a boat was skirting along the towering side of the galleon Michel grabbed a lighted linstock and moved it toward the touch-hole of a cannon:

"This folly has gone far enough," he said sharply. "We stand to lose everything. Give them the guns."

Hopfoot restrained him. "Give the lad his chance," he insisted. "If he fails, there's time enough."

Even as he spoke *The Black Pirate* caught his boathook in the cross-rod, let his fishing boat slide from under his feet, was jerked against the stern of the boat, climbed up to the cross-rod, went overhand along the rod and dropped to the rudder, which he fouled in such a manner as to turn the course of the ship.

Through my glass I could see the steersman thrown off his balance by the fouling of the rudder.

The Black Pirate was making his way from the rudder up to the stern of the galleon, clinging to the projections that formed the elaborate ornamentation of the ship.

The mate was still intent upon the aberrations of the wheel. *The Black Pirate* pinioned him and left him.

He whipped a knife from a sheath he had fastened to his wrist, slashed the sheet, caught the tip of the mizzen tightly in his two hands and flapped upward with the loosened sail, gaining a footage on the main topsail yard.

Again the knife came into play as he plunged it into the heavy canvas of the topsail and went down the sail with it, rending the fabric as he slid.

Treating the mainsail the like, he landed on the quarter-deck and vaulted to the main deck.

Except for the fact that his maneuvering was bringing the ship toward our boat, we could not see how he expected to make good his boast, even at this stage, so with unabated interest we watched for his next move.

He worked his way out on the foreyard, and while he was doing so the fo'c'sle watch—the same who had saluted him so cheerfully a short time before—was aroused by the shouts of the dangling sailor and fired his pistol.

Fairbanks as **The Black Pirate**, 1926 publicity photograph.

The Black Pirate was unhurt. He caught at a brace and swung himself to the forecastle, but not quite in time to intercept the watch, who disappeared down a hatch, screeching alarms as he went.

Now became apparent the point toward which *The Black Pirate* had been working.

He swiveled a pair of cannon about and lighted a linstock in his hand, and the cannon ranged to sweep the deck. *The Black Pirate* held them at his mercy.

With his foot he kicked loose from its bits a rope to which an anchor was catted and the anchor dropped into the sea.

The clumsy galleon, her sea-way lost, slid quietly into the cove and lay broadside to our ship.

Lined up along the rail and perched in the rigging of our own ship, we hailed *The Black Pirate* with shouts of approval.

"There is more to our trade than sword tricks," I said, addressing no one in particular, but taking care that Michel should hear me.

CHAPTER VI—RANSOM

THE BLACK PIRATE'S exploit had delivered the galleon into our hands and, dividing into parties, we pursued our customary tactics.

From the tail of my eye, I watched him.

The Black Pirate's face was somber. Mechanically he smoothed the blazoned ring on his forefinger.

Suddenly he sprang to his feet.

"Ahoy, you sea wolves!" he shouted. "There's something I would say to you."

There was a general slackening of activity as all eyes turned toward him.

He kept up this shouting until most of our Company was gathered about him.

"See!" he said. "Here's a ship captured without firing a shot—sound as the day it was built—not a spar broken. Why do we destroy it and lose the richest part of our adventure? Let's hold it for ransom."

I mounted the quarter-deck beside him.

"He's a lad of rumgumption," I told them. "It means fifty pound a head for every man jack of us."

Now what happened next was not in his plans because he could not have foretold it.

CHAPTER VII—THE LASS

B ABOON, clambering back and forth from one ship to the other, prying into odd corners in his search for loot, peered through a porthole into a seeming empty cabin.

On the bed, rich coverlids had been tossed aside as if by some recent occupant.

On either side of the bed the doors, made to enclose it, were folded back.

As Baboon peered closer to see if the coverlids were worth salvaging, he saw a pair of these folded doors move and a woman-servant stealthily came from behind them. Opening them, she disclosed a young woman, to whom she gave the drink.

Here was a discovery! Baboon dropped his bundle, ran through the passages leading to the cabin.

The serving woman struck him which halted him for a moment, then the panic-stricken lass ran down the passageway.

Here a half dozen others joined in the chase.

Michel, standing alone at the bulwark, reached out his arm and caught her as she would have run past.

Baboon and the half-dozen others who had joined in the chase gathered around and laid claim to her.

Mopp, and Baboon, and Hargot and the others pulled and hauled at her. But Michel held her tight in his arm and refused to budge.

The struggle was growing violent when Hopfoot interfered:

He waved some bits of rope. "Draw lots for her," he said, "and the short strand wins."

CHAPTER VIII—THE SHORT STRAND

S o, when I took over the speaking and *The Black Pirate* turned away, this is what he saw:

A lass—a lady by the look of her—with soft fair hair and soft fair skin and soft pretty garments designed to be worn in the privacy of her cabin, and she held in the cruel arm of Michel as in a vise.

In Hopfoot's fist, strands of rope.

Michel loosed his grasp on the lass and she crumpled against the deck-house, burying her head in her arms.

The hazarders each pulled a strand of rope from Hopfoot's fist.

Each looked to see what he had drawn and held it forward to compare with the others. All but Michel, who shut his fist until all the others had displayed their strands. Then he opened it slowly, and gloatingly, and disclosed the *Short Strand.*

CHAPTER IX—HOSTAGE

ALL this I got later. At the time of its happening I was bandying words with our company on the advantages of holding the galleon for ransom. *Ringnose*, as ever, was cross-grained.

"How do we know they'll send us a ransom?" he asked me.

The Black Pirate's attention had shifted alternatively to the drawing and to what was going on about me.

He heard Ringnose's question and it gave him his chance.

Leaning over, he lifted the shrinking lass to the quarter-deck and set her up before the men.

"Here's our surety," he told them, and held up a trinket that dangled from her neckchain. "This emblem marks her. She is a *Princess—a Princess of royal blood.* We'll hold her for hostage."

How much of this he was devising as he went along I could not determine. In any case, he was holding the attention of the Company.

Michel interrupted.

"The girl is mine," he shouted. "I won her by lot."

The Black Pirate countered him. "Shall we sacrifice the good of all for the benefit of one?" he asked them.

"Not so," one called out. "Riches for all of us. We vote with you, my bully-boy."

CHAPTER X—THE RANSOM SHIP

We gathered in the main cabin to draw up a paper that should stand as an agreement between us and the chief passagers of the galleon.

In it we set forth the amount of the ransom to be fifty thousand pieces-of-eight, as *The Black Pirate* had advised, and to that we added:

AND IF SAID RANSOM BE DELIVERED BY NOON TOMORROW, THEN WILL THE PRINCESS BE GIVEN BACK UNTO YOU SPOTLESS AND UNHARMED. BUT IF YE COME AGAINST US WITH SHIPS OF WAR AND SOLDIERS, THEN SHALL THE PRINCESS BE PUT TO DEATH AND HER BODY THROWN INTO THE SEA.

And to this we subsigned our names and we delivered it to the Chief Passager of the galleon.

And the Chief Passager accepted his mission and went away with his people in our ship, making farewell obeisance to the lady with great sadness.

Standing on the quarter-deck near the ship's dial, I shouted aloud, so that all on board both ships might hear me:

"We give you from noonday till noonday—by the ship's dial."

There was a great confusion—stripping our ship of its guns and the treasure we had already loaded upon it and putting these upon the galleon—and manning our ship with sailors from the galleon's crew—and setting aboard of her the Chief Passager, who was to go for the collection of the ransom.

And two things were done under the cover of this confusion, whereof the one was told me later, but the other one I guessed.

The one was the passing of the Powder Monkey in secret into the departing ship—sent by Michel with instructions to blow it up when night came. This I divined later.

The other was a communication which went, also in secret, from *The Black Pirate* to the Chief Passager. It ran in this wise:

SHOW THIS RING TO THE GOVERNOR. HAVE HIM SEND AGAINST US A DETACHMENT OF MY BEST SOLDIERS. THE "PRINCESS" WILL BE SET ASHORE THIS NIGHT.

And it was weighted with the blazoned ring.

CHAPTER XI—LETTER OF THE BOND

So soon as the ransom ship was well out of sight *The Black Pirate* joined me at the ship's dial.

"Show me your map," he said, and looked at it carefully, measuring the distances.

He looked away, thoughtfully, toward the sea. A second later he started and exclaimed. Following his look, I saw him we called Baboon. He was slipping over the side of the ship.

The Black Pirate moved swiftly and several of us followed. In the passage outside the girl's cabin Michel joined us.

The Black Pirate opened the cabin door. Over his shoulder we could see Baboon. He squatted in the open window. At the sound of the opening door he turned and drew his pistol.

There was a puff of smoke and he toppled over backward, disappearing from our sight.

The Black Pirate returned his own smoking pistol to his belt and stepped to the side of the lass, where she cowered against her serving woman.

He lifted her to her feet, bowed courteously and then came back to us.

"This was necessary," he said curtly, gesturing toward the open window through which Baboon had gone to his death.

"It was for the good of our Company. We must keep to the letter of our bond."

Michel looked at him blandly.

"I owe you thanks," he said smoothly, "for saving her—for me."

With a muttered word to me to make the lady's safety my charge, *The Black Pirate* followed.

At the door he paused and looked back. The lass' eyes were fixed on him. For a long moment they looked at each other.

CHAPTER XII—AN AFFLICTION OF THE HEART

I LEFT my position of trust at the door of the cabin just long enough to secure some simple food for the lass.

As I was returning with it *The Black Pirate* cornered me.

"Have you ever known about—," he began, "or heard about—or read about—a man falling in love at first sight?"

'Twas a right canny question, but I was forced to admit that such a condition was outside my experience.

So he explained to me that this thing had happened to him and asked me would I deliver a letter from him to the lady on whom he had set his affections.

He put the letter on the salver and I took it into the cabin.

"You are in constant danger," it read. "Set your plans to follow mine. This night I will come to set you ashore."

She pondered the matter, holding the bit of parchment in her hands and knitting her brow.

"Who is this *Black Pirate?*" she asked me.

"He's a sound enough lad," I told her, craftily, "but he seems to be suffering from an affliction of the heart."

She looked away from me absently. His eyes were fixed on space.

Unconsciously *she folded the letter, clasped it in her two hands and rested it against her breast.*

CHAPTER XIII—FRUSTRATION

BY the middle of the night feasting and drinking in the main cabin were at their height and the revelers were uproarious.

The Black Pirate came under the cabin window with one of the ship's boats and I had the two women ready and waiting.

I made fast the rope he threw me and he climbed up. I handed out the serving woman and he set her into the bobbling boat below.

Then I set the lass on the sill.

She checked him a moment, as he would have lifted her down.

"You risk your life for me," she said gravely.

"I would do more—I would give it," he told her.

She looked at him with that curious, questioning regard.

"Who are you?" she queried gently.

"A pirate who has found his treasure—and lets it go," he told her and, stooping, kissed her hand.

The boat pushed off and he started up the rope to the cabin.

Suddenly I saw him quicken. He signaled to the small boat to hasten and then, coming in through the window, gave me brisk orders.

"Open the door," he said. "Then hold me at pistol point."

So by that I knew that he had been seen.

They came into the cabin, Michel at their head. Michel it was who had seen him and called the others to witness.

But because of my drawn pistol and the raised hands of the *Black Pirate* they did not suspect me of complicity.

They stripped him of his weapons and bade him come with them. And through the porthole I could see Odell and Blodgett swimming toward the small boat, which they caught and brought back to the ship.

CHAPTER XIV—WALKING THE PLANK

WE shall walk the plank," said Michel and had much ado to conceal the pleasure he took in this announcement.

He flung a word to me to bind the culprit's eyes, the while he went to direct the preparation for the execution of the sentence.

I dare say I fumbled a bit in my search for a bandage.

Mullins jerked my arm.

"See that!" he hissed. "The jade would balk our plans."

I looked where he pointed.

The lass, her head held high, grand in her self-forgetting, walked bravely to the prisoner.

She put her lips against his cheek and reached to his hands, tied behind him. In them she placed a knife she must have abstracted from some pirate's holster.

I am never gleg at the uptake, but I did what seemed to be best.

I snatched the knife from his grasp and made a great to-do of admonishing the lass. Then, as *The Black Pirate* looked at me, I placed the knife, blade foremost, in my belt and crowded close upon him to make fast the blindfold.

I took my time to this and, as I tied, I could feel his hands working and knew that he was severing his bonds and twisting them so that the severance would not show.

A lane was made and the prisoner was walked through it.

His feet were placed upon the plank and Michel, prodding his back with the point of his sword, followed him to the end of the plank.

There they both paused and Michel whispered a word in his ear.

As I was to come to know later, he boasted that *the ransom ship was at the bottom of the sea.*

Urged on by the guiding sword *The Black Pirate* took another step—the step beyond which was space.

A splashing sound in the water. The tortured scream of the lass. Then stillness.

CHAPTER XV—COMFORT

THE lass was crumpled against the deck-house, sobbing like an ailing wean, all unconscious that Michel was watching her. I looked about for the serving woman and had a suspicion of the truth that Michel had had her taken below deck to leave the lass more lone.

I took the lass to her cabin. From her window I peered out into the darkness, hoping, yet misdoubting.

In the passage outside her door I met Michel. I locked the door and took the key.

Him I remonstrated with.

"Our men are in no mood for trifling." I told him. "The agreement read Spotless and unharmed till noon tomorrow." Break that and ye're in for a good downsetting. Ye'll walk the plank yourself."

For the sake of the bonny lass I resolved to bide with him and so I did for the night. *I propped up my chin with my knife and the prick of it, if I drowsed, set me wide awake at once.*

CHAPTER XVI—THE NOONDAY OF THE TOMORROW

OUR whole company crowded together to watch for the coming of noon. Some scanned the sky. Others watched the dial. Still others watched the high banks that hid the entrance to the cove in the hope of seeing the ransom ship come round them.

Michel stood above the dial, a mug of sack in his hand and listened, with an amused grin, to the disappointed oaths of the Company.

The shadow fell on the mark of noon.

Michel threw away his mug.

"The time is up," he said. "We wait for no man. Set all sails."

At the foot of the companionway I waited for him.

It was a sore stroke—the failure of the ransom ship to return—but I hoped to argue him out of his purpose.

He pushed me back toward the door till I refused to give ground longer.

Then he struck me over the head with the butt end of his pistol and I knew no more.

CHAPTER XVII—SCUTTLING

WHAT happened after that I have pieced together from what others have told me.

In the cabin, the lass, terror-stricken at the sight of Michel, sprang to the window. He caught her and jerked her to him, closing the window with finality.

There came the thunder of a cannon ball.

Michel, balked for the moment, tied the lass to the paneling and made for the deck.

The boat that had fired the shot as it came around the bend was now in full sight. It was a long galley, without sails and with a single bank of oars on each side. It was crowded to the full with men. It carried one gun.

On the deck of the galleon our gunners were running out their cannon and getting them trained on the galley.

The shots fired from the galleon seemed immediately effective.

The galley sank and its crew with it.

Again, our men could not know that this was but a trick. The galley had been scuttled from the inside and its crew, trained men in their line, were swimming under water in the wake of their leader.

So Michel—with a hasty order to heave up the anchor and set sail—returned to his purpose below decks.

CHAPTER XVIII—RESCUE

MEANWHILE Hopfoot found me insensible and revived me, and I, myself, went into the cabin.

I loosed the poor lass of her bonds and fetched her from the cabin.

I heard a sound behind me and turned.

Michel, with drawn sword, had made to stab me in the back, but he had been hindered in his purpose.

And the man who had hindered him was The Black Pirate!

The lass gave a gasp and clung to my shoulder.

The Black Pirate flung Michel against the wall and he fell in a heap. Then he sprang onto him and choked him.

The lass cried out a warning to him and we saw Mopp coming down the companionway, his pistol leveled. Behind him came others of our men.

The Black Pirate jerked Michel to his feet and made a shield of him to catch Mopp's bullet. Michel's head lopped forward in a queer, inert manner, and, still carrying him, *The Black Pirate* fought off the others.

A pirate crept up on him from the rear and he swung around on him with Michel's corpse. Both bodies fell through a hatchway to the hold below.

So, fighting, he protected the lass and me and Hopfoot and the serving woman who joined us, until he had set us on a companionway and started us toward the deck, holding a door against his pursuers until the way of our flight was hidden.

CHAPTER XIX—JUSTICE IS SERVED

WHILE this was the case with us, there had been great doings above deck.

The Black Pirate's men, by his orders, had kept under water long enough to allay any misgiving on the part of our crew.

When they came to the surface they swarmed up the side of the galleon like so many ants.

Our men were taken unawares.

There were plenty of guns, but they were useless within the ship.

It was a matter of a short time till all were under arrest, all but Hopfoot and me, and us, out of the goodness of his heart, *The Black Pirate* spared.

We came to the quarter-deck. Hopfoot and I and the two women and as we did so *The Black Pirate* was lifted to the deck by his men and he called out that all might hear:

"Justice is served."

There was a sudden flurry and someone announced:

"His Excellency, the Governor."

A fine gentleman walked through the lane that was made for him and saluted *The Black Pirate*.

"My Lord Duke," he said, in full, round tones, "we are much in your debt for ridding our seas of these villainous cutthroats."

I heard a bonny wee sound from the throat of the lass and she softly echoed the Governor's words.

"Lord Duke?" she whispered.

The Governor turned to her.

"Princess!" he exclaimed. Then, *"Your Highness,* we give thanks for your deliverance." And he swept the deck with his plume.

'Twas *The Black Pirate's* turn to feel amazed and I knew for certain that until that moment he had not really known whether she was gentle or simple—nor, for that matter, had he cared.

The Governor looked back and forth between them.

"You know each other not!" he exclaimed, and when they shook their heads he bowed low again.

"Your Highness," he said, "I present *His Grace, the Duke of Arnoldo."*

They looked at each other a long moment.

"Lady," he said, "I have just been made known to you—I pray you forgive this suddenness—in the presence of all these, and I would it were the whole world—I ask your hand in marriage."

He leaped to the quarter-deck and took her in his arms. She raised her face to his and their lips met.

The Governor was overwhelmed. He sat down on a convenient gun carriage and fanned himself with his plumed hat.

'Twas no small privilege to see a sight so bonny.

I fumbled in my pocket and found the map and the key to the *Secret Hiding Place.*

"'Twill make a grand wedding gift," I said to Hopfoot and made to offer it to them.

But they were that intent on each other they did not see me.

So I settled myself to bide their time and I propped up my chin with my knife, knowing well that if I drowsed the prick of it would wake me.

THE END

*Originally published in 1926 by the Elton Corporation (Fairbanks' own company), this program book for **The Black Pirate** consisted of 16 pages, featuring, in addition to the short story reprinted above, a complete cast list with star biographies, production credits, stills, and behind-the-scenes details about how this early Technicolor film was made. Lavishly printed on heavy antique linen paper in full color, the booklet has the look and feel of a real 18th Century pirate novel. Also included is the sheet music for the "Love Motive of the Black Pirate" from the original film score by Mortimer Wilson.*

If I Were Fifteen

By Douglas Fairbanks

A fter reading this article, you will not find yourselves set down upon a smooth highway leading unerringly to success and happiness, with all life's problems solved and nothing for you to do except to gather in the rich prizes it has to offer. That is to say, this is not in the ordinary sense a "success" article. It will not enable you to become forthwith a dominant figure in whatever sphere of life you choose to electrify with your prowess.

As I have said many times before, I hold no formula for success. There is no magic I know of that you can apply at fifteen or forty that will so lubricate the machinery of living that you will whirl gaily along, without hardship or misadventure, to your appointed goal. If I had discovered anything of the sort, I would have made use of it long before this. I distrust the usual prescriptions for success as I do all ready-made things designed for the human race at large. We can not take human beings as if they were factory products all cut to the same pattern. Each individual is a distinct and separate problem, with his own special equipment of traits, inclinations and capacities, subject to circumstances that have no precise duplicate in the case of anyone else, and to influences that he may bend to his own advantage but may not destroy. One does not have to be a fatalist to admit there is some force bigger than the individual that urges him forward in a certain direction. Whatever this may be, and whether we call it "destiny" or by some name less formidable, the best thing we can do is to get acquainted with it, cultivate it, co-operate with it, and then when it is realized we can look pleasantly backward upon our early struggles and decide with man's natural egotism, that we did it all ourselves.

Of course, there are general rules which apply to every one. Without a proper care and exercise of the body and a training for the mind and emotions, there can be no real enjoyment of life and nothing that deserves the name of success, but the special rules which shall govern our own conduct and guide our own progress, we must work out for ourselves. I make therefore no pretensions that what I have to suggest in this article is infallible. I offer no guarantee for its general use. And if anybody seized upon it as a sure recipe for success, I would laugh at him.

As a matter of curiosity, now that we and other people are talking so much about it, what do we mean by "success"? It is an odd fact that many of the words we use most glibly represent ideas that are vague and hazy in our minds, or at least mean different things to different people. You undoubtedly have listened to many arguments that have come to a deadlock simply because the opponents did not take the trouble to define what they were talking about.

Probably no two people reading this have precisely the same understanding of success. To one it may mean the acquisition of wealth and material possessions, to another, getting what he wants, whatever it may be, to still another, reputation. But there must be something faulty in these measures of success, because any one of them or all of them together often leave people unhappy and even miserable. And misery certainly makes a strange companion for success. Since there are so many and widely different conceptions, perhaps I may be excused if I take my own. Then, even if you do not agree with me, you will at least know what I am talking about. To me, success is not a destination but a journey. It does not consist in drawing into a station, getting off the train and settling down to a long rest. It lies more in striving than in accomplishment. There must be achievement, to be sure, but this achievement must not leave one satisfied and inert; it must furnish an impetus and quicken the desire for further progress. I do not believe that satisfaction makes a much better companion for success than despair. The man who is satisfied with success would be satisfied with failure.

This is not intended to be a perfect or even a profound definition. All I mean to say is that there will always be such a gulf between what anyone accomplishes and what it is possible to accomplish that one is not entitled to stop at any given point and proclaim himself a success. I once met a very young man on a trip to New York, who seemed despondent and out of sorts about something. When curiosity moved me to ask him his trouble, he explained that he found it depressing to consider that at his early age he had accomplished all that one could do in this world, and that there was nothing left ahead. I can think of several terms I might apply to this young man, but "success" is not one of them.

At fifteen, I did many things that I would not do again, if some miracle threw me back to that age and let me keep the experience I have gained since. But I am not going to discuss them. You will make the same or similar mistakes anyway, and reading a few printed words of advice will not stop you. It is possible to magnify one's failings and faults into an importance which they do not deserve. If a young man forms the habit of dwelling too much upon his weaknesses, of examining himself reproachfully and saying, "I am a weakling," "I can't do what others can," "I have no strength of will," or "I have this or that failing," he is doing his best to make these doubts about himself come true.

I do not believe in this gloomy contemplation of faults, thereby cultivating and augmenting them. Anyone who gives his mind and energy to building up his assets will not have to worry much about his liabilities. If you lay out an arduous enough program of what you can and should do, there will be no necessity for a list of "don'ts." A mind and body pursuing an interesting objective, absorbed and pleasantly fatigued by the pursuit, does not wonder off into byways and detours. I mean that it is better to govern one's self by positive than by negative thoughts, to develop strength instead of bolstering up weakness, to think in terms of benefits to be gained instead of pitfalls to be avoided.

The necessity for physical or mental medicines is a confession that there is something basically wrong in the system of living, and I would rather change the system than become dependent on remedies. It is better to pursue health than to nurse and pamper illness. The venerable French statesman, Clemenceau, sitting at an office desk in the midst of his daily work while rumors were cast abroad that he was dying, was quoted as saying that he was too busy to die. There is a lesson in this. The thought or fear of illness or death does not commonly cast a shadow over active people.

I can take myself as an example of this doctrine without immodesty for there is nothing heroic about it. I am not waging a terrific battle against illness, weakness and temptation. I am simply ignoring them. They do not enter into my calculations at all. My life is so crowded with positive interests that there is no room for them. There is no time to court illness or any other form of disaster. A daily routine that is a continuous performance of mental and physical gymnastics and is enlivened with diverse interests and small adventures aside from the great adventure of watching one's main purpose climb a little nearer to completion, provides me with an armor against most infirmities. If I were idle, Heaven knows what ills would descend upon me, what new ways of wasting time and energy I would invent.

There is one very simple habit of mind I formed at fifteen or earlier, that has been of real help to me. It has saved to minimize the discouragements that come to everyone and enabled me to proceed from one task to another with enthusiasm. Briefly it consists in having a goal ahead of me that is not too distant, an immediate objective that I know it is in my power to reach. I do not know how it is with you, but if I am starting out on a long walk, I do not fix my mind on a distant point that I hope to reach. I first focus on the nearest range of hills, and having gained this immediate goal, I look forward to another. Each step reached is an encouragement and I proceed with confidence and enthusiasm to the next. Viewed as a whole the journey would have seemed tedious and perhaps impossible, but taken in the manner I have suggested, it is easy. In all athletic pursuits, I have followed the same principle. If I am in a hurdle race or an obstacle race, I do not think of the dozen or so barriers I have got to meet. I concentrate upon the first one.

Lofty ambitions that know no restraint or boundary are no doubt commendable, but for the practical purpose of accomplishment, it seems wiser to tie these ambitions to something in the foreground that is attainable in the near future. At least so I have found it. One must take measure of ambition and find that it is not running beyond the capacity to fulfill it. For nothing is more discouraging than to have high aspirations and great prospects turn into vain hopes, to entertain constantly marvelous intentions and consequently abandon them, until we have formed the habit of dreaming of future triumphs without doing anything to make them come true. On the other hand, the attainment of a definite object, even if it lies only a short distance away and does not represent a great advance, gives one courage and confidence and points the way ahead.

At any rate, I have always found some object in the foreground that beckoned to me more strongly than vague prospects in the distance. I can not remember that, as a small boy, I wanted to be president, or even a member of cabinet. I wanted something which did not hide uncertainly behind the mists of the future but which lay temptingly at hand. I wanted very much to be the boy who was two years ahead of me in school. He, with his superior knowledge and his greater privileges was hero enough for me, and my desire to be in his place was fortified with the practical certainty that in a short time I could gratify it. It was something directly in the line of vision whereas the White House was as dim and legendary in my mind as the heights of Olympus. Of course, when I reached this goal, another one immediately presented itself, more glittering, more to be desired. But I do not believe that from fifteen on, I have ever lived more than two years at a time. Beyond that, I have had fairly distinct intentions, but my ambition focused upon the thing directly ahead.

If anyone asks me to-day what I shall be doing ten, or even five years from now, all I can do is to look wise, for I have only the vaguest idea. I do know, however, what I shall do next year and that when that is passed, a new objective will present itself, which I will attack with fresh enthusiasm.

I do not particularly wish to recommend this attitude of mind to others. In my case it has brought fair results, and that is about all I can say for it. You may hit upon something better. I will admit that this piece-meal progress from one stepping stone to another does not fire the imagination like the meteoric and flashing journeys through life that one often reads about. But you will probably find that in most cases a long period of careful painstaking preparation preceded the time when these careers began to "flash" and throw off sparks. If the method of progress which I have mentioned seems prosaic, certain compensating advantages can be claimed for it. One is that it furnishes constant small encouragements, without which ambition falters and hope is more likely than not to give way to despair. It likewise provides you with an opportunity, having reached one stepping stone, of getting your wind, collecting your thoughts, and determining whether you are taking the direction in which you really want to go. For ambition often changes its course between fifteen and twenty-five.

I would, therefore, hold myself always ready for such changes, prepared to weigh anchor from the past and set my sails to catch the new and brisker winds of the future. I would never set so fixed a course that I could not alter it to suit changing winds and currents. Life, as a philosopher remarked, is a process of adjusting internal to external conditions. When new conditions arise, instead of fighting against them, it is far better to adapt ourselves to them, respond to them, make use of them. Nor do I believe in the formation of any habits that become so confirmed that they shackle us and prevent us from being always pliant, mobile, and ready for some new form of activity. The best progress has always been made by men who, realizing that there must be a better reason for doing a thing than the fact that it has always been done before, throw off the shackles of the past, walk boldly in the present and accept eagerly the gauntlet thrown down by the future.

*This article originally appeared in the April 1926 issue of **Boys Life**, official magazine of the Boy Scouts of America. Fairbanks was a regular contributor to this publication throughout his career.*

When Will We *Really* Have Talking Movies?

Within the next ten years we may expect many new developments in the picture business. There is no doubt that music and sound will play a very important part in these developments. When I say sound, I do not necessarily mean talking motion pictures. Dialog may and may not be the ultimate result of experiments with sound in pictures. The proper synchronization of beautiful music may mark the end of all our present-day experiments in talking pictures.

Along this line of new developments I believe we may expect much in the way of improved colored pictures. There is beauty in color, music, composition and movement, and these things may all be combined.

These changes represent definite forecasts as to what can be expected of pictures ten years hence. No one can say for sure that all these things will take place, but it is reasonable to assume that they will. I feel certain that present-day experiments will result in sound being combined with motion, but this will not become the commonplace thing for some time.

Of course, production methods will have to be changed as new devices are introduced, and new stars will have arisen by the time many radical changes are made permanent. Inventions cannot be perfected overnight, so we may not expect a revolution in the picture business. It will be a slow process of development of new scientific ideals.

—**Douglas Fairbanks**

*In their June 1927 issue, **Motion Picture Magazine** asked film industry leaders to submit their thoughts on the advent of sound technology in the movies. Fairbanks is found here, along with Sam Goldwyn, Irving G. Thalberg, director Clarence Brown, producer Al Christie, and others. Their statements reflect clear skepticism about "talkies;" most agree that talking pictures will probably be little more than a passing fad. Even Fairbanks, whose predictions were usually right on the money, seemed to underestimate the importance of sound in the future of filmmaking.*

MOTION PICTURE ARTS & SCIENCES

◆

THE ACADEMY'S PLANS

By DOUGLAS FAIRBANKS

*O*UR *purpose is positive—not negative. We are formed to do, not undo.*

Our first positive effort should be directed toward the founding of a magazine. We have certain things to tell our constituency and we have, without doubt, ready to hand, in the flood of friendly, interested and sympathetic inquiry and comment that daily pours into our offices from all quarters of the known world, the greatest mailing list ever provided for this purpose.

The man who handles this project and solves the problems connected with it, who brings together the right people and directs their efforts, must have world-knowledge and world-wisdom. The right man will be big enough for the job and he will recognize that the job is big enough for him.

Our second positive effort should look to the construction of a fitting building, call it a club-house for want of a better term, to house our varied interests, give us headquarters, a meeting place for our Academy and our branches, a publishing house for our magazine, a repository for our research library and technical laboratory. The enterprise to be covered by a bond issue to which all of us can subscribe according to our desires.

Then we have a film to make. The giving of an entertainment for charitable purposes has always been a more or less hazardous undertaking. "After all, I'm giving this away," says the artist, and sings his most often-sung song or presents his best-known sketch. But our film is to be made for the benefit of all of us. We're all going to participate in the results and the little selfish something that is in the best of us will give more under those circumstances—harder work and greater creative effort. The great thing about this project is that fifty percent, coming to the Academy and fifty percent, going to the Motion Picture Relief Fund means that the Relief Fund will receive a much larger sum than would accrue to it from an entertainment given with only the charitable end in view.

These are immediate things for us to do. Let's do them.

*Introduction to the very first issue of the **Academy Magazine**, Vol. I, No. 1, November 1927. Fairbanks had recently co-founded the Academy of Motion Picture Arts & Sciences in May of that year, and was serving as the Academy's first president at the time this article was written. Fairbanks hosted the very first Oscar ceremonies in the Hollywood Roosevelt Hotel, where the Academy kept its business offices for several years. He continued as Academy president until 1931.*

Autographed photo, circa 1927,
from the collections of the Douglas Fairbanks Museum.

Douglas Fairbanks

(Letterhead)

Hollywood, California
December 6, 1927

Dear Mr. Pengelly:

Thanks so much for your letter. It was a great pleasure for me to take it home to give to Mary and I'm sure that if she has any vague ideas of retirement, such encouragement and whole-hearted praise as that given by you and Mrs. Pengelly will prove a powerful deterrent.

With best wishes from us both, I remain

Sincerely,

Douglas Fairbanks
(Signature)

Mr. W.J. Pengelly,
616 Hartman Building,
Columbus, Ohio.

DF:KD

This letter appears to be a personal reply to a piece of fan mail in which Mr. Pengelly implored Mary Pickford not to make good on her latest promise of retirement. Note the initials of "K.D." at the bottom, referring to Kenneth Davenport, Doug's secretary and friend of many years. Doug had known Davenport since they were both struggling actors on Broadway; Davenport appeared in a 1904 play with Fairbanks called **The Pit***.*

The Big Adventure

By Douglas Fairbanks

S peaking of adventures, which I have been asked to do, I have learned that it is not the number of thrilling experiences you go through but what you get out of them that counts. You can seek new thrills until there seem to be no new ones left, travel until the mind grows dizzy with the changing scene, turn life, if you will, into a series of lively skirmishes with death, but unless there is some meaning, some object sought, some goal to be discovered in all this mad adventuring, it does not seem very profitable. What is left in the mind, after the excitement of the moment has worn off, and you begin to view your experience in the light of knowledge gained, of benefit received—that, it seems to me, is the test of true adventure. You do not have to discover the South Pole or add to the wisdom of nations, but unless you have definitely contributed to your own fund of useful experience, your adventuring will seem rather empty and purposeless.

In general, I believe that it is a tendency to-day to swallow too much and digest too little—and this applies equally well to food, books, and experiences. You can devour all the new books, take in all the new plays, taste every adventure that the passing moment offers, and in general, attack life as if it were a feast to be eaten as rapidly as possible for fear the table might be cleared before you finish, but you will not necessarily enrich your minds by so doing. Unless you choose from this menu of life rather carefully, eliminate what is useless, take a little time off to assimilate and digest things as you go along, you are more likely to suffer from mental dyspepsia and end up by losing your appetite altogether.

This is one reason, I suppose, why I like to write these occasional articles for BOYS' LIFE. They represent a digestive process, an opportunity for reflection, for reviewing past experiences to see whether they have created any fund which yields present dividends. In this sense, I am not writing so much for publication, as I am talking to myself. If any lesson emerges from my random observations, it is pointed chiefly at myself, and intended for the reader only if it happens to hit him.

266

This reflective mood—one which a fairly busy life does not permit me to indulge in too often—was caused by a question just asked me by a visitor to the studio.

"What," he asked, "do you consider the biggest adventure you have ever had?"

I am pretty well trained in the trick of answering questions, for I seem to be a constant target for the curious to shoot at, and these questions are usually so similar that answering them is merely a mental reflex, requiring little thought. But this was a new one and needed thinking over. What has been my greatest adventure?

There came into my mind the memory of a wild night long ago when I was stranded in a howling blizzard in the Rocky Mountains. My companion and I were lost. We had no guide, and the darkness and swirling snow made an impenetrable blanket through which we could see hardly a foot ahead. We were far from food and shelter and the odds were terrifically in favor of our freezing to death before we were rescued. This was an adventure of a sort, but it does not seem to stand the test of time very well. It leaves me with nothing but a fading memory of a rather foolhardy walking trip across the Great Divide, which might have ended in disaster but didn't.

I can think of numerous incidences in my work of making motion-pictures that were thrilling enough at the time. I remember a fight we staged in "The Mollycoddle" in which the villain and I rolled, tumbled and fell down the greater part of a steep mountain side, and I narrowly escaped having my skull crushed. As it was, in protecting my head, two of my fingers were broken. But this somehow doesn't seem very important to-day either. A stirring moment and nothing more. Certainly adventure is made out of different stuff from this.

It was not half so exciting as an incident that happened when we were making "The Americano" many years ago. On the location we had chosen, there strolled an evil-looking Mexican who was the exact type I required for a certain part in the picture. When they told me that this fellow had had no experience whatever in acting before a camera and didn't even know there was such a thing as a motion-picture, I was all the more determined to engage him, for, under certain conditions, the naturalness of the untrained actor is just what you want.

Into this Mexican's brain there percolated only vaguely what the business was about, but when he got it into his head that one of the crazy Americans into whose company he had stumbled wanted to fight with him and was willing to pay for the privilege, he showed signs of genuine interest. Although this fellow whose villainous face made him so suitable for the part didn't know anything about acting, it turned out that he knew *all* about fighting.

So, when I cuffed him lightly on the side of the head, as a sign that the frolic was on, he went me one better by drawing a huge knife and made at me like a wild man. I spent a few very interesting minutes in trying to ward off the spirited attack of this man, who proved very skilful with his knife, and in trying to convince him that it was all in a spirit of play. But there was no such thing as a make-believe fight with this earnest Mexican. A fight was a fight and there was no fooling about it.

The other members of the company were going to interfere, but feeling that I could handle him and thinking we could get a very realistic scene in this way, I told the camera man to go on cranking. The fight covered quite a lot of territory indoors and out, and the camera man had some difficulty in following us. I came out unhurt, except for a few superficial jabs. The odd thing was that this fight did not register as well on the screen as if it had been "acted" in the usual way. Which may or may not prove something about the art of making pictures.

But I don't seem yet to have hit the trail of real adventure. Such little incidents as I have recorded are all very well as lively interludes in the sometimes dull routine of living. Exciting moments, to be sure, but after all little more than items in the day's work. I could recount dozens of them, for I have had my full share of such minor adventures and I have done many foolhardy things, of which I have no inclination to boast at present. They do not come up to the requirements I mentioned.

I like to feel that the spirit of adventure is something above sheer recklessness and bravado—a quest undertaken in a cause, with the high hope of discovering something greatly to be desired, leaving one with some fund of experience that one can draw upon later. About all you can learn from rolling down a rocky mountain-side is that it is a most uncomfortable kind of locomotion, to be avoided if you have any other means of travel.

So let me come to what I consider my real adventure, and I want to warn you that it is not particularly sensational or even unusual. On the contrary it is one on which every human being must embark. If this makes it sound commonplace, let me assure you that I have not found it so. This is an adventure not in flirting with death but in meeting life, a much more important undertaking, and in the long run, just as exciting.

When I was about eighteen, I was seized with a restless spirit which I do not have to explain because it is a common symptom of maturing youth. I wanted something that life was withholding from me, and the fact that I didn't know exactly what it was made me want it no less badly. All I knew was that it didn't exist in Denver, Colorado, where I lived. My surroundings did not live up to my bright expectations. At eighteen they seldom do. I wanted something bigger and better, more adventurous and alluring than I could find at home.

As I say, I do not have to explain this mood of revolt against life as I found it, for I do not believe a person has lived who has not felt it acutely at one time or another, who has not cherished the illusion that the great things of life are not to be found at home, that the surroundings and conditions in which one lives are like confining walls holding one a prisoner while adventure dwells merrily outside and beckons from far horizons. At eighteen, life is a bright promise and one does not care to have its fulfilment too long deferred. If life had some prize package for me, I wanted it tied up and delivered at once.

So I went to New York, having no doubt that here I would find some kind of treasure worthy of my exalted expectations. In an effort to find it, I tried college, business and many other things. But adventure seemed carefully to avoid each new path of life I chose. I got a glimpse, now and then, of the mysterious thing I was pursuing, but it always seemed to have moved on. I felt as one does who comes upon the charred camp-fires of the party he is following; during the night it has stolen away, and the trail must be taken up again. My surroundings were still in a conspiracy to cheat to me of what I wanted. Then I thought of London. Of course! One could not expect adventure to dwell in this prosaic land. One must cross the Atlantic.

With only fifty dollars in your pocket, it is one thing to plan a trip to London and quite another thing to get there. But I was determined to complete my search. I worked my passage on a cattle-ship sailing for Liverpool. There were many little adventures on the way, but on the whole I would say that a ship full of odorous cattle on a heaving ocean came about as far from presenting the perfect life I sought as anything I had yet encountered. I walked from Liverpool to London earning food and lodging along the road by hauling lumber, crushing rock, anything to reach my greatly desired goal of London—the dwelling-place of true adventure.

But this goddess of adventure must have heard I was coming, for when I arrived, she had again skipped away, leaving only a stir in the air and faint footprints in the streets. All I found was another big city, different from New York, but not necessarily better or more alluring. Something was evidently wrong with the world, for it persistently refused to meet my expectations. This roving life, was, of course, not without thrills. There were plenty of them. Journeying in a strange land, never knowing what lay beyond the next bend in the road or how or where you were going to eat and sleep next, knocking up against strange types of people and getting to like them, breathing deep, walking fast and eager to meet any situation that presented itself—in all this there was the breath of adventure, but the real thing seemed to be

missing. I felt as if I had picked up a number of pieces in a jig-saw puzzle in my wanderings, but I couldn't fit them together into the complete and perfect adventure.
The key to the puzzle always lay somewhere beyond.

As a last resort I decided to try Paris. I didn't want to come to the pessimistic conclusion that this world was incapable of coming up to my
requirements, that it was unworthy of my high expectations. So I determined to give Paris every chance. I would creep up on it in the dark, when the
glamor of night rested on the city, and it appeared at its adventurous best. I
would give the world one last opportunity to redeem itself.

When Paris failed me, an uncomfortable suspicion began growing in my
mind. This was that there was just a chance that something was wrong—not with
the world, but with me. When one discovers that he is out of harmony with his
surroundings, there is always this bare possibility. Youth is generally a pretty
harsh judge of everything except itself. This suspicion deepened into certainty
one evening as a friend took me to a performance of a French play in which a celebrated French beauty took the leading role. The performance, which seemed to
take an audience of perfectly intelligent people by storm, left me cold and unre-
sponsive. This raving beauty seemed more raving than beautiful, and I saw nothing in her to justify her reputation.

"Have you ever thought," my friend asked me, when the show was over, "of
trying to view people and things here in Paris through French eyes, of trying to
get into their mood and adjusting yourself to them instead of expecting them to
change themselves to suit you?"

This thought was something of a jolt, but I had it coming to me. Could it be
the unwelcome truth that the shortcomings for which I had been blaming the
world dwelt in myself? Had my disappointing surroundings simply reflected an
emptiness within? In other words was I like a man with defective eyesight who
blamed what he saw rather than his distorted vision because things didn't look
right? The answer to these questions was, I had to admit, an emphatic affirma-
tive. Apparently I had traveled thousands of miles in search of high adventure,
only to find that adventure is not a matter of geography at all, but lies where the
seeing eye can find it. I had traveled to New York, crossed the Atlantic, peered
into the fogs of London, searched the wonders of Paris, and what I had been
looking for all this time, without knowing it, was—myself.

Having come to this strange ending of my great quest for adventure, I
promptly shipped as a sailor on a passenger steamer for New York, for I wanted
to get home as quickly as possible. The voyage was far pleasanter than the one

over, not altogether because I found human beings more interesting companions than cows, but because I had a new slant on life and I was eager to try it out. My adventure had not yielded the fine treasure I had expected, but it had at least left me with a little better sense of how I stood in relation to life. Thus far my attitude had been that of an eager spectator challenging the world to start performing without realizing that I was expected to play some part in this performance. I had expected wonders from my surroundings and very little from myself. I decided to reverse this: to cast a more lenient eye outward and a more critical eye within; to measure myself to meet these surroundings instead of expecting them to adjust themselves to fit me. For it had dawned upon me that what I needed was not a bigger and better environment but a finer perception with which to view it.

Seen from this new angle, New York showed me a more friendly and inviting countenance, and I knew that adventure lurked in every part of it. Since I had decided upon the stage as a career, I tried to perfect myself in every capacity that would be of value, however indirectly, to the actor. I concerned myself not with making any more extravagant demands upon life, but with fulfilling the demands that life made upon me. And it was astonishing to find how warmly my surroundings responded to this overture on my part and leaped up to my expectations. With the discovery or development of each new faculty in myself, with the acquisition of each new interest, the world became a brighter, better and more adventurous place to live in. For I was no longer a critical and exacting outsider, demanding entertainment, but a contributor, realizing that the mutual adjustment between me and my surroundings required that I have something to offer. When they failed to give satisfaction, I learned to seek the reason within.

This may not sound like a very rollicking adventure, but life holds nothing more interesting or important than this first sharp clash with the world and our final adjustment to the conditions it prescribes. You *can* change your surroundings, if they fail to suit you. But you can't do it by running away from them, for they have a mysterious way of tagging around after you. Nor can you do it by turning a hostile or defiant eye upon them. You can do it only by looking first within and equipping yourself to meet them. Then, when you approach them properly, you will find them friendly and eager allies ready to serve you in any reasonable demand you may make of them.

*Originally published in the June 1928 issue of **Boys Life**, official magazine of the Boy Scouts of America.*

A Message to Young Men

By Douglas Fairbanks

You may have heard this by radio

I have no message in the ordinary sense—no doctrine, no magic formula that will light the way to happiness, success, and prosperity. There are enough people delivering such messages.

But there *is* something I want to say to the young men of this country. And, incidentally, may I suggest to you older people that you won't feel nearly so old if you stop figuring your age by the calendar? It's not the mere passage of time that makes us grow old. It's the settling down in the rut of fixed habits and set ideas and saying to ourselves, "We are now such and such an age and we must act with appropriate stiffness and restraint." It's not hardening of the arteries that makes us old. It's hardening of the ideas.

I want to talk particularly to that group—and I know it's a large one—that is interested in the Junior Olympic competitions now going on the country over, the winners of which get a trip to Holland to see the Olympic games. These Junior Olympics will also develop material for the American team for the major Olympics of 1932, to be held in Los Angeles.

What applies to athletics applies to everything. The method of attack is exactly the same whether it is competition in athletics, competition in scholarship, in business and art, or competition with yourself in overcoming the obstacles of life.

The fellow writing a poem is up against the same problem as the fellow doing a high jump. The important thing is to get over the top.

You may say that you can't expect to be as good as So-and-so because you're handicapped in some way or other—weak lungs—poor endurance—you can't be a Nurmi because you haven't the right stride. Well, I'll bet you there never was a champion at anything who didn't feel at some time or other that he had some unconquerable handicap.

Don't tell me that strong legs and a good heart and lungs make a great runner. There is something else. You might say that because Paddock was handicapped with fat or the Norwegian Hoff lacked certain bone structure and muscle development, they hadn't the material to make them champions.

The thing that puts them over the top, gives them the added half inch or the fraction of a second less, is the thing I want to talk about now. The all-important thing—whether it's the poem or the high jump—is spirit. And in nine cases out of ten this spirit has been born in the fight against bitter odds, in some one's trying so hard to overcome a fault that he turns weakness into strength and snatches victory from defeat.

The man with the weak biceps is likely, in his effort to correct them, to acquire much stronger ones than the average. There is no courage quite so terrific as the courage of the timid man who has conquered his timidity. The world is full of strong, vigorous men who began life as weaklings, of orators who once were tongue-tied, of business giants who once had trouble with the multiplication table.

Beethoven was deaf when he wrote some of his best music. There was spirit! Lindbergh does not seem to have any unusual capacities. I am sure there are a great many people who can sit up nights better than he can. It looks to me as if he were too tall to be comfortable in an airplane, anyway. How has nature favored him? It hasn't. But he has spirit.

Thank Heaven for your handicaps, for they are benefits in disguise. In struggling to overcome them you develop a strength you couldn't possibly get in any other way, a strength that will enable you to take future barriers with a laugh.

Take adversity as a bitter but healthful tonic which when once gulped down puts new blood and strength into you.

The worst thing that happens to you may be the best thing that happens to you, if you don't let it get the best of you. Sounds complicated, but it isn't. Think it over. Say it over. Say it over after me. Are you ready? Come on, fellows: *The worst thing that happens to you…may be the best thing that happens to you…if you don't let it get the best of you!* That's fine!

I don't pretend to be a second Coué, but if you will say this over the next time you face a bad situation, with the odds apparently all against you, you may see things in a different light. Beneath the severe handicap may lie victory. Under the frowning mask of failure, success may be smiling at you.

This is the spirit that will bring victory in Amsterdam this year or in Los Angeles in 1932. You young Americans have a heritage of spirit—one that has been bred in you by generations of pioneers. Now use it. An older American is looking at you with pride and confidence.

*This "Message to Young Men" was originally a radio address broadcast nationwide during the Junior Olympics of 1928, and was published by **Youth** Magazine that September.*

Douglas Fairbanks

(Letterhead)

Hollywood, California
January 10, 1929

Dear Mr. Bosqui—

Thanks for writing and for the pleasant tribute you pay my work.

Yes, as you surmise, we have debated the subject of the Conquest of Mexico both as historians and fiction writers have treated it. Our production is so limited, however, we must neglect much that we should like to do.

Best wishes.

Sincerely,

Douglas Fairbanks
(Signature)

Mr. F.L. Bosqui
125, Lecarne House
Loveday Street
Johannesburg,
Transvaal

DF:LW

Francis Lawrence Bosqui was an expert on metallurgy, and wrote several books on the subject. He resided in Johannesburg, South Africa, where he was consultant to the South African Townships Mining and Finance corporation. Unfortunately, Mr. Bosqui died just a few months after this letter was written, on May 4, 1929. Note the initials at the bottom of the page "L.W.," indicating that the letter was typed by Lotta Woods, his secretary at the Douglas Fairbanks Pictures Corporation.

Douglas Fairbanks Says Talkies Will Become Better and Cheaper

✦

Declares Sound Pictures Bring All Actors Closer to Audience and Widen Their Opportunities—Also Record Best of Several Performances

By DOUGLAS FAIRBANKS
Special to the Christian Science Monitor

BEVERLY HILLS, Calif.—There is no question about the fact that we are living in a mechanical age, and for that reason it is only natural and right that the theater, as well as other activities, should benefit from mechanics.

Talking pictures are a long step in this direction. They are the heaviest blow which has yet been dealt the legitimate theater, for they not only bring to the screen the living, breathing actors of the stage, but they intensify their acting, and form a new medium of expression farther reaching than the stage itself.

By this I do not mean that talking pictures will do away with the stage, for I believe the legitimate theater will always obtain. Nor do I imply that they will harm the legitimate actor. Far from that, they will give him an opportunity to reach wider audiences and therefore to earn more than he has ever found possible in the past. All the best actors of the stage will find a place waiting for them in this latest development of the screen.

Facial Expression

Talking pictures bring the audience closer to the actor than the stage ever could. Facial expressions, which form one of the most important parts of an actor's art, have been largely lost over the footlights, but in talking pictures these expressions, as well as the slightest whisper of the voice, are carried naturally and undiminished to the farthest corner of the galleries. I have an indelible impression of Eddie Cantor rolling his eyes when he got the wrong number in a talking picture, while the many times I have seen him actually on the boards have no such vivid memory for me. I feel that I saw the Prince of Wales more intimately when I heard him speak in a talking picture than on any occasion when I met him personally.

Never have I been so moved in the theater as I was in seeing Miss Pickford's recently completed talking picture; and the fact that I say this about my wife is more significant than if I said it about anyone else, because in her case I am probably more highly critical. Stage hands and theater workers who saw the preview wept, while at another test, when we heard the voices without seeing the picture, people were moved to tears by the intensity of the dialogue alone. To me this indicates that the voice, even more than the picture, grips an audience.

Duplicating a Selected Program

In the past, great actors have been able to reach only limited audiences. With a single print of a talking picture they can reach more people in one day than in a week of personal performances. Duplicate prints increase the figures to fabulous proportions. This means that their earning capacity is enlarged, and at the same time their working efforts are minimized. Also, the performance which reaches the public is unquestionably better than would be afforded by personal performances. In 10 performances by any actor or cast there is certain to be one that stands out above the others, and in making a talking picture this one best performance is selected out of the many scenes shot. Thus the quality of the production given through talking pictures transcends that of the stage, and is, moreover, uniformly maintained.

International Aspects

The international aspects of talking pictures are an especially interesting angle. We have supposed that these pictures would have to be remade for foreign bookings. Miss Pickford, for instance, has expected to make a silent version of her latest picture to be shown abroad. But the more we think of it the less we contemplate such a move. More than one European actor of prominence has used his own language when acting in the United States, and it is possible that talking pictures in English may be shown throughout the world, with something in the nature of a synopsis of the plot, similar to the argument of an opera, given audiences which do not understand English. If this is done, it will be a wonderful boon to the English language, and aid greatly in bringing about world friendship.

The scope of talking pictures, however, is far from limited by the more usual type of screen play. Almost everything which people now gather in halls to see and hear can be presented through this medium, and within a very short time, I believe, symphony orchestras and opera companies as well as stage productions will be coming to Hollywood to be "boxed" for wider distribution than they could obtain otherwise.

Mechanical Merits

The time has already come, for me at least, when I prefer to hear an orchestra over the latest and finest radio than in reality, for the tones are gathered by a battery of microphones, "mixed" properly, and delivered to the hearer more complete and uniform and, I believe, more pleasing than they could be caught from any single portion of an auditorium. The same should be true of a talking picture recording. Mechanical imperfections are being corrected almost every day, and before long the scope of talking pictures should be almost limitless.

The general environs of Hollywood will, it seems to me, be the natural place for most of the work in connection with this "boxing" of all forms of entertainment. If one wishes to manufacture steel he goes to Pittsburgh. Hollywood has long held pre-eminence as a film center simply because everything necessary to motion picture photography is more convenient to this locality than to any other. The desire of managers to draw it nearer New York has not affected this economic fact.

A New Efficiency

When the production of talking pictures becomes more nearly standardized, they will be made more cheaply than silent films are now, even though more technical skill and mechanical operations enter into the work. This is partially because there is a marked tendency within the industry to do away with great multiplicity of facilities and to centralize production on a sound, businesslike basis. The writer of film stories will be left free to evolve talking pictures untrammeled by the routine of the studio, but once the script is in the mill, it will be turned out much more systematically than has been possible heretofore. Better pictures for less money will be the result of greatest interest to the public.

There is a close connection between the development of talking pictures and radiocasting. A natural movement within this mechanical age is to avoid congestion through facilitated distribution of all commodities, from groceries to amusements. Traffic problems will be greatly lessened when people will not have to crowd into the city to attend the theater, but through television and radio can have a talking picture in the home.

Details at this time are only conjectural, but there is no reason why one cannot drop a quarter in a slot for talking pictures as readily as for illuminating gas or a telephone call. There will always be enough of those who prefer going to a theater to keep that institution alive, but there will be vast numbers of others added to the motion picture audiences of the world who will not have to leave their homes to get exactly the same entertainment.

This article originally appeared in the April 9, 1929 **Christian Science Monitor**. *Note how Fairbanks speaks of television, a new and very experimental medium he was actively involved with in its early stages of development. He participated in several TV "test" broadcasts in the 1920s, and was obviously very enthusiastic about this technology being the wave of the future. Of course, TV would not become widely available to the general public for another 20–25 years after this article was written. His "quarter in the slot" movie idea is an interesting glimpse into future innovations such as home video rentals, "pay-per-view" cable/Satellite TV and downloading movies from the internet for a fee.*

How Douglas Fairbanks Keeps Fit

◆

"The keynote of health is regularity," he says. "Combine moderation with this regularity and you have an unbeatable team."

By Eleanor Parker

I t was four o'clock, tea time on the Douglas Fairbanks set at the United Artists' studio in Hollywood.

Under the glare of the huge lights, Mr. Fairbanks was playing his favourite role, D'Artagnan, the gay and dashing seventeenth century musketeer of "The Iron Mask," a continuation of the story of "The Three Musketeers."

Promptly at the stroke of four a white-jacketed waiter appeared in the semi darkness of the behind-the-set confusion, and deposited his tea service on a convenient medieval table. When his scene was finished, the twentieth century D'Artagnan stepped out of the world of make-believe and received his cup of tea, standing.

Beside the silver pot were plates heaped with slices of rich chocolate cake, thin sandwiches and petit fours. But Mr. Fairbanks touched none of these viands, which, it was noticed, were left for others on the set. He drank only one cup of hot tea, without cream, sugar or lemon.

"This will keep me going until dinner time," he laughed, gaily gesticulating with his cup. "D'Artagnan's a strenuous fellow and it's a long stretch between twelve, noon, and eight p. m."

"Don't you ever eat sweets?" I asked, marvelling at this living picture of glowing vitality in the romantic garb of King Louis XIII's France.

"Occasionally," was the reply, "when I feel like it, and when my weight is below normal. I like candy and sweets as well as anyone, but not in big doses. Too much sweetstuff slows you up, and no one can afford to lag behind the procession in these fast moving days. In order to function properly every human body requires a certain and regular amount of food. Excess and irregularity are wrenches thrown in the machinery. Mental and physical speed depend upon perfect health, and perfect health relies upon regularity for its foundation."

There you have the health credo of the human dynamo which is called Douglas Fairbanks. He is the screen's greatest disciple of the doctrine of speed and efficiency, mental and physical. Not for one moment does he permit himself to slow up or to be slowed. With a physical fitness which would do credit to a high school athlete, and a mental alertness which keeps him always one jump ahead of the other fellow, he grows younger and speedier with the passing years.

"I think that the keynote of health is regularity," Mr. Fairbanks went on. "Eat regular means, sleep regular hours, exercise, work and play with regularity, and you will acquire an efficiency which will never fail. Combine moderation with this regularity and you have an unbeatable team."

Doug practices what he preaches. He arises at the same hour every morning, whether or not he is working. He eats breakfast, luncheon and dinner at their appointed intervals. He sleeps his self-allotted quota of eight hours every night. Should work interfere with his rest schedule, and often during production he is before the cameras until long after midnight, he makes up for the lost time by snatching an hour or two of sleep the next day. He exercises and takes his recreation, which are almost synonymous terms, with the same systematic regularity.

"What do you eat?" I asked him, as he set down his tea cup.

"Almost everything," he answered, "so long as it is properly cooked. Meals and food don't mean a great deal to me except as they afford a respite for interesting companionship and conversation. I eat a great many vegetables and fruit, not only because they are good foods, but because I like them. We, who live in California, sort of feel honor bound to like our native fruits and vegetables, you know." There was a twinkle in his eye.

"Of course, I have to watch the scales. If I add a little extra weight, I cut down on my day's rations, and vice versa. Breakfast is always light, luncheon varies according to the morning's verdict of the scales, tea is just tea, and at dinner I eat according to the degree of my hunger, but it's never enough to overload my stomach."

"Do you ever take anything between meals?" he was asked.

"Very rarely," he replied. "Once in a while I drink some orange juice and occasionally, on a hot day the wiles of the ice cream man tempt me beyond resistance. I don't believe in eating between meals. It upsets the regularity of the digestive apparatus. Another wrench in the machinery, that's all."

And he was gone to perform some more of his breath-taking stunts. A few moments later he returned, and perched himself on a high stool where he could peer through the lens of the camera at the preparations going forward for the next scene.

"Don't you ever tire, Mr. Fairbanks?" I asked somewhat bluntly.

"Not often," he flashed a smile. "It is too interesting, all this," his gesturing arm included the vast studio, on every beat of whose pulse he keeps a constant finger. "When I am interested and busy, I am never tired. But, you see, I don't go beyond the limits of my physical energy. If, though, I should feel the least bit tired, I obey the signal and rest."

Mr. Fairbanks is rarely, if ever, ill. When asked to explain his immunity, he answered rather tersely. "Right living habits—that's all."

From boyhood Doug has been vitally interested in sports and athletics of all kinds. The story is told that he lost his first job as an office boy at the age of twelve because he kept the office in a constant state of upheaval with his athletic proclivities. Imbued with an inherent energy and vitality, which know no bounds, he naturally turned to physical sports as on outlet.

On the studio lot is a large gymnasium with the words, "Basilica Linea Abdominalis" above the door. Mr. Fairbanks translates it freely as "The Temple of the Waistline." Here every evening Doug and his friends engage in a half hour of the fast and speedy game of "Doug," named after its inventor. It is a combination of modern tennis and ancient badminton, played with racquets and feathered balls of cork. When Bill Tilden and Bill Johnson played "Doug" with Mr. Fairbanks, they moved with a speed they had never known in any tennis championship contest. The game is speedy, fast, and just the sort of game Doug would play.

After his evening game, he plunges into the pool in his dressing apartments. A rapid turn or two in the tepid water, a steam bath, a brisk rubdown, and he is ready for anything—work or play. This same schedule is carried out every day that he is in Hollywood, for whether or not he is in the midst of actual production, he is to be found at the studio.

Mr. Fairbanks enjoys golf, and slips away now and then for a brisk and friendly eighteen holes. When Doug plays golf, the game assumes a new energy.

No sauntering from green to green in this Fairbanks game. He is off with the ball. The caddies will tell you he plays the fastest game of golf at the country club.

Doug's recreation is—life, and the living of it. He enjoys every minute of his work, every phase of his many activities. Perhaps his happiest moments are those spent in the seclusion of his gracious, hilltop home, surrounded by his friends, dispensing the hospitality for which he and Mrs. Fairbanks are famed throughout the world. Then he comes the nearest to complete relaxation which it is in his power to reach.

Regularity is the fountain of youth from which Douglas Fairbanks drinks. Regular habits, combined with an intelligent moderation, are the open sesames to the doors of his success and zest for life.

*

This interview by Eleanor Parker was published in the April 1929 issue of **Correct Eating** *Magazine, and gives a great deal of insight on Fairbanks' daily routine along with some idea of how he managed to maintain peak physical condition at the age of 46.*

Douglas Fairbanks and Mary Pickford in London, May 1931.

The Inside of the Bowl

✦

Or, How to Be Happy Though Famous

By
Mary Pickford
and
Douglas Fairbanks

T he editor of this magazine asked us if this could be advertised as the first article which we have ever written together. We feel tempted to answer that he can go further than that and say that it will be the last one.

In other words, there have been difficulties. We first tried dictating it in relays, one taking up the burden when the other had lost his breath. We got along all right until it developed that we were writing on totally different subjects. As a piece of writing it possessed distinct originality, but it lacked the kind of clarity that magazines and readers demand.

The procession of "I's," which is bad enough in any personal narrative, becomes particularly awkward when it is impossible to tell to which co-author the pronoun refers. So we started using "we," but when we had written this sentence: "We spent the afternoon in having our hair dressed and exercising on the parallel bars," we decided that this method, too, had its weaknesses.

We offer the result, therefore, with misgivings and with a blanket apology to cover its shortcomings. It furnishes conclusive proof that in some things, at least, two heads are not better than one.

Our decision to write this article together was the result of a discovery that without knowing it we were bent on the same errand. The discovery was not a remarkable one, since the errand is the same on which every mortal is busily engaged from birth till death: the quest of happiness.

The reader will please not infer, simply because we have chosen to indulge in this innocent speculation, that we take ourselves to be authorities on the subject of success and happiness, or that we hope with a few deft words to settle the question once and for all.

It is our belief that no one upon whom fortune has heaped a full measure of success has really the slightest idea of how it all happened. One can always, when pressed for reasons, dig back into one's early life and discover sterling traits of character, fine habits, and indomitable perseverance that pointed like arrows to future achievement. But we would be great hypocrites if we did not acknowledge that luck has played a leading part in our lives. So, if we were writing one of those little homilies to youth that are so popular these days and wished to be logical, we should have to say, "Be as lucky as possible and nothing can prevent your ultimate success."

To be slightly more serious, there is something, of course, in knowing how to handle and extract full advantage from luck when it arrives. Otherwise luck will be something that happens to somebody else.

Without the sudden (and for us very lucky) growth of the motion picture as a popular medium of expression, where would we be today? The reader can guess this as well as we can. Our guess is that we would not now be asked by magazines to account for our success.

If there is one thing that exceeds the futility of telling people how to be successful, it is telling them how to be happy. By following the usual rules, and by unusual diligence and luck one may achieve success (in the common sense of the word, which is purely a material one), but the very term "pursuit of happiness" is a misleading one, for it implies that, like some kind of game, it should be chased to its lair. Whereas everyone knows from common experience that the harder you go after it, the less chance you have of finding it.

History and fable are full of accounts of men who set forth on adventures into foreign lands on the assumption that anything so rare as happiness must dwell in some far-off place. But they have usually returned empty-handed and disillusioned, to find what they were seeking resting quietly and unobserved on their own doorsteps.

But as we said before, it is not our intention to grow wise and informative on the subject, for we are in possession of no special secrets. By way of introduction to what follows we would like to make a few simple observations born of our own experience in trying to derive the greatest possible enjoyment from living. To us, it is the direct result of learning to be contented with conditions that cannot be remedied, and discontented with conditions that can be improved—and then striving to improve them.

This almost exhausts our total stock of wisdom on the subject. Happiness seems to be a kind of by-product of careful and thoughtful living—nothing that one can set out definitely to produce, but something that is added if the other ingredients are combined in the proper proportion.

Or, looking at it more fancifully, it is a perverse quality that appears when one stops searching for it too eagerly—like a name that one strives in vain to recall but that pops gayly into the mind the moment one has ceased thinking about it.

We invited a newspaper writer to our home in Beverly Hills for the week-end. Although he politely did his best to conceal it, it did not take a mind reader to detect that he had come to study us. He might as well have announced, "Here are two people who are popularly supposed to be examples of success and prosperity. I am going to find out how they manage it and pass on the secret to others."

He left us with an air of bafflement, almost of reproach. It was plain that we had been a grave disappointment to him. One does not know exactly what he expected—whether he had fancied that we would eat our soup with theatric gestures, register high emotion when the doorbell rang, talk in subtitles, or what not.

At any rate it was evident that he had expected something different from ordinary human behavior, something atmospheric and above the commonplaces of everyday life.

The evening was so completely lacking in any element of the unusual that we could not help feeling sorry for our visitor. It almost seemed that we were entertaining him under false pretenses—that we should have rehearsed some bizarre performance for him, and if we had no especial eccentricities to exhibit, that we should at least have assumed a few for the occasion.

As a matter of fact, after a hard day's work at the studio we permit ourselves at home the luxury of being natural and doing exactly what we want to do. There is enough acting and working for effect to be done at the studio. Before dinner, we all walked out on the broad lawn and watched the yellow full moon popping up over the hills and dimming the myriad lights of Los Angeles in the distance. We examined it with binoculars and observed that the top was dented with a huge crater, and there ensued a lively discussion whether the moon had an atmosphere like the earth, no one in the least daunted by a complete ignorance of the subject.

Going indoors, we sat before a log fire in the living room while George Ade and Charles Chaplin, who were among our guests, engaged in a spirited contest to see who could remember and sing the oldest songs.

This started other kinds of reminiscences. Someone had brought up an old scrapbook with newspaper clippings and pictures of theatrical stars of twenty and twenty-five years ago, showing John Drew, Ada Rehan, Olga Nethersole, and many others in the early days of their careers, and there followed many anecdotes of the theater and the inevitable argument as to whether the good old days were really any better than the present ones.

During dinner, we fear, the conversation did not soar to any greater heights. It could hardly have furnished our inquiring guest with the secret for which he was searching. We talked of the usual things: the future of California and the motion-picture business, our next productions, building an extension to the house so that we might accommodate more guests, a recent mysterious burglarizing of the house in which the burglar had contented himself with a few suits of clothes, our hopes and fears, Coolidge, prohibition, and cross-word puzzles.

T he same things probably, or at least the same sort of things, that were being discussed at the same time by millions of people in a million homes. No bright lances of thought were caught and shivered into sparkling words and phrases, there were no explosions of temperament and not a single symptom of genius. In fact, so far as the inquiring reporter was concerned, we were a dismal failure. We were just an ordinary group of people eating dinner.

Later, someone made the assertion that no one in the company could walk naturally through the dining room, without exhibiting a particle of self-consciousness, precisely as if no one were watching him. We all tried this in turn with only indifferent success. This led to other simple pastimes. One person absented himself from the room and the others decided upon some adjective whose meaning they acted out upon his return, and which he tried to guess. Not a very intellectual diversion, no doubt, and perhaps a strange game for actors, who might be thought to have enough of this sort of thing in their work, but everyone seemed to enjoy it and it caused endless merriment.

It is fashionable these days to deride such simple pastimes, although it is questionable whether those provided in their stead are any more sensible or amusing. At any rate we are starting no reform movement to bring them back. It is understood that we are not prescribing for other people but for ourselves.

Still later, our behaviour, which was beginning to win the complete disfavor of our guest, became more ordinary than ever. We spent a few minutes at the radio, trying to find some far-off stations but always discovering that we had located nothing more distant that KFI or KHJ of Los Angeles. Tiring of this, we put one of our latest pictures on the screen at one end of the living room, with easy-chairs drawn up at the other end so that one might choose between watching the picture and taking a nap.

We found things in it to admire, to question, to condemn, as people will; wondered what the motion-picture industry was coming to; took another walk outdoors, with the moon now riding high in the heavens; uttered a few banalities about life in general; planned a picnic breakfast on a mountain top at sunrise; and went to bed before 11.

As we said before, our newspaper friend, when he left us Monday morning, looked disappointed and a little hurt, as if he had been tricked. He had been looking for thrills and had found the commonplace. Finally he exploded. "Why, you," he said, "are just like other people—just like others, only more so! You do the ordinary things in the ordinary manner. There is nothing in the least extraordinary about you."

We could not possibly quarrel with this statement, because we believe it to be correct. It is true that our amusements are simple ones and that we derive our greatest enjoyment from ordinary things. There is no great philosophy in this attitude. It is chiefly a matter of personal taste. But it does seem to stand to reason that since life is mostly composed of the ordinary and is not a succession of high moments and great climaxes, one is distinctly better off if he can extract enjoyment from the everyday stuff of life than if he keys himself up to a pitch where he needs constant excitation and thrill.

The most unhappy people we have met are those who are constantly seeking new and more extraordinary ways of gratification, who feverishly follow every new cue to pleasure, and careen madly after happiness, as if it could be roped with a lasso. The pleasure-seeker is nearly always a discontented person, finally deserted even by the illusion of happiness, and the man who makes a business of pleasure is the last person to find it.

What one notices about this fierce pursuit of pleasure is that those engaged in it are not following their own inclinations but are allowing other people to dictate and prescribe their forms of amusement. They are keeping social engagements which are really irksome, going through a dismal round of so-called pleasures which society has imposed on them, playing games they do not want to play, eating and drinking things they do not want, listening to conversation which does not interest them, simply because the fashion of the hour or the tyranny of social habit is too strong.

It would be interesting to make a canvass of persons gathered at any one of a dozen social functions and ask each one confidentially how he was enjoying himself. Unless we are very much mistaken, three out of four would say something like this: "To tell the truth, this is the last place in the world I would like to be. I am going through the motions of having a good time, but I am extremely bored. I am deadly sick of the host's stories, and the antics of the woman who has had at least one cocktail too many make me a potential murderer. I wish I had the courage to stay home."

Pleasure, under these circumstances, assumes a kind of compulsion much more painful than that which labor imposes, for in the latter there is always some compensation. Even at its worst, there is something disciplinary and strengthening about it: a pleasant consciousness of earning a livelihood, an honest gratification at producing something, even if it is nothing more important than candlesticks. But in the grind of pleasures there is no compensating quality whatever, unless satiety, dyspepsia, and weariness of soul can be classed as such. We can think of no greater punishment to inflict on anyone than a life of uninterrupted pleasure.

Co-authorship now seems to be leading us into a pitfall which in writing singly we have always managed to avoid: the temptation to preach, to moralize, which was far from our original intention. We seem to be saying, "We know how to live. We have freed ourselves from the shackles that bind others. We are big enough to be simple, and courageous enough to live as we want to."

This would be a kind of arrogance of which we are really not guilty. But it is hard to speak about happiness except in the terms of one's own experience. Since this preachment, if such it is, is our only offense, is voiced with the most sincere conviction, and comes from two people who have practiced it with fair success, perhaps it may be forgiven.

It is not very original either. Disguise it as we may, it is only another plea for simplicity, a brief for the simple and ordinary pleasures—a suggestion that the feverish rush after enjoyment is carrying us way past our goal into a land of satiety and boredom.

This experiment we would recommend because we have found it successful: that those whose lives are crowded with amusements look over their list of social engagements for the week and ruthlessly cancel three-fourths of them. We think they would be surprised to find with what a quickened sense of enjoyment they would greet the ones that remained and with what a feeling of relief they would welcome a few evenings in which they could do exactly as they liked.

hen once the adjustment is made—and that is always difficult—one is sure to find that, for no other reason than force of habit or some social coercion more fancied than real, he has been doing things that not only did not add one jot to his general happiness, but actually bored and depressed him.

It has been our experience that one can come closer to a full enjoyment of life by this process of simplification and elimination than by adding and multiplying one's forms of amusement. There are a lot of nonessentials, many of them masquerading under the heading of pleasure, that one can dismiss without the slightest sense of loss. It sounds paradoxical, but it is really a fact that one of the best ways of adding to our happiness is by decreasing the number of our pleasures. The needs of life, the requirements for happiness, are so few and so simple that they are within the reach of everyone.

And we can truthfully say that, so far as we are concerned, neither money nor reputation has much to do with them.

Good digestion, which means good health, plenty of fresh air and exercise, occupation with some worthy purpose, even if one does not get very far with it, and the zest of life and peace of mind that go with these things—this, so far as we know, boxes the whole compass of human enjoyment.

Take away one item, and you may chase happiness to the ends of the earth and not find it. Add to them ad lib.—set the cumbersome machinery of pleasure running full speed, introduce every new device for enjoyment that the ingenuity of man can invent—and you will have added nothing important.

We are not speaking with any greater wisdom than comes from personal experience. This philosophy, if anything so simple deserves the name, may not be palatable in general, because it runs against the restless current of the times. All we know is that it suits us. We discovered long ago that what we liked best were simple things, ordinary enjoyments, the freedom from all social compulsion, the right to live and act without dictation. And here at home, resting quietly after a day's work, seeing the people we want to see, affecting nothing we do not feel, refusing to do things because someone else finds them amusing, looking backward a little into the past but mostly forward with great hope and enthusiasm into the future—this is the best way we know of being happy.

Being ordinary is, under the conditions of modern life, something of an art. One of the commonest illusions is that in order to make an impression on other people we must assume qualities we do not possess, adopt airs that sit but poorly upon us, and in general try to sustain the fiction that we are more gifted, important, and splendid than we really are. The temptation is greater than the average in the case of the person who is in the public eye and feels that he must live up to the popular impression that he is an exceptional and superior being.

To cite ourselves immodestly as examples, we must admit that we have gone through with this ordeal. When millions of people conspire to make you believe that you are a marvel, it is sometimes easy and pleasant to accept this generous verdict and behave as nearly as you can in the way in which you think a marvel would act. The motion-picture star is in constant danger of believing what his press agent writes about him and trying to behave in a manner to uphold the illusion.

The best corrective, as we have said somewhere before, is to keep your sense of humor as active as possible. When someone tells us that we attract larger crowds, when we appear in public, than the President of the United States, we reflect that a white elephant walking down Main Street would draw a larger crowd than any one of us.

The strain of acting up to people's expectations has grown too great. We have fallen back on the simple expedient of being ourselves and reserving our acting for the screen. If visitors are disappointed, this is a risk that we must take. One may lose some prestige of doubtful value when he decides to be his ordinary self, but one discovers a tremendous relief and peace of mind that is worth any price.

Incidentally, living and thinking in ordinary terms, cultivating a taste for simple, primitive things, has been a great benefit to us in our work. It enables us to meet the tastes of our audiences, which fortunately are also simple and ordinary ones, without any necessity for adjustment.

There is only one universal language and that is the common human language of hope, love, fear, and the other elemental emotions. If we fancied for a moment that we were sitting on the heights of Olympus, looking down with superiority and condescension, wondering how we might interpret our soaring thoughts so that they would be intelligible to the herd, and to what depths we would have to descent to suit the ordinary public taste, we would be in a bad way.

We do not know a great deal about other forms of expression, but in the making of pictures we are sure that nothing worth while will ever be accomplished by those who have to struggle to bend their high talents down to the level of the public. And we are inclined to believe that nothing great of any kind can be achieved with a feeling of superiority to what one is doing or for the people for whom it is done—that nothing notable has ever been written, composed, chiseled, or acted with the tongue in the cheek or with a sneer.

THE END

This is the first (and only) article Fairbanks ever co-authored with Mary Pickford. The complete article above was originally published in the November 9, 1929 issue of **Liberty** *Magazine. An abridged version was included in the December 1929 issue of* **Reader's Digest***.*

Douglas Fairbanks

THE THREE MUSKETEERS, ROBIN HOOD, THE THIEF OF BAGDAD, THE GAUCHO, THE IRON MASK—titles like these always remind us of one name—Douglas Fairbanks!

This actor has made many a dashing hero seem very, very real to us all. Long ago he sent a message to your older brothers and sisters to read in CHILD LIFE. This month he sends you one. He not only writes to you about enthusiasm, he also writes about moderation and says:

Moderation

A great many religious teachings point directly to the physical well being. Through some spiritual channel out of old China comes these words of wisdom that can be aptly applied to any race or generation: "Eat little, bathe often, so that your body may rest lightly on your soul."

(Signed) DOUGLAS FAIRBANKS

---

*Published in the February 1931 issue of **Child Life** Magazine.*

While traveling through the East to make the film **Around the World in 80 Minutes**, Douglas Fairbanks befriended everyone from the King of Siam to the Shanghai Superintendent of Police. He even wrote the foreword to a book on self-defense later published by Mr. Fairbairn. This advertisement for the book comes from an American newspaper dated November 15, 1931.

ROBINSON CRUSOE

✦

1932–1933

By Douglas Fairbanks

I n September 1704, a sailor by the name of Alexander Selkirk was ship-wrecked on the island of Juan Fernandez, in the Pacific Ocean off the Coast of Chili. Five years later, he became "Robinson Crusoe." His experiences served as the foundation for that famous story, written in 1719 by Daniel Defoe.

Judging by the early date of Alexander Selkirk's adventures, he was probably the first civilized white man ever to apply the knowledge and principles of wood-craft, handiwork, fire by friction and other methods of meeting emergencies which are taught nowadays to the Boy Scouts.

In the story, "Robinson Crusoe," which is not history but fiction, very likely Defoe enlarged upon the real adventures of Selkirk. However, the underlying principle of the book is based upon fact, and it is a story which has delighted and fascinated readers for several generations. With this in mind, when we decided to make a new photoplay and were groping about for a subject, the happy thought occurred that we might combine much of the activity which is so essentially a part of Scouting and Scout Law, with the adventures depicted in "Robinson Crusoe," and thus create a very novel and entertaining picture.

At first, my idea was to make a literal translation of "Robinson Crusoe" which is a regular mine of Boy Scout activity, but I soon saw that the book is really not adaptable to the screen, because when analyzed it lacks variety, and also it would not offer the opportunity I sought to accent the true value of Scout lore which, when conscientiously undertaken and thoroughly absorbed, gives a boy not only physical and mental training, but also a foundation in character that will stand him in good stead all through life. Of course, we were greatly disappointed at first over not being able actually to film "Robinson Crusoe," for I had intended to take the picture on the island of Juan Fernandez, where Selkirk actually had his experiences. This is undoubtedly one of the most beautiful spots in all the seven seas, and would have lent itself to screen treatment most admirably. However, we found just as good spots in the Society Islands and among the other groups that compose French Oceania, so our disappointment was comparatively short-lived. And when we finally reached the island of Moorea, where the Robinson Crusoe penthouse scenes were taken, I don't mind saying that my knowledge of Boy Scout methods came in very handy. In fact, I don't know what we would have done without it, for although the natives were very adept at implement building, it was hard to make them understand through an interpreter just what kind of implements we wanted. So the result was that in most cases we had to show them by making the first implements ourselves.

A great deal of interest and amusement was aroused among many of the chiefs and tribal rulers with knot-tying as practiced by the Boy Scouts. For instance, they were amazed at the simplicity and efficiency of the square knot, which they quickly learned to tie. Also the bowline piqued their curiosity, and they regarded it much as we might look upon a puzzle.

A few of the more primitive, of course, were superstitious about the whole process of knot-tying, considering it a sort of witchcraft which might prove harmful. While a very simple and kindly people, nevertheless the Polynesians are very superstitious, and knot-tying to many of them was new, for they accomplished the same result by twisting and tangling or braiding fibers together.

A very amusing incident occurred while we were making some scenes near the lovely spot on the island of Tahiti where Robert Louis Stevenson once lived.

Walter Pohlman, the chief technician of the company, had made an imitation skull from a natural chalk-stone which is found to some extent on a few of the South Sea Islands. This skull was to be used on Friday's war canoe, to denote that he was a head-hunter. When properly mounted, it did, as a matter of fact, give the canoe a very awesome and sinister look. Whenever we would haul this canoe along the roads through the jungles from one location to another, the natives would give it a wide berth as it passed, usually hiding in the jungle. And one day, after several of them had seen the canoe resting on the beach in the hot sun for several hours, the rays shining brightly on the skull, one of the tribal ceremonial conductors approached the chief technician and, talking through an interpreter, said: "Please do not leave that skull out in the sun all day because if you do it will walk around all night!"

A great many of the thatched huts in the South Seas are infested by giant spiders, some of them almost as large as a good sized crab! They are perfectly harmless, however, and the natives seem to think they are an omen of good luck.

There are also giant land crabs, some of them fourteen inches in diameter, counting their long legs, which climb the trees. They go right up the bole of a cocoanut tree, agile as the natives themselves. And to get rid of them, the Polynesians make them commit suicide! This is done by putting a collar of clay around the cocoanut tree near the top, say about sixty or seventy feet from the ground and just below where the nuts form. When the collar hardens, it sticks to the tree and the crab climbs over it to get at the cocoanuts, too hungry and eager to pay attention to it. With his powerful scissors-like claws, he cuts the stem of a nut and it falls to the ground, whereupon he backs down the tree, bent on finding the nut and eating it. But when his legs strike the clay collar he thinks he is on the ground, so he lets go and falls to his death below.

Everything about the South Seas is tremendously interesting, and I only hope that we have caught some of the charm of the region and spirit of the people and novelty of their customs in our interpretation of the adventures of "Mr. Robinson Crusoe."

However, I want to make it clear that our photoplay is entirely a work of fiction. For instance, cannibalism is now very rare in the South Seas, and is extinct in the Society Islands.

*Originally published in the January 1933 issue of **Boys Life** Magazine (Boy Scouts of America).*

A later portrait of Douglas Fairbanks, around the time of his retirement from the
screen in 1934.

Biography of Douglas Fairbanks

Revised January, 1933
From the Douglas Fairbanks Pictures Corporation

Douglas Fairbanks was born in Denver, Colorado, May 23, 1884. His father was a New York lawyer who went West to look over some mining property and remained there. Doug performed his first stunt at the age of two. When his nurse's back was turned he climbed to the roof of a shed in the yard and jumped to the ground. A gash was cut in his forehead and the scar is plainly visible to this day. You can see it in his close-ups.

The elder Fairbanks was a profound Shakespearian scholar and the study of the poet's dramas was included in Douglas' earliest curriculum. He began learning the famous speeches of Hamlet and Othello at seven and by the time he was ten, knew by heart all of the familiar passages. This was, of course, merely a memorizing of the words without a comprehension of their meaning. Understanding came with further study and today Fairbanks can quote almost verbatim page after page of the master dramatist. There is hardly a subject that comes up that he cannot tell you just what Shakespeare had to say regarding it.

The interest of the elder Fairbanks in Shakespeare had gained him a wide acquaintance among the exponents of the playwright's works and when these players visited Denver they were invariably entertained in the Fairbanks home. Right in the foreground would be found the future King of the Movies, then aged ten, energetically spouting, "To be or not to be"—undoubtedly the youngest and peppiest Hamlet on record.

"Of course I didn't know what the words meant," says Mr. Fairbanks, "but I could recite them all."

When Douglas was 17 the family moved to New York. Here he took his first fling at theatricals in the company of his father's friend, Frederick Warde, famous Shakespearian actor. At first the young Thespian had only bits, but when the troupe played Duluth something happened to one of the principals and Doug was promoted to the roles of Cassio and Laertes. He says the audiences were uncertain whether it was Shakespeare or Rubenstein's Melody in F he was giving.

One of the newspaper critics remarked that "Mr. Warde's company was bad but worst of all was Douglas Fairbanks as Laertes." Similar press notices were plentiful. Doug at once set about determining what was holding him back and decided it was lack of education in its broader phases.

So after his season with Mr. Warde he went to Harvard. His credits from the Denver city schools and the Colorado School of Mines were not sufficient to enroll him as a freshman, however, so he became a special student with courses in elementary Latin, French and English literature. That was cultural enough to satisfy anyone and what with liberal courses in freshman caps, bulldog pipes and Blumenthal posters young Fairbanks kept himself interested for five months. Then he grew restless and decided that 'education in its broader phases' was a lengthy process, so he returned to the stage—this time in support of Effie Shannon and Herbert Kelcey in "Her Lord and Master". When that engagement was over, the wanderlust—always a throbbing reality in his life—seized him. With two pals he started for Europe on a cattle-boat. Each had $50 in cash. They worked their way safely across, had a glorious time and were back in the shadow of the Goddess of Liberty at the end of three months.

The next jump was into frenzied finance. It was quite the thing to become identified with the Street even in those days when leaks were unknown, and he went in because most of the young men he knew were becoming brokers rather than because of any aptness for figures or finance. Within six months after invading Wall Street, he became head of the order department of the brokerage house of DeCoppet & Doremus,—a considerable position for a young man. He might have continued as a broker had not the fear that his employer would discover his ignorance of high finance caused him to resign.

Next he thought he would like to become a captain of industry, and in the approved manner of books he put on overalls and learned all about the manufacture of bolts, nuts, and hinges in a downtown hardware manufactory. When he had mastered the secrets of all the floors of the factory he began investigating the other departments. One of the first things he discovered was that the head of the concern only drew $10,000 a year after devoting most of his life to bolts, nuts and hinges. Shortly after that the embryonic captain of industry folded up his overalls and returned to the stage.

For a year he played in Alice Fisher's support in "Mrs. Jack", following Edward Abeles in the role Abeles created. His engagement ended prematurely, however, after a duel of words with the company manager. It was only natural that youth and vitality such as Mr. Fairbanks possessed should not be confined to the limits of one role, and on many occasions it overflowed in the form of interpolated lines and business. After an unusually exuberant performance the manager "called" him before some of the other members of the company. The result of the riot that followed was the resignation of Fairbanks and its immediate acceptance.

This episode so discouraged Doug that he decided to become a lawyer and for all of three months he read law in the offices of E. M. Hollander & Sons. He might now be influencing juries with his irresistible smile had not a wave of Japanese operetta just then submerged the local stage. At that period no musical comedy was complete without its geisha girls fanning 'neath the shade of cerise-blossomed cherry trees. To the impressionable young counselor at law far-off Japan seemed one huge tea party of geisha girls, and he was consumed with a desire to taste of its exotic delights. The time fuse of his wanderlust had about burned out anyway, and when the spark reached this desire Mr. Fairbanks was hurled across the Atlantic en route to the Orient by way of Europe with an idea of disposing of the rights to a patent electric switch for enough to enable him to spend the rest of his life riding in a rickshaw with room for two. But in London he stumbled upon a New York girl with whom he was violently in love, and he forgot all about the geishas.

When he returned home he went under the management of William A. Brady, an association which lasted on and off for seven years. He appeared under Mr. Brady's direction a season in New York in "The Pit," and at the end of the engagement following a disagreement over a reduction in salary he was again at large. In London again (whenever he was in doubt he invariably went there, he says) he met Lee Schubert, who engaged him for a part in "Fantana," his first role in a musical play. During another one of the "off" occasions from Brady, Doug appeared in a melodrama called "Two Little Sailor Boys"—a lineal descendant of "The Two Orphans".

By this time Mr. Brady's plans had matured and he sent Fairbanks a wire offering him a five-year starring contract. Recalling their parting, Doug was so astonished that he wired Brady asking if the offer had really come from him. A few months later he enjoyed the pleasure of seeing his name in electric lights as the star of "Frenzied Finance", presented by Mr. Brady. This play was a failure and while waiting for Brady to secure a successor to it Fairbanks appeared in support of Mrs. Brady (Grace George) in "Clothes" and played leading comedy parts in "The Man of the Hour", and "As Ye Sow". By this time Mr. Brady was ready with another vehicle and Fairbanks made a second stellar bow in "All For A Girl". It was during the short run of this piece that the Fairbanks smile first suggested its possibilities. Most of the critics mentioned it in their reviews, and the following morning all papers carried large advertisements inviting the populace to come to the matinee that day and bask—at $2.00 a bask—in the radiance of the famous Fairbanks smile. Exactly eighteen people accepted the invitation!

Mr. Brady happened to have at this time "The Gentleman from Mississippi" ready for production and he made a berth in this piece of Fairbanks, co-starring him with Tom Wise who played the title role. This play had a year's run in New York and did a great deal to establish Doug as a player of juvenile comedy roles.

Followed "The Cub" and "A Gentleman of Leisure", both successes. The latter received excellent newspaper notices and a long run was expected. These hopes were not realized however, and one night, after the performance, Mr. Brady summoned Doug to his office and with his cigar at its lowest angle of depression asked if he would be willing to cancel his contract which still had some time to run. The suddenness of this appealed to the star—it being his own method, precisely—and the arrangement was immediately concluded with great good feeling. The bond was signed at 2 a.m., and at 10 o'clock the next morning Mr. Fairbanks had been engaged by Cohan & Harris, to be starred by them for the next five years.

"This is immense, Doug," said George M. Cohan, in high glee, through the southeast corner of his mouth and the left nostril. Mr. Cohan reserves the northwest corner and the right nostril for ordinary conversation. "I've always wanted to write a play for you. You're the typical young American. We'll open Thanksgiving night." It was then late October.

Thanksgiving came without the play, and to kill time the typical young American went to Cuba with a comrade and walked across the island, then took a ship for Yucatan and walked from Progreso to Merida. When he came back the play was still unfinished.

"I've got the young man in the drawing-room," said George M., "and I can't get him out."

While he was still trying to rescue the hero his star put on a vaudeville sketch called "A Regular Business Man", and after that he was sent to play the leading role in "Officer 666" in Chicago. In the Windy City the late Lewis Waller told him of a play he once did in London that he thought would be suitable to Fairbanks. When this play reached the local stage it was called "Hawthorne, U.S.A.". Mr. Cohan eventually succeeded in extricating Broadway Jones from the drawing-room—for the hero was none other than the young chewing gum manufacturer—and, because his new star was occupied, he broke his own vow and returned to the stage.

Not only had Fairbanks always indulged in every form of sport, in fact athletics had actually been a part of his daily life. He was never known to enter a room or ascend or descend a stairway in the orthodox manner. Invariably he would mount three steps at a time or scale the balustrade. In "Hawthorne" he first employed to any great extent his athletic prowess in the theatre. He made his entrance in this play by vaulting a wall and at the finish of the third set he sprang from a balcony to the throat of his adversary and staged one of those spectacular melees for which he afterward became so famous.

Following "Hawthorne" came "He Comes Up Smiling", "The New Henrietta" and in the season of 1914—his last in the theatre—he appeared in "The Show Shop". These three plays were successes and firmly established Fairbanks as a Broadway star.

Like other stage stars, Doug had regarded the "movies" as more or less of a joke and it required "The Birth of a Nation" to open his eyes to the real possibilities of the screen. But he was in no hurry to "go movie". His motto was—"He leaps best who leaps last". However, when D. W. Griffith came along with a tidy offer of $2,000 a week for a period of 10 weeks the time seemed propitious, and the summer of 1915 found Doug facing the camera while this astounded instrument did its best to record his rapid-fire impersonation of "The Lamb". The picture was an instantaneous success and offers from picture producers began to pour in. Triangle—of which Mr. Griffith was the head—wisely came forward with a three year contract at a salary commencing at $2,000 a week and with an increase of $500 a week every six months. Fairbanks accepted this and settled down to a career of picture-making.

His success was due largely to a fast tempo—an innovation which eventually revolutionized the entire process of motion picture acting, and thus made screen history.

For Triangle, Fairbanks made "The Lamb", "Double Trouble", "Reggie Mixes In", "His Picture in the Papers", "The Americano", "The Habit of Happiness", "The Matrimaniac", "Flirting with Fate", "The Good Bad Man", "The Half Breed", "Manhattan Madness" and "American Aristocracy".

The athletic actor holds an interesting theory about his capacity to perform feats of physical prowess. He believes that the possession of a certain nervous force is as much a part of this ability as the muscular force itself. When he is about to undertake a stunt that requires unusual strength this nervous force manifests itself in a vocal outburst, as if he were under the influence of some violent emotion. While he does not underrate his physical strength, he believes that he possesses this nervous force in such a degree that he can perform feats of strength in excess of his physical capacity. It is a sort of an athletic version of the Kantian philosophy of the will to do, and when he has developed it to a still higher degree Mr. Fairbanks says he believes he can overcome the laws of gravity and fly if only for a distance of a few feet. As for climbing over buildings and doing stunts at high altitudes, that is possible through complete absence of the fear born of elevation from the ground.

Nearly two decades ago now, when Mr. Fairbanks was earning $800 a week, the maximum he received on the legitimate stage, he used to think if he could ever save $100,000 he would retire and never speak another word of work. With the prospect of making many more times that amount within the coming year he knows that he would Houdini out of the strongest chains that might seek to restrain him to idleness.

This, then, is the life of Douglas Fairbanks, and through it all his smile has grown wider and wider, until now, when beyond all doubt he possesses the sunniest, most infectious, most celebrated American smile.

This 1933 biography was the "official" word from Mr. Fairbanks, via his personal publicity director, Mark Larkin. This press biography is a Revised Version of an earlier bio Fairbanks routinely gave out to the media. Note that he gives his birth year as 1884, not 1883.

Grand National Is Captured
By Golden Miller

❖

Douglas Fairbanks, Sr., film star for many years, has written the following exclusive dispatch, giving a spectacular colorful picture of the running of the Grand National steeplechase, one of the turf's most exciting horse races.

By DOUGLAS FAIRBANKS, SR.
Wire Story

AINTREE, Eng., March 23.—When I return home I think I will lay out a hazardous riding course like the Grand National on my ranch in Southern California, where my cowboy friends may visit me. I will test their skill, or at least teach them to take their falls gracefully.

I experienced the greatest succession of thrills possible to pack into 10 minutes, and the quarter of a million persons who witnessed today's Grand National will agree with me.

This greatest steeplechase in the world over four and one-half miles was run under 10 minutes. While I prefer to leave statistics to men with long white beards, it is significant that nearly $10,000,000 was won by holders of Irish hospitals sweepstakes tickets, and more than $50,000,000 changes hands as a result.

The prize money won approximately by a horse named Golden Miller was under $40,000—a mere fraction of the $5,000,000 spent by the huge crowd. Yet the race didn't take any longer to run than a Mickey Mouse movie.

I laid 10 pounds (about $51) on Lone Eagle, one of Jock Whitney's pair, for sentimental reasons, not only because the horse was American-bred, but because

Mary once gave me a horse by that name. Unfortunately, he broke a blood vessel, but Jock's other entry finished third.

The race was not exactly an American triumph, but at least we were in at the finish. After all an American horse won in 1933 (Mrs. F. Ambrose Clark's Kellesboro Jack), and it is too much to expect another miracle of these materialistic times.

The day upset a series of preconceived ideas I had concerning the race. In the first place I was warned that it usually rains. However, not a drop of rain fell, and the sky was sunny.

In the second place, not a single horse fell at Becher's Brook, supposed to be the most cruel of all jumps. Twice the horses leaped this famous fence without unseating a rider. While several were thrown, only one jockey was injured, thus answering the critics who protest the alleged dangers of the course.

On my arrival I immediately walked around the course. At first glance most of the fences appeared less formidable than I had imagined, but when I saw a policeman standing at Becker's Brook with the top of his helmet a good foot below the hedge, I revised my ideas about it.

What the classical rodeo is in western America, the Grand National is to Great Britain. It is second to the annual derby in interest and affection for all horse-lovers, be they prince or pauper, for here, unlike in the United States, the sport of kings is also the sport of relaxation and solace for the poor.

*The museum's copy of this wire service article appeared in the March 24, 1934 edition of the **Nevada State Journal**. A rare and interesting find, this is Fairbanks' only attempt at sports writing. It would also prove to be his last widely published article. Within the year, he would announce his retirement from acting and stopped making movies altogether. He ceased publishing articles after that, limiting his writing output to a few rough story ideas scribbled on paper. These scenarios remained unfinished at the time of his death from a heart attack on December 12, 1939. Douglas Fairbanks was 56.*

AFTERWORD

✦

On Friendship

"…I remember you and recall you without effort, without exercise of will; that is, by natural impulse, indicated by a sense of duty, or of obligation. And that, I take it, is the only sort of remembering worth the having.

When we think of friends, and call their faces out of the shadows, and their voices out of the echoes that faint along the corridors of memory, and do it without knowing why save that we love to do it, we content ourselves that friendship is a Reality, and not a Fancy—that it is built upon a rock, and not upon the sands that dissolve away with the ebbing tides and carry their monuments with them."

For Further Study

Books

The titles listed below are available in the Douglas Fairbanks Museum archives, many public libraries, and through used booksellers:

Laugh and Live by Douglas Fairbanks. (Britton Publishing Company, New York, 1917)

Making Life Worthwhile by Douglas Fairbanks. (Britton Publishing Company, 1918)

Youth Points the Way by Douglas Fairbanks. (D. Appleton and Company, New York, 1924. © Boy Scouts of America, 1923)

Young Lawyer U.N. Truth's First Case by Emory Washburn Ulman. Foreword by Douglas Fairbanks. (Cullinan Publishing Company, Brooklyn, New York, 1922)

Douglas Fairbanks—The Making of A Screen Character by Alistair Cooke (The Museum of Modern Art Film Library Series No. 2, New York, 1940)

Mary Pickford and Douglas Fairbanks—The Most Popular Couple the World Has Ever Known By Booton Herndon. (W.W. Norton and Company, New York, 1977)

Doug and Mary by Gary Carey (E.P. Dutton, 1977)

His Majesty, The American: The Films of Douglas Fairbanks, Sr. by John C. Tibbetts and James M. Welsh (A.S. Barnes, 1977)

Douglas Fairbanks—The First Celebrity by Richard Schickel (Elm Tree Books, Great Britain, 1973)

Douglas Fairbanks—The Fourth Musketeer by Ralph Hancock and Letitia Fairbanks (Henry Holt and Company, New York, 1953)

The United Artists Story by Ronald Bergen (Crown Publishers, 1986)

United Artists—The Company Built by the Stars by Tino Balio (The University of Wisconsin Press, 1976)

The Fairbanks Album by Douglas Fairbanks, Jr. and Richard Schickel (New York Graphic Society, 1975)

The Salad Days by Douglas Fairbanks, Jr. (Doubleday and Company, New York, 1988)

A Hell of A War by Douglas Fairbanks, Jr. (Doubleday, 1993)

Knight Errant—A Biography of Douglas Fairbanks, Jr. by Brian Connell (Doubleday, 1955)

The Mark of Zorro by Johnston McCulley published serially under the title of *The Curse of Capistrano,* illustrated with scenes from the film. The book is dedicated "To Douglas Fairbanks, The Zorro of the screen" by the author. (Photoplay novel, Grosset & Dunlap, 1924)

Don Q's Love Story by K. and Hesketh Prichard, illustrated with scenes from the Douglas Fairbanks film, *Don Q, Son of Zorro.* (Photoplay novel, Grosset & Dunlap, 1925)

The Thief of Bagdad by Achmed Abdullah, based on Douglas Fairbanks' *Fantasy of the Arabian Nights,* illustrated with scenes from the film. (A.L. Burt Company, New York, published by arrangement with the H.K. Fly Company, 1924)

The Black Pirate by MacBurney Gates. Based upon the story written for the screen by Elton Thomas and retold in short story form by Lotta Woods, with color illustrations of scenes from the film. (Photoplay version, Grosset & Dunlap, 1926)

The Gaucho by Eustace Hale Ball, novelized from the screenplay by Elton Thomas and the short story by Lotta Woods, illustrated with scenes from the film. (Grosset & Dunlap, New York, 1928)

United Artists presents Robin Hood featuring Douglas Fairbanks. Adapted from the film by Austin Gilmour, Alex Gottlieb. (Engel van Wiseman Inc., New York, 1935)

VIDEO/DVD

Many Douglas Fairbanks films, particularly his early comedies for Triangle and Artcraft, are regrettably absent from the home video marketplace. Below is a listing of the titles that we know to be available on VHS or DVD at the time of this writing. A complete Fairbanks filmography, including titles not yet available on home video and "lost" films can be found on the museum's website at: *DouglasFairbanks.org.*

Documentaries

Intimate Biography Series: Douglas Fairbanks—The Great Swashbuckler (90 minutes, 2005)

The American Experience: Mary Pickford (90 minutes, 2005)

Star Power: The Creation of United Artists (60 minutes, 1997)

Douglas Fairbanks and Mary Pickford: The Birth of a Legend (25 minutes, 1966)

Fairbanks Films

FOR TRIANGLE FILM CORPORATION

1915
Martyrs of the Alamo (various uncredited extra roles)
Intolerance (uncredited extra)
The Lamb
Double Trouble
1916
His Picture in the Papers
The Habit of Happiness
Reggie Mixes In
Flirting With Fate
Mystery of the Leaping Fish
The Half Breed (* incomplete print)
Manhattan Madness
American Aristocracy
The Matrimaniac
The Americano

THE ARTCRAFT FILMS

1917
Wild and Woolly
Down To Earth
The Man from Painted Post
Reaching for the Moon
1918
A Modern Musketeer (* incomplete print)

THE UNITED ARTISTS YEARS

1919
His Majesty, The American
When the Clouds Roll By

1920

The Mollycoddle

The Mark of Zorro

1921

The Three Musketeers

The Nut

1922

Douglas Fairbanks in Robin Hood

1924

The Thief of Bagdad

1925

Don Q., Son of Zorro

1926

The Black Pirate

1927

The Gaucho

1928

The Iron Mask (original silent version with "talking" sequences)

The Iron Mask (1952 re-release "sound" version, narrated by Douglas Fairbanks, Jr.)

Show People (cameo)

1929

The Taming of the Shrew (The only version of this film available on home video is the 1951 re-release, heavily edited by Mary Pickford with revised/overdubbed sound and music tracks.)

1930

Reaching for the Moon

1931

Around The World in 80 Minutes with Douglas Fairbanks

1932

Mr. Robinson Crusoe

1934

The Private Life of Don Juan

ALSO RECOMMENDED

The Douglas Fairbanks Collection

An excellent DVD box set of Fairbanks films, bonuses and rare footage, including:

The Mark of Zorro
The Three Musketeers
Douglas Fairbanks in Robin Hood
The Thief of Bagdad
Don Q., Son of Zorro
The Black Pirate

For more information about Douglas Fairbanks, please write, call, or visit us on the web:

The Douglas Fairbanks Museum

Postal Mail: P.O. Box 685082
Austin, Texas 78768-5082
Phone: (512) 233-2214
Email: FairbanksMuseum@cs.com
Web: *DouglasFairbanks.org*

Our mission is to collect, preserve and interpret artifacts and archival materials relative to the life and influence of Douglas Fairbanks, Sr., by utilizing the collections and exhibits to provide cultural and educational programs and publications to historians, film scholars, and the public.

The museum's collections contain photographs, artwork, movie posters, autographs, rare documents and correspondence, audio/video recordings, films, books and periodicals dating from the 1860s to the present. Our collection is growing rapidly, and currently consists of approximately 1100 artifacts in addition to thousands of pages of published materials in our newspaper and magazine archives.

Our collections have been featured in a wide variety of media, books, documentary films, and live presentations worldwide. Credits include projects and exhibits produced by the National Mariners Museum, PBS *(Public Broadcasting System—USA)*, BBC2 *(UK)*, The National Portrait Gallery, The Gerald Ford Presidential Museum, The Martin and Osa Johnson Safari Museum, The San Francisco Silent Film Festival, Delta Entertainment, and the Douglas Fairbanks Memorial at Hollywood Forever.

In 2005, the museum provided interviews, photographs and research materials to a new documentary film titled *Douglas Fairbanks—The Great Swashbuckler*, available on DVD.

The Douglas Fairbanks Museum was founded in 1998 by a small group of Fairbanks fans, and is operated by a volunteer conservation and research staff. The museum is located in Austin, Texas.

978-0-595-39776-1
0-595-39776-X